The LIVING Supply Chain

The LIVING Supply Chain

The Evolving Imperative of Operating in Real Time

Robert Handfield
North Carolina State University
Raleigh, NC, USA

Tom Linton
FLEX^{TM}
San Jose, CA, USA

This edition first published 2017
© 2017 by John Wiley & Sons, Inc

The right of Robert Handfield and Tom Linton to be identified as the authors of this work has been asserted in accordance with law.

Registered Office
John Wiley & Sons, Inc., 111 River Street, Hoboken, NJ 07030, USA

Editorial Office
111 River Street, Hoboken, NJ 07030, USA

For details of our global editorial offices, customer services, and more information about Wiley products visit us at www.wiley.com.

Wiley also publishes its books in a variety of electronic formats and by print-on-demand. Some content that appears in standard print versions of this book may not be available in other formats.

Library of Congress Cataloging-in-Publication Data

Names: Handfield, Robert B., author. | Linton, Tom (Thomas K.), author.
Title: The living supply chain : the evolving imperative of operating in real time / Robert Handfield, North Carolina State University, Raleigh, NC, USA, Tom Linton, FLEX, Milpitas, CA, USA.
Description: First edition. | Hoboken, NJ : John Wiley & Sons, Inc., [2017] | Includes index. |
Identifiers: LCCN 2017012501 (print) | LCCN 2017022127 (ebook) | ISBN 9781119307198 (pdf) | ISBN 9781119307228 (epub) | ISBN 9781119306252 (cloth)
Subjects: LCSH: Industrial procurement–Management. | Business logistics–Management.
Classification: LCC HD39.5 (ebook) | LCC HD39.5 .H364 2017 (print) | DDC 658.7–dc23
LC record available at https://lccn.loc.gov/2017012501

Cover image: © Riccardo Vallini Pics/Gettyimages
Cover design by Wiley

Set in 10/12pt WarnockPro by Aptara Inc., New Delhi, India

10 9 8 7 6 5 4 3

To Lise and Rodney, my dear parents
Robert Handfield

*To my wife Cheryl whose encouragement gives me strength and whose
wisdom the courage and curiosity to explore new ideas.*
Tom Linton

What the Experts are Saying About This Book

Handfield and Linton reveal the "secret ingredient" to leveraging the power of a well managed supply chain. The emphasis on visibility is key to turning companies that simply react to their environments into proactive champions for their customers. This book is a "How To" guide to leveraging the untapped power of a well managed supply chain. It will teach you how to turn from a reactive "firefighter" into a proactive champion for the customer. The book will revolutionize the way companies approach supply chain management. It turns conventional wisdom on its ear, and is timely and relevant to tomorrow's business environment.

—Frank Crespo, *Vice President, Global Supply Network Division (CPO/Logistics/IoT Analytics), Caterpillar Inc.*

The LIVING supply chain is a wake up call to any enterprise that depends on suppliers and contractors. Be fast, be nimble and make supply chain transparency the nucleus of your operations or become endangered.

—Paul Massih, *Vice President, BP PSCM*

Tom Linton and Robert Handfield's book is a fascinating journey through the future of supply chain management – the LIVING supply chain. Such future involves speedy supply chain networks leading to high customer satisfaction, high asset velocity and high profits. Such future is based on real time information and connected systems between trusted partners. Rather than a theoretical manuscript, the book is based on the experience and work of Linton, who is Chief Procurement and Supply Chain Officer at Flex. He is actually building and evolving such a supply chain and thus the book is a must read for every supply chain professional.

—Yossi Sheffi, *Professor, MIT Center for Transportation and Logistics*

The book on The Living Supply Chain is itself a great "living" reading on how to bring supply chain to a powerful living state. The idea of Live–Interactive–Velocity–Intelligent–Networked-Good is the foundation of how supply chains can be agile, adaptive and aligned. The book brings the AAA supply chain concepts to life. I congratulate the authors for producing this book that would be of value to every supply chain executive and practitioner.

—Hau Lee, *Professor, Stanford University*

The concept of the supply chain had a short but useful life. Much value has been unlocked in the last 30 or more years in the recognition that functions once thought of as discrete – procurement, logistics, materials management, etc. – were not only linked but also had mutual dependencies. However, as a practical matter, we have reached the limit of new insights from this one-dimensional model. Handfield and Linton's book explores a multi-dimensional model based on the biological concept of an ecosystem. This new way of thinking promises to yield vast amounts of additional insights that will enable the next wave of innovation in supply management.

—Tom Derry, *President, Institute of Supply Management*

Supply chains are the nervous system of the material world, a living universe of flows that propels the world economy forward. As this lucid book reveals, Flex is the supply chain's brain, evolving the global production system through technologies that promote transparency and trust. No matter what political obstacles emerge in the years ahead, supply chains will flourish and optimize the world economy for everyone's benefit.

—Parag Khanna, *Author of "Connectography"*

In an age when most organizations and functions are focused on the transition from human labor to AI and smart machines, Handfield and Linton looked at the modern supply chain and realized that it has come alive! Their global ecosystem view of the "living" supply chain emphasizes the need for speed, transparency, and alignment — particularly when there is a high level of dependency on suppliers for the creation of customer value.

—Kelly Barner, *Owner & Editor, Buyers Meeting Point, LLC*

Successful businesses are those that support the success of their customers. This book captures the essence of our volatile, uncertain world and the opportunities that exist for the commercially astute, organizationally integrated business. More important, it offers insight to the recipe for 21st century operations and the management of complex supply ecosystems.

—Tim Cummins, *CEO, International Association of Commercial and Contract Management*

A LIVING supply chain requires a living company. The authors make a great case for how Flex is creating a living company to thrive in the living supply chain.

—Tom Choi, *Harold E. Fearon Eminent Scholar Chair of Purchasing Management, Arizona State University Executive Director, CAPS Research*

As it becomes more important to move faster and respond effectively to change, this book starts to explore some of the principles organizations can adopt to succeed in our "real time" world ...

The world we're living in means it's more important than ever for companies to build hyper reactive supply chains. This book plots the path to success in our "real time" world ...

—Alex Martinez, *CEO, Procurement Leaders*

Linton and Handfield chart the future of supply management from the perspective of an exemplar best practice in a winning firm that links a myriad of stakeholders in real time. Winners must move beyond restrictive chains to enlightened networks that understand and implement supply network speed, transparency and trust. The authors show you the why and what of such interdependent ecosystems. Simply put, supply networks resemble nature since success results from mutually beneficial, fast, autonomous, balanced and fair interactions. The future is here, but as William Gibson observed, it's not evenly distributed. A must read with a caution: This book is not for the faint of heart – you'll be exposed to radically new ways of thinking that, once accepted, can never be turned back.

—Joe Sandor, *Hoagland–Metzler Professor of Purchasing and Supply Management, The Eli Broad School of Business, The Eli Broad Graduate School of Management, Michigan State University*

A great book to understand the impact of today's digital transformation on global supply chains. Data is the new natural resource that is changing how Enterprises operate. When you consider that data is not only growing at incredible rates, but almost 80% of data is unstructured (think text, pictures and sensor data), getting your arms around all this data can be daunting. However, what is so exciting is that we now we have systems that can understand unstructured data and draw insights from all these vast data sources. This is where we are focused within IBM's Watson Supply Chain business. Leveraging cognitive systems to provide insights, intelligence and improved visibility.

—Jeanette Medlin Barlow, *Vice President of Watson Supply Chain, IBM*

This is one of the most inspiring and conceptually innovative books that I've read about supply chain management in a long time. It fuses the experience and ideas of a top supply chain executive with those of an academic guru on the subject to create a vision of the real-time, intelligent, collaborative and hyper-responsive supply chain. The term "living" nicely encapsulates the very essence of this supply chain about which the authors write with great erudition, eloquence and enthusiasm.

—Alan C. McKinnon, *Professor of Logistics, Kühne Logistics University*

Over my career in multiple large corporations I have often heard the term "End State Design" used in the context of Supply Chain design and technology enablement. The reality is that there is no "End State". To survive we need to have an adaptive supply chain and capability to both optimize and adapt simultaneously. Today the rate of change is just too fast, and those that master the ability to adapt their supply chains in response to the rapidly changing environment will be the winners. We need to embrace the rapid change in business models, embrace the fact that innovation by companies such as Uber & Airbnb can shift an entire industry on its back with minimal startup capital. This book begins to describe the ability to shift from functional silos to E2E Frictionless flow with the maturity to make E2E tradeoff decisions as a key enabler for success. Striking this balance whilst still keeping the technical depth and expertise in functional teams is a critical success factor and will only enabled through a transparent supply chain.

—Wayne Rothman, *Vice President, Enterprise Supply Chain Planning, Johnson & Johnson*

This book combines supply chain theory and practice research from Professor Hand-field, one of the leading Supply Chain professors, with the real world experience of Tom Linton, leader of Flextronics supply chain a business that had to be agile to survive in a fast changing industry. This book blends insight with practical case study that will benefit supply chain professionals in their journey to excellence.

—Phil Priest, *SVP GBS, Smith & Nephew*

A fantastic read and excellent stories from Dr. Handfield and Tom. Years ago IBM embarked on a journey to develop our Transparent Supply Chain solution, to provide visibility, alerting and disruption management across our global supply chain. This journey has been incredibly transformational for IBM. Transparency leads to velocity and velocity is paramount in supply chains! In order to delight our clients everyday, acting with agility and speed in a complex and ever-changing global chain has been a critical success factor for IBM.

—Joanne E. Wright, *Vice President, IBM Supply Chain*

Contents

Preface

On a wet morning in January 2016, I sat next to a cozy fire in a Portland coffee shop, with a warm cup of black coffee and an open Apple laptop. I thought about what I had seen the day before, on a tour of the Flex Pulse Center in Milpitas, California, and the discussion I'd had with Flex's chief supply chain officer, Tom Linton.

I've known Tom for over a decade. Tom worked at IBM from 1981 to 2001 before moving to e2Open during the dot.com years, then to Agere Systems (now LSI), then to Freescale, and then 3 years in Korea as the head of procurement for LG in 2008. He started at Flex in 2011. We had kept up with one another over the last 20 years, and Tom had visited NC State on two occasions. A month earlier, Tom had urged me to come out to California and see what he was doing with something he kept calling the "Pulse." Since I was traveling to the West coast to visit Nike in January 2016, I agreed to drop by and visit.

And what a visit! My brain was still reeling, trying to absorb it all. What I had seen in Flex's Pulse Center, and at Elementum, its startup company, which created the software "wrapper" that made the Pulse available to everyone, had made such an impression on me that I believed it was the start of something that seemed both organic and very, very new and uncharted. Flex was deploying an experiment of sorts, one that took everything we ever knew about supply chains, tossed it out the window, and started from scratch.

I had left Tom with a parting comment: "I think we need to write a book about what you're doing here." Tom had smiled, and nodded knowingly.

So as I sat in the coffee shop that early morning, I thought about whether there indeed was a book to be written. I didn't have much time, as I was scheduled to meet with the Nike Global Sustainability & Manufacturing team in nearby Beaverton later that morning.

But I gave it a shot. Typing quickly, I came up with a list of 10 key points that had jumped out at me in the brief hours I had spent at Flex. I wrote down ideas for eight chapters, copied them into an email to Tom, and asked him what he thought.

Within an hour, Tom wrote back:

> I think you captured some of our thinking exactly. A tighter economy requires a new way of optimizing how supply is managed. Maybe we can set up some regular calls and flesh this out?

And that's how this book was born.

I am a college professor who has been hanging around supply chain executives for 25 years. I have witnessed the popularizing of the term "supply chain management," though many people still think of it as "something that has to do with logistics, right?" Over this period, I've also witnessed the Internet bubble in 2000, and heard people say it would "change everything." I've seen enormous organizational change, including shifts such as the "logistics renaissance," "world-class procurement," "the Internet of Things," "Big Data analytics," and many other buzzwords that populate the lingo of executives worldwide. What I saw that winter day at Flex, however, seemed truly revolutionary. And I was determined to write about this phenomenon.

In the months that followed, Tom and I put together our thoughts and observations, with Tom sharing his stream of consciousness as he launched the Pulse Center, while I recorded my observations from the perspective of an academic working in the supply chain field for years. I decided to start each chapter with an observation taken from my remarkable tour of the Flex facility.

Another important part of the story is several books that we both read during the writing of this work. These include *The Serengeti Rules* by Sean Carroll, *NonZero* by Robert Wright, *Team of Teams* by Gen. Hugh McChrystal, *Connectography: Mapping the Future of Global Civilization* by Parag Khanna, and *The Homing Instinct* by Bernd Heinrich. These works were diverse: one was on biological evolution, the second on world history, the third on military campaigns in Afghanistan, the fourth on the future of global economics, and the last on the migratory patterns of wildlife. But a common thread runs through these books, which ultimately helped shape our thinking in developing the "new rules of supply chains," which readers will discover for themselves.

As you read this book, bear in mind that three major shifts are shaping the new digital economy.

1. Data is foundational to everything we do. Data is a natural resource – those who capture data and learn how to exploit it will be those who succeed in the new economy.
2. The Cloud is transforming information technology and moving business processes into digital services. Understanding how to make data available to make decisions is foundational to how we operate.
3. The shift to cognitive computing is unlocking new insights and enabling optimized outcomes. Human–machine interaction will change everything about the way we work.

We are truly moving to a critical inflection point where the management of multi-tier supply chains is driven by the evolution of new hardware devices and software possibilities, but which is held together by a concept which we call "federation." These changes are both evolutionary and revolutionary. New combinations of cloud, mobility, and human–machine interaction are pointing to a great leap forward in the supply chain profession and its impact on the company performance.

The story is still being written. The narrative that follows gives you an idea of how exciting this ride is going to be. It may be different by the time you are reading this – so you'll have to keep up in "real time" on your own from that point on.

Rob Handfield

Introduction

Supply chain management is an evolving field. While logistics, sourcing, planning, materials management, and data and systems have existed for generations, the combination of these disciplines is less than 40 years old. The incorporation of data and real-time systems in the way we operate supply chains is just emerging.

This book is about re-imagining what supply chain is, and what it's becoming. The premise of the book is that supply chains are ecosystems that adjust and evolve in ways similar to the way the natural world behaves. We have used our creative imagination to envision how supply chains will evolve and adapt to the emerging complex new business environment of the future.

This book also introduces the topic of balance to supply chains, not in the classic context of supply and demand but as it relates to the values companies increasingly are placing on healthy, honest, and transparent supply chains. What is "good" in supply chain management has been an area of inquiry that has expanded in ways both unforeseen and consistent over the last 100 years.

So if, as Abraham Lincoln suggested, we are to rely on the "better angels of our nature," forgive us. In addressing the LIVING supply chain and the common purpose and federated forces behind them, we are merely disclosing what is happening in the world today. Even though forces and flows also exist within illicit supply chains, we believe companies driving good supply chains are becoming increasingly prominent and are improving the state of the world. The Dodd–Frank Bill, for example, regulates American companies' use of so-called "conflict minerals," the UN Global Compact calls on companies to support internationally proclaimed human rights, and numerous international agreements now regulate carbon emissions and trade. All these consensus actions align with a win–win approach to integrating global corporations on common standards of behavior.

The new rules of supply chain management do not eradicate the old rules. The fundamentals of value chain, supply–demand, and customer-centric solutions driven by mass customization, omni-channel solutions, and globalization are only a back story to the rising wave of Big Data analytics and cognitive supply chains that will eventually make supply chains intelligent enough to accurately predict outcomes. For decades, supply chains have been about nodes and processes that define both the design and network of how things move. We have targeted revenue benefits, income statement cost improvements, and procure-to-pay cash lifecycle benefits through to inventory contributions to balance sheets. We have pushed globalization, driven cycle time improvements, and focused on leaning out and leaning in as we pushed for recognition as a "C-level" function. Each contribution over the decades by industry leaders and organizations such as the Institute for Supply Management the Council of SCM Professionals, and APICS have helped define supply chain today.

The central argument of this book is that balanced supply chains will win and selfish supply chains will lose. The challenge we face is that supply chains are selfish by nature. The success of our new rules lies in making sure they allow business practices that balance the profit motive with healthy supply chains. We use an analogy to Sean Carroll's *The Serengeti Rules* to offer insights into how nature and business are more parallel than previously thought.

Dr. Robert Handfield and I have worked together for over a decade. I often reference his widely used and respected *Purchasing and Supply Chain Management* (written with Robert J. Monczka, Larry C. Guinipero, and James L. Patterson and initially published in 2001), one of the most widely used supply chain textbooks of our time. My personal copy has been annotated and dog-eared multiple times, and its fundamentals are essential learning in supply chain courses and companies worldwide. When Rob suggested we put down in a book, the innovations we were developing at Flex, where I serve as the chief procurement and supply chain officer based on my career in supply chain management, I could not say no.

I hope this book becomes a starting point for a new wave of innovative conversations about what supply chain *IS* versus what it *DOES*. When we start to understand the underlying values we are promoting and the time we are disrupting, we are on our way to a new understanding of how supply chains affect business outcomes. Whether our function becomes part of the autonomous new fabric of business in the coming decades will be rooted in how LIVING principles and new supply chain rules are adopted globally.

Time is on our side. After all, in business, we own it.

Tom Linton

1

The LIVING Supply Chain

New Rules for the New Normal

It was raining hard in San Jose the morning I walked from the A-Loft Hotel to meet Tom Linton at the Flex offices.

"We don't usually get this much rain," several locals had informed me, "but we are sure glad, because we need it. Four or five years of droughts have really depleted our water supply."

I had driven by the site of the 2016 Super Bowl the night before – a site where the favored Carolina Panthers offense would be decimated by an attacking Denver Broncos defense, a reminder that a great defense can beat a good offense.

Our meeting began with a broad overview of Flex. The name change from Flextronics to Flex had occurred in July 2015, in response to the fact that the company was no longer a "contract manufacturer" in the traditional sense of the word.[1] Contract manufacturing was Flextronics' original business, during the boom years of the 1990s and the Internet boom, when the company largely manufactured PCs for big names like HP, Dell, and others. Contract manufacturing was a volume business, with razor-thin margins, and it relied on a company's ability to scale up a new product assembly line anywhere in the world. I had written about Flextronics in one of the first-ever supply chain books, *Introduction to Supply Chain Management*, published in 1999.

"We are no longer a contract manufacturer," Tom emphasized, "but we are in full transition to become a company that, when I think about it, hasn't ever existed before. In each of the organizations I've worked in, I like to experiment with organizational models. This is the biggest experiment of them all, and I believe we are achieving an essential alignment of procurement and the supply chain organization that is unique. We are influencing and shaping Flex's corporate strategy, but we are also totally supporting it.

---

[1] The terms Flextronics, Flex, Sketch-to-Scale^{TM}, Intelligence of Things^{TM}, the Pulse Center^{TM}, and other terms in this book belong to Flex International Ltd., or its affiliates.

The LIVING Supply Chain: The Evolving Imperative of Operating in Real Time, First Edition.
Robert Handfield and Tom Linton.

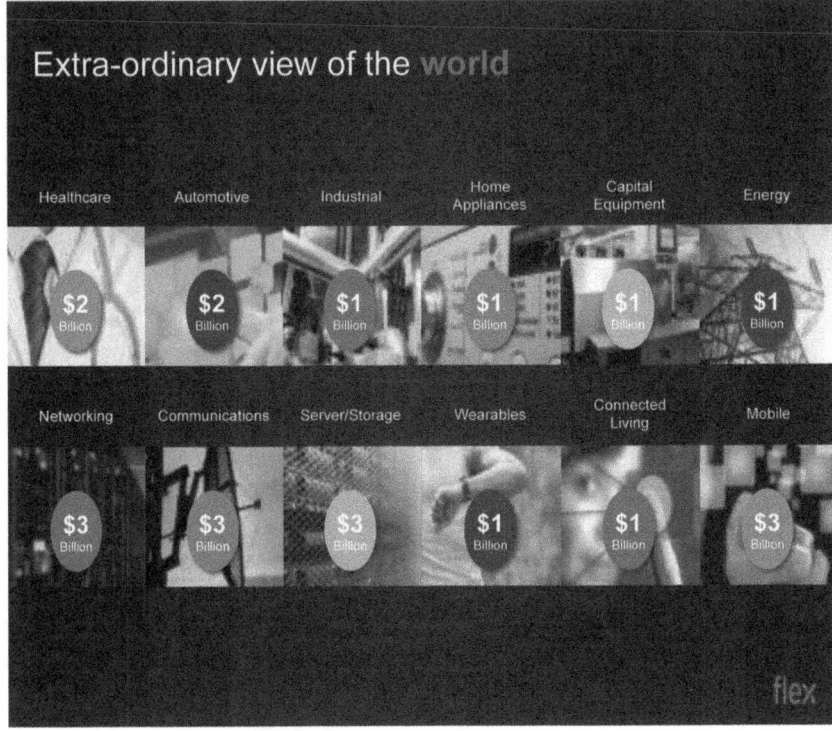

Figure 1.1 Flex's Business Divisions. *Source:* Reproduced with permission of Flex

"We are a capability supply chain company," Tom said. "Supply chain is our business, but it is supply chain on steroids. We have over 200,000 employees and over 1000 customers in 18 different industries, and produce $1 billion or more in at least 12 of these verticals", referring me to a chart showing all of Flex's business verticals (Figure 1.1). "I'm involved in the downstream supply and manufacturing side, as well as the upstream, quoting to our customers when they come to us for a new product. We call it 'Sketch-to-Scale™' to represent what we do from design through manufacturing. We incubate start-ups and drive scale for large original equipment manufacturers. We don't just make PCs anymore – but produce just about every electronic product you can think of that's out there. We make cell phones, Nike footwear, industrial products, Wink networks for the connected home, Bose speakers, Apple servers, Microsoft X-boxes, Fit-Bits, drones, and dozens of devices for the emerging connected world. We produce medical products for J&J, Cisco products, and automotive products for Ford. We're a significant player in everything from floor care (Dyson, Bissell) to industrial test equipment and solar energy and are running billion dollar businesses in each of these sectors. But you won't ever see our name or our brand on these products. We are one of the biggest companies nobody has ever heard of, and we are continuing to expand in other areas." In late 2016, Flex announced that they are partnering with a company Rib Software to form a joint venture, YTwo Formative, to digitize the acquisition of building materials in a revolutionary set of solutions for the $9 trillion housing industry.[2]

Droughts and Super Bowl outcomes are just two of the many uncertainties facing the population in our global ecosystem. One-in-a-thousand-years rain like the one that hit South Carolina in October 2015, the Tianjin explosion, the Bangkok monsoon flooding, and the Japanese earthquake/tsunami and resulting devastation are just a few of the natural disasters to hit global supply chains in the last few years. These disasters create disruptions, but nothing like the disruptions brought about by global terrorist events, political foment and civil unrest, worker strikes, increased challenges in border crossing, and labor issues that are part and parcel of the global supply chain. As any student of business history knows, globalization has brought about a huge number of discontinuities and disruptions. These disruptions are no longer unique and rare; they are ubiquitous, and the time between disruptions seems to be shrinking. In fact, it is a rare day when no disruptions of any kind occur.

Managing volatility would be an acceptable strategy if the return on this level of risk were high. But that doesn't seem to be the case. The press continues to talk about stock market volatility, with pundits predicting that the economic downturn in China will impact the global market. Low oil prices, low commodity prices, and low food prices had everyone worried, as this indicated that demand was also low. Growth rates were predicted to be anemic. A collection of CEOs in Davos, Switzerland, predicted doom and gloom,[3] as validated by a Deloitte survey of 1700 executives who all felt that there would be negative growth in the year ahead. Britain's 2016 vote to enact Article 50 and exit the European Union ("Brexit") has caused panic and uncertainty for Europe and the UK, with UK officials running around frantically and interest rates reaching new lows. Indeed, there seems to be no upside. Worse, experts noted that volatility "is the new normal," and that there isn't much hope for stability.

In January 2016, economists predicted that United States and global GDP growth would hover between 1.9% and 2.4% based on slowing growth in China. The outlook in January 2017 also hovers around 2% in the face of a Trump presidency, while global GDP is predicted to be at 2.9–3.4%.[4] Lower investment, unfavorable demographics, and weak productivity growth are the hallmarks

2 http://www.prnewswire.com/news-releases/flex-and-rib-software-join-forces-to-transform-building-and-housing-industry-300367092.html
3 http://www.pwc.com/gx/en/ceo-agenda/pwc-at-davos.html
4 Doerfler, S., "The Big Unknown," *Inside Supply Management*, January 2017, pp. 17–21.

Table 1.1 Real GDP Growth (%)

Country Groups	2013	2014	2015	2016	2017	2018
Aggregates						
Advanced economies	1.1	1.7	1.8	1.7	1.9	1.9
High-income economies	1.2	1.7	1.6	1.5	1.9	1.9
Developing economies	5.3	4.9	4.3	4.3	4.9	5.1
Low-income economies	6.5	6.1	4.5	5.3	6.3	6.6
BRICS	5.7	5.1	3.8	4.2	5.1	5.3
Emerging market and developing economies (EMDEs)	4.7	4.2	3.4	3.5	4.4	4.7
World	2.4	2.6	2.4	2.4	2.8	3
Regions/Economies						
Europe and Central Asia	2.3	1.8	−0.1	1.2	2.5	2.8
Latin America and the Caribbean	2.9	1	−0.7	−1.3	1.2	2.1
Middle East and North Africa	2	2.9	2.6	2.9	3.5	3.6
Sub-Saharan Africa	4.8	4.5	3	2.5	3.9	4.4
East Asia and Pacific	7.1	6.8	6.5	6.3	6.2	6.1
South Asia	6.1	6.8	7	7.1	7.2	7.3

Source: Reproduced with permission of World Bank

of the global economy[5] – certainly nothing that anyone is looking forward to. Business confidence is lower, manufacturing is "quiet," and rapid changes in this environment are causing many supply chain executives to scratch their heads and wonder how to deal with an economy that is at best subdued. Hopes that the Trans-Pacific Partnership might boost production due to removal of the more than 18,000 taxes on American exports were dashed when President Trump withdrew from the agreement. There are increasing signs that the once-popular trend toward open borders and globalization is moving toward regionalization and protectionism (Table 1.1).[6]

Increased complexity in the global economy is adding another layer of malaise to supply chain executives. As customers are increasingly demanding "customized" solutions, companies are forced to produce in smaller quantities, leading to what is known as "mass customization." Increased regionalization of

---

5 Siegfried, M., "2016: A Year of Transitions," *Inside Supply Management*, January 2016, pp. 22–24, http://www.worldbank.org/en/publication/global-economic-prospects
6 https://scm.ncsu.edu/blog/2016/07/08/the-growing-fragmentation-of-global-trade-guest-post-by-tim-barnes/

product regulations and even localization requirements are driving increased scrutiny of shipments across borders, as well as new packaging and traceability requirements. The move toward e-commerce and shipments to end consumers via Amazon and Ali Baba is driving smaller packages, increasing congestion on city streets due to more deliveries, and escalating the potential for logistical malfunctions. How will companies survive?

One approach that many companies have sought in order to reduce risk in this environment is to *outsource* to third parties like Flex. Outsourcing involves divesting your company of processes that once were done internally, and have, them done by third-party suppliers. Because Flex works as a contract manufacturer across 18 of the largest global industries, it essentially acts as an absorber of global risk for many customers, including Apple, Ford, Amazon, and others. On the other hand, this structure also provides companies like Flex with the power of global insight. Each of the 12 verticals to which Flex contributes represents more than $1 billion in business. But, this value only represents the cost of goods sold for the end customer; since brands in electronics and other industries often mark up their products, the real revenue impact is often two, three, or four times higher. In each one of these business segments, Flex typically has 30–50 customers and often builds the newer technology products that, while cutting edge, require low-cost manufacturing in order to maintain market-friendly pricing.

As a result, Flex can triangulate across operations strategies, geographic strategies, and product strategies like no other company. It also can begin to predict how technologies, consumer behavior, supply chain innovations, or digitalization that are emerging in one sector – say the consumer products segment – may appear in automotive or medical products tomorrow. For example, who ever thought people could one day play music in their cars from their portable phones?

Learning More About Flex: A New Business Model

In his role as Flex's chief supply chain officer, Tom Linton runs an end-to-end supply chain. But end-to-end *really* means end-to-end – including customer-facing flows, supplier and material-facing flows, and all the sourcing and logistics in between. One organization manages all of it – because all these processes have to be so tightly linked. This is tricky, because non-disclosure agreements between customers may prevent Flex from spanning boundaries in the business with other customers who are their competitors!

Flex's supply chain organization controls sourcing on electrical, direct, and indirect procurement, and also oversees all materials at over 120 global site locations, including all the intellectual property, inventory, cash cycle, days sales outstanding, days payable outstanding, and the entire financial workflow of the organization. When their Chief Supply Chain Officer (Linton) presents to leadership, he is effectively talking to them about managing the balance sheet and the income statement, as well as supporting incoming revenue.

The biggest advantage of this level of oversight is that it allows Linton to align organizational capability and financial outcomes with procurement and supply chain strategy. In so many supply chains, the different pieces of the supply chain are often misaligned. Information systems have, for years, tried to "integrate" these disparate pieces, but this has still resulted in misalignment of decisions, primarily for political reasons. Every function has its own agenda, its own performance measures, and its own culture, and operates in a silo. Installing an ERP system to "Integrate" these parts does little to address these disparities.

Linton puts it this way: "All of the pieces, for the first time in my career, are fully aligned. I'm fortunate that Flex is an organization that readily welcomes change and adaption to a change ecosystem, and is able to attract and retain very talented people because of that. It is like a big chiropractic alignment, and when it happens, it is truly the secret sauce of successful organizations, versus those that remain functionally aligned with functional strategies that aren't aligned. We have true visibility to all financial flows, which ensures that we are profitable."

The Milpitas site that we visited later that morning was the location for much of the R&D in the company. We were traveling to Building 2, where many of the prototyping and new technology start-ups were experimenting with prototype and design-scaling efforts. Once these new processes are developed, Flex scales them up in different parts of the world – Brazil, China, Mexico, or wherever they are appropriate for a Flex customer.

Companies like Cisco, Microsoft, and Apple all have a huge market cap, but their manufacturing activities are unlimited. Flex manages all these activities for them, which means Flex must run a top-notch end-to-end supply chain. So even though you won't see a "Made by Flex" label on these companies' products, Flex is in the background, ensuring that everything is coming together. This is one reason that Flex and other contract manufacturers are emerging as the fabric of the emerging trend toward what Flex calls the "Intelligence of Things[TM]."

The other interesting anomaly is that "top 25" lists of the "best supply chains" at Gartner[7] often list these very companies: Fitbit, Amazon, Apple, Cisco, Nike, Inditex, Samsung, Intel, H&M, Lenovo, and others. Tom noted, "We manufacture for many of these companies, and actually hold a lot of their assets for them. So when Gartner measures the top supply chains, one of the criteria they use is the ratio of the company's revenues to its assets. All these companies are asset-light – because Flex is holding their inventory for them!"

---

7 http://www.gartner.com/technology/supply-chain/top25.jsp

Now my interest was really piqued. Flex and others like them hold a lot of the inventory and material and manage the shipping flows for these big companies. How does that work? How can one company manage so many supply chain processes and so many customers?

A Brief History of Supply Chain Management (The New Rules of LIVING Supply Chains)

The new Flex supply chain structure in this book is part of a massive evolution in today's supply chain world. These changes will occur sometimes quickly, sometimes slowly, but will undoubtedly come into being in the next decade. The changes we write about in this book are not just about technology – they are about true evolution, in a biological sense. In fact, many of the changes we are seeing have been captured in a set of statements we call the "Rules of LIVING Supply Chains." These new rules are aligned with many of the rules that dictate how species, human beings, and genetics have evolved, and represent a natural, rather than a radical evolution. They are occurring because the world of global trade is reshaping the way we operate. In a sense, this world has reached the limits of growth. The new rules will require a new set of management approaches, as the traditional approaches to managing the supply chain will no longer apply.

To understand this, a brief history lesson is in order. Supply chain management as a field continued to evolve as large organizations saw the need for dedicated functions responsible for management of materials, which included purchasing raw materials, managing manufacturing processes, and moving materials (logistics). The mid-1960s witnessed a dramatic growth of, and interest in, the materials management concept. Still, the concept's origins date to the 1800s. Organizing under the materials management concept was common during the latter half of the 19th century in the US railroads, which combined related functions such as purchasing, inventory control, receiving, and stores under the authority of one individual.

External events directly affected the operation of the typical firm. The Vietnam War, for example, resulted in rising price and material availability pressures. During the 1970s, firms experienced material problems related to oil "shortages" and embargoes. The logical response of industry was to become more efficient, particularly in the purchase and control of materials. Widespread agreement existed about the primary objective of the materials concept and the functions that might fall under the materials umbrella. The overall objective of materials management was to solve materials problems from a total system cost perspective rather than from the viewpoint of individual functions or activities. Functions that fell under the materials umbrella included material planning and control, inventory planning and control, materials and procurement research, purchasing, incoming traffic, receiving, incoming quality control, stores, materials movement, and scrap and surplus disposal.

Rob Handfield witnessed the evolution of the management field now known as "supply chain management" as a young assistant professor at Michigan State University (MSU). Handfield was part of a group called the Global Procurement Benchmarking Initiative, led by Dr. Robert Monczka. During his time at Michigan State (1992–1999), the GPBI benchmarked more than 300 global companies, and set forth many of what became known as the principles of "World Class Procurement." Many of these principles became the foundation for consulting practices at Accenture, Deloitte, Booz Allen, and others. At the time, these principles were appropriate. The idea was that procurement needed to establish a position not just as a "buyer of stuff," but as a centralized function that tabulated spending across both direct and indirect categories of spending, leveraged this volume through purchase power, and sought to achieve significant cost improvement. Business consultants also began looking at procurement as a vehicle for measuring supplier performance, improving suppliers through development activities that needed help, and acknowledging that some relationships with suppliers needed to be more strategic than others. As purchasing became more efficient, the term "strategic sourcing" was coined, which involved combining volumes of requirements from across the business, grouping them into large bids that went out to suppliers, and driving down costs due to larger quantity discounts achieved. This also led to the use of "reverse auctions," in which suppliers would bid on these quantities online. In logistics, the focus became on centralizing distribution centers and warehouses to drive optimization in transportation routing and reduce inventory across the system.

Many of the traditional concepts that evolved from this perspective of "driving cost of materials lower" focused on increasing the efficiency of operations in the supply chain from supplier to end customer. Many of these principles also coincided with the introduction of "lean manufacturing," based on the "just-in-time" thinking pioneered by the likes of Toyota. For example, the "Theory of Constraints"[8] emphasized that to optimize an end-to-end system, "bottlenecks" had to be addressed by adding capacity at this operation. "Just-in-time" and "lean manufacturing" focused on standardizing products, improving coordination between different enterprises to reduce inventory, and only delivering the exact amount needed, in quantities that could be immediately consumed by the follow-on operation.

Another group at MSU, led by Dr. Donald Bowersox, also spurred new thinking on the "Logistics Renaissance," proclaiming that the role of logistics was to add value and drive market penetration through technology integration. All the

---

8 Goldratt, E., *The Goal*, 2nd ed., North River Press, Great Barrington, MA, 1992.

work done in this period highlighted many important issues, encapsulated in a "maturity model" that identified how organizations could develop these capabilities over time toward a truly "world class supply chain" organization.

However, "world class" still emphasized distinctions in the field. Purchasing, operations, and logistics were still viewed as disparate functions, and arguments broke out over which area should dominate. The three groups involved in these activities (purchasing, operations, and logistics) were lumped together as "supply chain" functions, but never stopped working independently of one another. Professional disputes emerged among the logistics, operations, and purchasing trade associations over who was really in control of the supply chain; purchasing felt they were calling the shots, while logistics professionals claimed that they had oversight over all movement of material in the chain. All the while, they claimed to be driving "world class procurement" or "world class logistics" practices, implying that these practices are the best of the best. "Technology integration" was intended to bring these groups together; however, lingering tensions, discontinuities, and waste in the end-to-end supply chain of many organizations still exist. Sure, they could buy things more efficiently and ship things more efficiently – but were they really linked? Hardly.

In the end, there are some real problems with the "world class" view of the supply chain. Although transactional excellence and efficiency is certainly an operative element that forms the basis for excellence, there is a shift away from the idea that "world class" applies to every situation. A supply chain executive at BP stated this very well: "World class is simply a set of tools on a tool belt – but the real wave of change involves understanding the business well enough to apply the tools that will drive a total cost view of end-to-end value stream. Supply chain analysts are too focused on getting an answer that is cost-optimized, rather than focusing on an outcome. And a centralized world-class solution is not always appropriate in every operation globally, because a single model may not work for every small, medium, and large operation. And so we need to approach the problem with a different tool belt, and be ready to use a number of different tools depending on the different business drivers and geographic components that are in play in different situations."

So, if "world-class supply chain management" is no longer the objective, what is the next generation of supply chains going to look like? To answer this, it is important to emphasize that managing supply chains is no longer just about cost optimization, but about deep understanding of the components of customer value, and making decisions quickly in response to sudden shifts in customers' requirements. While cost optimization may well be one element of this equation, value has many meanings. Managing the supply chain first and foremost requires that managers act as internal consultants who spend most of their days listening closely, not just to the explicit needs of internal customers for materials, information, services, knowledge, and capability, but also to the intangible elements customers need. In a sense, real-time supply chains involve understanding and predicting what internal users and customers will need right now, even before they themselves recognize that they need it. And velocity/speed is an integral capability that requires quick response to customer needs to create the right capability.

The New Rules of the LIVING Supply Chain

Attention to speed and velocity is also an idea promulgated by evolutionary economics and biologists, who emphasize that organisms and creatures that are quick to respond will evolve more quickly, and will survive. Those who don't will die out. One of the best books to cover this concept is "The Serengeti Rules" by biologist Sean Carroll. Carroll explains how and why entire ecosystems can get "sick" when the populations of certain members are too low or too high. In fact, these rules provide an excellent set of guidelines for thinking about how supply chains operate as an ecosystem; instead of applying the rules to animals or biological entities, we have applied them to enterprises. In this manner, we propose the idea of a "LIVING" supply chain as one of a set of networked enterprises that are subject to biological rules.

Biologists have observed that systems of animals, birds, insects, and bacteria depend on one another for survival, and in fact can be characterized as "food webs" (Carroll, p. 39). An example of one of such food web links nitrogen, bacteria, plants, spiders, gulls, dung, puffins, arctic foxes, polar bears, seals, and other animals based on observations by Charles Elton in the 1920s. Elton visited the Arctic Islands and created a "food-cycle" schematic that showed the interconnected set of chains and webs that existed between species on the Bear Island (see Figure 1.2).[9] In this figure, one can trace the chain that begins with nitrogen and bacteria at the upper left, and traces the link all the way through land birds, which provide food for the arctic fox. Other scientists (Smith, Hairton, and Slobodkin, going by the acronym of HSS) suggested that there are four general "trophic levels" of biological communities[10]: decomposers (fungi and worms), producers (plants and algae), herbivores (birds, insects, etc.), and carnivores (sharks lions, etc.). In this framework, the well-known HSS hypothesis emerged that "predators regulate herbivore populations," and that the removal of predators can lead to an explosion in herbivore populations. The reverse has also been shown to be true: Sea otters "induce" the growth of kelp by repressing the population of sea urchins. Other examples of "trophic cascades" include bass–minnows–algae, wolves–moose–fir trees, and armadillos–leafcutter ants–trees.

---

9 Carroll, S., *The Serengeti Rules*, Princeton University Press, 2016, p. 39.
10 Hairston, N., Smith, F., and Slobodkin, L., "Community Structure, Population Control, and Competition," *The American Naturalist*, vol. 94, no. 879, November/December 1960, pp. 421–425.

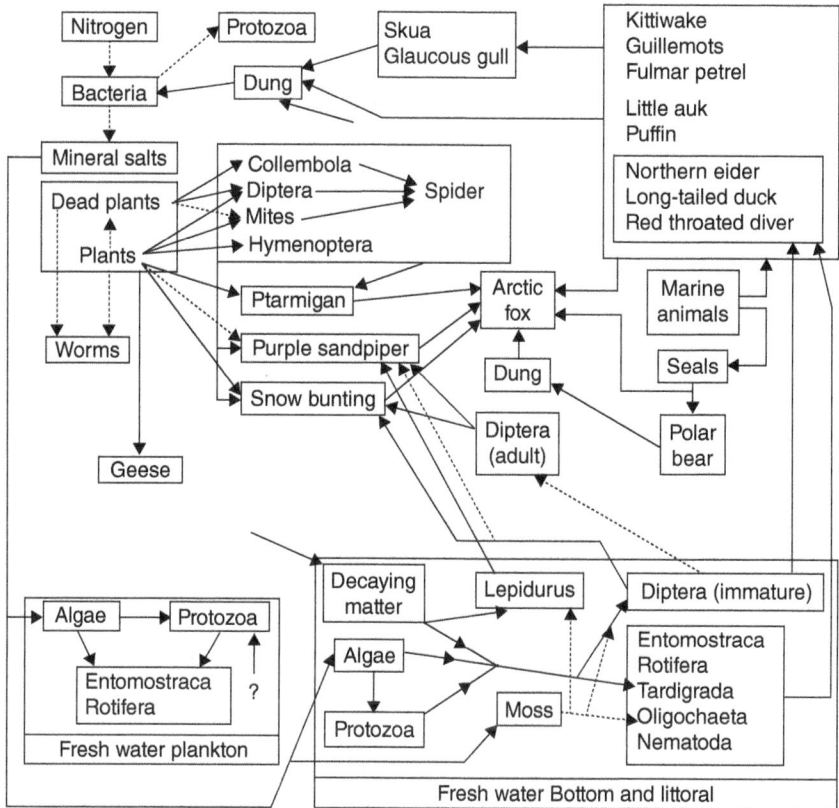

Figure 1.2 Charles Elton Figure of the Arctic Island Food System. *Source:* Reproduced with permission of Princeton University Press

These observations comprise the elements of the *Serengeti Rule 1* summarized by Sean Carroll in the book by the same name:

Serengeti Rule 1: Not all species are equal. This rule proposes that some species exert effects on the stability and diversity of their community that are disproportionate to their numbers or biomass. These are termed "keystone species" based on the magnitude of their influence on the food chain.

We have applied this biological rule to create a rule for the emerging supply chain network ecosystem.

New Supply Chain Rule 1: Not all enterprises are equal. Firms that adopt more quickly by embracing *real-time data, velocity, transparency, and rapid response* to change in the ecosystem will adapt more quickly, and will survive. Those that do not adopt these principles will become extinct. Hyper-reactive and predictive supply chains have a competitive advantage.

Companies need to influence their supply chains as a responsibility. Every company has a supply chain and they need to know their position in it and play their position.

Why is velocity and real-time transparency so important in the supply chain? There are many reasons, but an anecdote Tom told me in our first meeting made it very clear.

> I was driving alone, stuck in traffic when the three lanes of the 101 were blocked, with an empty HOV lane next to me. There was a fifth lane used by police cars and fire trucks, who ripped off toward the accident which was blocking the highway. I wasn't allowed to use the HOV or police lanes, but it suddenly made me think: rather than trying to weave in and out of traffic in the blocked lanes, it would be much faster to get into a lane that is moving quickly, which would mean adding a passenger. And the analogy was clear: rather than focusing on how to optimize the constraint through lean manufacturing and six sigma, why not just change the game so you can move quickly? And if you focus on speed by thinking differently, then you can go around constraints and won't have to pass through them. So now when people come to my office and tell me about some supply chain problem they're having, my response is to just keep the momentum, switch to the HOV lane, and move quickly around the problem!

This analogy points out a simple concept: in the new global era, *speed and velocity are more important than everything else!* Speed drives business value and inventory turns, reduces working capital, produces cash (monetizes) assets, and makes customers happy, which in turn further drives top line revenue (see Table 1.2). Supply chain optimization typically involves turning the knobs on a supply chain design that is broken. But creation of real-time supply chains provide a means for creating value that the customer cares about, and in today's rapid environment, velocity has customer value. Late deliveries, substandard quality, safety incidents, damaged shipments, and multiple other problems do not alleviate the benefits offered to a customer for lower price, as many logisticians and planners will tell you. In many cases, speed not only reduces costs – it also creates customer value (Table 1.2).

To summarize, companies with speed enabled by real-time visibility will see improved customer satisfaction. What customer doesn't want his or her product more quickly? Speed also reduces costs, as agility and nimbleness allow companies to move quickly to address situations that may end up costing them a lot of money. Speed also reduces inventory, as working capital moves more quickly, and reduces obsolescence and excess inventory. Inventory is a substitute for lead time, so as lead time shrinks, so does inventory. Finally, speed frees up cash flow in a firm's global operations. Companies with more cash flow can reinvest in the business, acquire another company, or buy their stock. All these

Table 1.2 Speed Wins! Pros and Cons of Speed

Pros	Cons
Customer satisfaction improves as revenue is increased	Quality issues may occur through speed
Profits rise as more goods are produced	Growth is challenging
Assets move faster; improving drives productivity	Risk of making the wrong decision
Net working capital and free cash flow improve	Requires increased information visibility which may be perceived as risky

outcomes make the company stronger, and more able to withstand the challenges of the global ecosystem. As predicted by the New Supply Chain Rule 1, enterprises with higher velocity are not equal to slower companies; they are stronger, more nimble, in better financial health, and growing by leaps and bounds, while the slower firms will slowly go extinct (similar to the health of keystone species as defined in Serengeti Rule 1).

Amazon's Flywheel Effect

One company that "gets this" more than any other is Amazon. Amazon not only developed the world's largest online marketplace, but has moved to create features like Amazon Prime that promise free shipping in two days. Speed is continually being improved on, as Amazon seeks to create same-day shipping capabilities, to make customer satisfaction even faster. In his book *The Amazon Way*, John Rossman writes about the "flywheel effect."[11] This effect is the opposite of the "bullwhip effect," a traditional supply chain "theory" that states that rational decision-making based on limited human views of phenomena drive excess inventory in the chain. The flywheel effect is a core element in the rise of Amazon. John Rossman notes, "Allen Mandelbrot founded the field of fractal mathematics, which studies, among other phenomena, how patterns in nature have a tendency to repeat themselves at different scales – for example, the way spiral galaxies resemble whirling sea shells which in turn resemble tiny unfurling fern fronds. In a similar fractal fashion, the virtuous cycle is replicated throughout Amazon.com at macro and micro levels. It generates a set of self-reinforcing energies that continue to flow even when the energy source is discontinuous – much like a flywheel, which is the favorite metaphor for this phenomenon at Amazon." (p. 8)

---

11 Rossman, J., *The Amazon Effect*, 2nd ed., CreateSpace Independent Publishing Platform, May 9, 2014.

The flywheel is a metaphor for the emphasis on speed and velocity of decision-making driving flow and interàctive speed, or the "anti-control tower" phenomenon. Supply chains are proposed to flow to the point of least resistance, very much like the Chinese proverb that states that cost, like water, will always flow to the lowest point. Similarly, supply chains will always find the fastest way. Route maps have evolved into works of lean architecture in which time is treated as waste, as waste equals cost. The impact of new, responsive supply chains, especially around interactive objects and the "Uber-ization of trucking" poses a radical threat to traditional premium services such as UPS and FedEx, which were founded on traditional point-to-point supply chains with large discontinuities.

Visibility Drives Velocity

Two key concepts reflect the core elements of real-time supply chains. Velocity is the ability of an organization to enable the flow of working capital rapidly through its end-to-end supply chain. Working capital generally comes in the form of inventory, which is an asset that doesn't produce any revenue or cash. Thus, the object of the real-time supply chain is to achieve velocity in every aspect of how companies run their business. This includes how inventory is tracked and monitored, how much to produce, how much to ship, what modes of transportation to use, how to organize distribution, how to move product through logistics systems, and most importantly, how quickly people in all areas of the supply chain (suppliers, distributors, customers) are able to react and make decisions related to unexpected events and disruptions that impact the supply chain. This is defined by a simple set of principles:

• Real-time data increases visibility
• Increased visibility results in improved velocity
• Velocity increases flow and decreases friction
• Visibility increases prediction accuracy

The key to enabling the ability to have velocity is through visibility – defined as the relative transparency of events, material, and flows to all key decision-makers in the extended supply chain. Visibility allows individuals to see what is going on, and in empowered ways, allows these individuals to interpret information and rapidly make decisions in response to data. The opposite of visibility is opacity, which refers to a complete lack of visibility regarding what is happening in one's upstream and downstream network. When individuals have visibility that results in velocity of decisions, the system becomes frictionless. Speed of decisions increases not just the flow of information, but also the flow of materials, shipments, production, and all activities in the chain. This reduces friction, which increases flow. Friction includes all the typical delays and problems that slow flow and cause inventory to build up. This includes multiple layers of approvals, delays in decisions until more information becomes available, or even operating as normal when a major disruption has occurred unbeknownst to you. It can produce bottlenecks in production systems and shipments, which delays material and causes inventory to build.

These principles are not new. Many of the concepts around "lean production systems" emphasize flow and visibility. However, in the context of the digitization of the supply chain, these concepts have a new meaning and impact. It is also the case that many organizations have invested in very expensive systems called "control towers." In a control tower, information from all of an organization's logistics systems, production facilities, inbound shipments, outbound shipments, and inventory levels are dumped into a massive data warehouse. The information is then centralized into a "control tower," where individuals scan what is going on, and senior executives "call the shots," sometimes using complicated algorithms and automated ordering systems. The fundamental assumption behind control towers is that the people at the top "know best" on how to optimize the entire supply chain, because they are the only ones who have access to all the data. Much of the data pulled are from ERP systems, transportation management systems (TMSs), warehouse management systems (WMSs), distribution requirement systems (DRPs), and material requirement planning systems (MRPs). Because many of these systems are in a "batch mode," which means they are updated on a weekly, or perhaps daily basis, the information being viewed in the control tower is always lagging. As a result, decision-makers in the control tower are making decisions based on what happened a few days ago, and are determining what to do next, based on what they think will happen next. This scenario embodies the "old" themes of "supply chain integration": batch processing, information updates, "control-tower" thinking where only some people see the information, and decisions requiring signoffs by the "higher ups." Linton notes that

> Real time supply chains are the anti-control tower. Real-time visibility of information is a driver of velocity, and the two are linked in business and the supply chain. Think about visibility in the context of driving your car. If you are watching your speedometer, you don't want information on your vehicle's velocity from a week ago, an hour ago, or even a minute ago. You want to know how fast you are moving right now! The same principle applies to the supply chain. To make informed decisions based on insight pulled from data, we need the data to be as fresh and as current as possible! In this way visible real-time information drives increased supply chain speed.

Traditional enterprise software accumulates silos of data. Managers call upon this data and pull it up in reports that can be used to make decisions. It provides information in chunks or batches, which, by definition, are historical. In fact, almost all decisions in current supply chain systems are based on information about things that happened in the past. It's as if your car speedometer told you how fast you were going yesterday. This is our current scenario. We know how much we quoted, sourced, contracted, and paid yesterday. What if we could make all our decisions in real time? What would happen to our performance if we had data in real time?

The opposite of flow is friction. Friction occurs when layers of decision-making are introduced into a process, slowing it down. Friction also includes disruptive events, or workers that don't feel empowered to make a difference in their operation, or who feel pressured to say and do things that they don't agree with. Flow is not just about material, it is about the enablement of individuals who work in the entire supply chain to contribute their ideas, thoughts, and observations to their work, with the end customer in mind, and who are allowed to provide feedback and shape the outcome in a positive way.

Visibility is only possible to the extent it is today because of the evolution of technology. Clearly, the establishment of the Internet led to the explosion of information and the subsequent supply chain tools and applications that are now harvesting data, and leading to the evolution of "cognitive" computing. But the disruption has not yet fully matured; in fact, it is only beginning. As organizations begin to operate entities that mediate impacts that are upstream and downstream, the power of this force will become evident as those companies who understand how to deploy this approach survive and thrive.

I had heard this sentiment 20 years ago, when I was working at Michigan State. At the time, Dave Nelson, the CPO of Honda, shared with me a vision that stayed with me for many years.

> Think of the number of individuals working in Honda's supply base. Say it's 20,000 people. What if we were able to get each of those 20,000 individuals to go to work every day, and be thinking about how to make Honda's products more innovative, how to improve quality, how to improve flow, and how to be more efficient at doing it? Think of the collective power that resides in the gray matter between the ears of 20,000 individuals, all working toward making Honda better! How can we harness that force!

As those organizations who grasp the viability of this approach expand their approach to influence the ecosystem, the ecosystem will thrive. Enabling people through visibility drives velocity which drives flow. But do people intervene when friction is present? It depends.

Changes Driving LIVING Supply Chains

A focus on speed is essential to the real-time supply chain. Every action should be focused on driving increased velocity of materials through the system.

Linton notes "I tell my people, if you wake up and go to work, and are confused as to what you should focus on that day – focus on speed. Speed will drive all other financial benefits that we need to be paying attention to. It will drive up customer satisfaction, as customers get their products sooner, and get new innovations that come to market sooner. It will drive out excess inventory, and improve our balance sheet. And it will speed up our cash-to-cash cycle, which makes our shareholders happy."

Tom recalls that this wasn't always the case. "This is my fifth year at Flex," he said. "When I arrived, lead-times were in excess of 40 days, in some cases. We set a goal for everyone of getting our lead times to under one month. Through our real-time information efforts, we've cut many lead-times by 25% or more. Because the focus in the electronics industry is on shipping everything at the end of the quarter, production is always heavier at the end of the quarter. But if you think of a quarter being only 12 weeks, and recognize that the material can drive 75% or more of your revenue, you need to plan lead times with the ability to pull material quickly. We have a big problem if they don't align. Speed is essential when moving materials. If the material is not in a supplier management inventory (SMI) hub or Kan Ban, we can't get material in time to drive revenue. The opposite of this kind of integration is guessing what you think the customer is going to do, and when they don't do it, you are stuck holding all this inventory. So velocity is the only way to be agile."

Important issues follow from the principle of emphasizing speed in all areas of the supply chain.

1. The first is that the *centralized control tower is giving way to a new layer of capabilities.* It's now a mistake to "control" a supply chain – which by definition means to introduce a series of decisions that limit its performance. We need to rethink what we mean by control towers; so we add visibility to increase velocity and not add decision-making gates to slow things down. Supply chains are become more virtually vertical, which means that as we become more reliant on our partners, we need to create a virtual form of vertical integration. This boils down to dramatically increasing the connectivity we have with companies in our supply chain. If you look around, there is a flattening of labor costs, which means that the only way to drive down total cost is through regionalization, through regional or local sourcing. This also drives down an organization's carbon footprint, by reducing transportation output. Whole Foods has the same idea when they use regional sources of produce, seafood, and meat.

2. The second big change that is coming is that *cloud computing is becoming the singular most important component of running a global supply chain.* Cloud computing is allowing something very special to happen, which I like to call business process convergence. In the past, we automated separate business processes that were each operating with one another based on commercial

invoices, purchase orders, and transactional documents. As these automated processes now start to link with one another in the cloud, these traditional transactional documents become obsolete. If you have a strategic supplier with a life-long contract to produce for you, and you know how much you are paying them per unit of output, why do you need a purchase order? You simply pay them electronically as products are shipped in the chain.

Cloud computing allows for the various steps in the business process to be linked in a single view, from multiple companies in multiple devices (mobile). As Cloud computing gets faster and software is developed to optimize for intercompany transactions, supply chains will find new ways to add layers of transparency to traditional business processes.

3. The third big change is that labor arbitrage will no longer be relevant, and that raw material costs and oil prices will eventually go back up. When this occurs, proximity will gain new advantages as commodities held up in long global supply chains will cause balance sheets and other logistics costs to rise. Global labor costs are quickly becoming regionalized, in that manufacturing will increasingly also become regionalized. That's why we believe manufacturing to satisfy demand in North America will return here, as manufacturing for China and Asia will stay over there. The same scenario will hold for the European continent. Because all labor costs will eventually become equal, we are running out of places to find lower cost labor. By the same token, there is a limited quantity of raw materials, whether you are talking about rare earths, metals, or precious metals. Because of the growth in population, demand will go back up, there will be scarcity, and costs will go up. We are in a "golden time" of low oil and commodity prices – but it is only a matter of time before they go up. Our only solution in the end will be to find alternative raw material sources, including bio-based fuel and other products, as well as substituting things like aluminum for copper. But this will take time and engineering.

4. The fourth big change is that *unpredictability is the only thing that is predictable*. Risk is always present and will introduce itself in unpredictable ways. Which means that we need to be more influenced by the use of tools that respond to unpredictability. Tom said, "I recently spoke at MIT and I challenged the engineers to come up with algorithmic models that could better forecast disasters. Now once they occur, we are able to react quickly within less than 24 hours. But forecasting when and where these disasters will occur is impossible. But what we can do is to build models that can tell us the disabling network impact of ANY disaster – something called the "Kill Shot." I'll talk more about that later. In our opinion, the focus on disaster response is like quality was 30 years ago. People are trying to predict where problems will occur – and it is pretty much impossible using the standard

probabilistic models that we are applying today. It is like trying to improve product quality by inspecting every PC we made, instead of designing products for quality.

5. The rise of real-time information allows for enhanced predictability from live visibility. This is one of the reasons Flex created the Flex Pulse Center. It is designed to create a model to take both physical and information latency out of the supply chain process by using real-time information around exception-based management to improve operational outcomes. The system should let you know when you are over your minimum order quantity – and creates a signal to the pulse center. This is like a tire pressure light on your car that only lights up when something is wrong. You have to be notified if there is a problem in your supply chain, whether it's a late delivery, a quality spill, a capacity problem, a transportation delay, a holdup at customs crossing a border, or even a major earthquake at a site. Your supply chain should run on an automated basis, and people are introduced into it only when needed.

6. The final big change we need is to overturn our entire cultural and psychological mindset when it comes to the supply chain. I recently read *Non-Zero* by Robert Wright, which I consider one of the most important books of the decade. It starts with a premise that the world is NOT moving to a zero-sum game, but to a non-zero sum outcome. For example, when a tribe of Inuit people killed a whale for food, they shared it with all the other tribes. All the tribes were trying to survive, so they formed alliances and states, worked together, and were able to march through time together based on collaboration. I started thinking about it – we need to adopt non-zero approaches to supplier management, if we are all to survive. But then I thought: collaboration is good, but it needs to be in balance. And so you need to ask those you respect, and that deserve it, and that you can trust, to join your supply chain.

For the uninitiated, *Non-Zero* explores the non-zero concept behind game theory, which suggests that over the course of history, zero-sum games are not as common as non-zero-sum games. In the latter case, non-zero-sum games involve collaboration between the parties in an eco-system, and emphasize how parties that work together – whether they're cells from multicellular organisms, multi-village policies with centralized rules, or hunter–gatherer societies – tend to mutually benefit. Wright has a positive view of the world, and suggests that positive correlations in non-zero-sum games produces two winners, and that this occurs in economics a good deal. Wright does not deny the existence of exploitation, but is intrinsically upbeat on history moving more toward win–win than win–lose. This is a fundamental concept underlying the LIVING supply chain. Unless organisms work together as a network with full information, applying this characteristic we call "trust," survival in a complex, constantly changing world is not possible.

This doesn't mean that you don't compete hard to win. When the ocean supply chain (plankton, fish, sharks, and other predators) is all in balance, it is beautiful. But when you take out one of the predators in the chain, it gets all screwed up, and fish and sharks start to starve and die out. So you need a balanced supply chain, and when you are in a balanced set of relationships, you will all survive.

The Big Change: Driving the Need for Real Time

An increasingly common set of discussions also revolves around the digitization and active tracking of product and materials in the network – and not just in the boardroom at Flex. In conversations with several executives at other companies, we discussed the increasing focus on the digitization of supply chains that were moving toward becoming live, fast, and intelligent. We have also presented this theme in several public and private forums, where the conversation inevitably turns to the need to understand the Internet of Things, in which smart and connected objects are driving the digitization of the supply chain. Here are a few examples:

- John Deere has formed an Enterprise Analytics Leadership Council which seeks to build a strategy for analytics for the enterprise, to provide leadership across the enterprise for analytics, and to identify opportunities for adopting analytics techniques.
- Continental is discussing how automobiles will increasingly be automated and connected to the Internet, resulting in an era of driverless vehicles.
- Drone technology is being explored for logistics, inspection of pipelines, and an increasing number of tasks.
- IBM is rolling out cognitive analytics as a base for creating Watson Buyer Assistant, BlueHound, and other technologies for assisting and eventually replacing procurement buyers.

Clearly something bigger is going on here. The role of supply chains is becoming increasingly important in what we believe is our next industrial revolution. The World Economic Forum is calling digitization the Fourth Industrial Revolution.[12] They characterize it as follows:

---

12 http://www.weforum.org/agenda/2016/01/the-fourth-industrial-revolution-what-it-means-and-how-to-respond

The First Industrial Revolution used water and steam power to mech-anize production (~1784). The Second used electric power to create mass production (~1870). The Third used electronics and information technology to automate production (~1969). Now a Fourth Industrial Revolution is building on the Third, and is producing the digital revolution that has been occurring since the middle of the last century. It is characterized by a fusion of technologies that is blurring the lines between the physical, digital, and biological spheres. ... The possibilities of billions of people connected by mobile devices, with unprecedented processing power, storage capacity, and access to knowledge, are unlim-ited. And these possibilities will be multiplied by emerging technology breakthroughs in fields such as artificial intelligence, robotics, the Internet of Things, autonomous vehicles, 3D printing, nanotechnol-ogy, biotechnology, materials science, energy storage, and quantum computing.

But how will this revolution impact multi-enterprise networks of organizations working in the supply chain? How did this digitization manifest itself? The idea, of course was compelling, but how to operationalize this big, fuzzy concept into practical approaches? This is what the analytics council at Deere and other companies were trying to figure out.

Linton thought hard about what was going on here in our discussion at the Pulse Center.

We are at an inflection point in the history of the field. Real-time will change the way we think about operating in a global economy, and how we produce things and interact with them in the digital world. The new supply chain is an interdisciplinary system that is driven by real-time information, and which will transform the way companies operate with one another. We need to make people aware of the importance of how real-time data and information will interact with managers of the future. We want them to think about velocity, not about statistical process con-trol, lean manufacturing, or the theory of constraints. This will also require a new kind of manager – one who is much more savvy about working with data and who is comfortable gleaning information from multiple sources of information.

This was the thinking that led us to begin this book. To begin to think about how digitization can be exploited to drive competitive value, we have concluded that the "intelligent" piece of the real-time supply chain needs to be combined with a number of other cultural values within the organization and with the upstream and downstream supply chain network. A good acronym that captures these concepts is the LIVING supply chain, which forms the basis for the remaining chapters in this book.

Characteristics of the LIVING Supply Chain

The principles of the LIVING supply chain embody this book's key themes:

Live: Do you have a real-time (LIVE) view of your information?

Intelligent: Are you able to connect the essential leverage points in your network through cloud, mobile, and other mediums to provide a platform for analytics? Can you track the DNA of your supply chain at a part number level, globally? Can the system evolve to link the objects in your supply chain?

Velocity: Is your entire enterprise and network focused on moving assets faster than ever in its history?

Interactive: Is there a common governance structure that defines how observations are translated into issues, how they are monitored and validated, and how they are translated into specific actions and responses?

Networked: Is your multi-enterprise supply chain networked so that a common and aligned view of business priorities and actions corresponds to trusting relationships common to everyone?

Good: Is your network truly good, with a common cultural understanding that transcends borders and views as strong principles integrity, doing the right thing, and being transparent about your intentions and actions?

The idea of a LIVING network is a powerful metaphor for what is going on at Flex. Flex recognizes that the "Intelligence of Things," not the "Internet of Things," is the key driver for change in the new era. The Internet is just the utility that keeps data flowing in the system. The emergence of more automation, 3D printing, hyper regionalization, and omni-channel customer service needs will be explicitly considered within an organization's technology roadmap, with the implicit assumption that these technologies will bear fruit in the next 2–5 years. This is not an unreasonable assumption, as the World Economic Forum predicts a "supply-side miracle, with long-term gains in efficiency and productivity. Transportation and communication costs will drop, logistics and global supply chains will become more effective, and the cost of trade will diminish, all of which will open new markets and drive economic growth."

The idea of an organic, LIVING supply chain suggests that not only is the supply chain an evolving, living organism, but that every product, and indeed every worker who toils in our networked factories, suggests a part number and human genome with endless requirements for transparency, in the same manner that the mining of conflict minerals demands visibility to the nth level backward into our material supply chains.

What's Next?

The rain was still pouring down as we stepped out of the building that morning.

"Oh, and there is one more big change," Tom said. "We are going to need increasingly specialized skills for people working in the supply chain. Generalists won't cut it anymore. We need people who have deep knowledge of procurement, analytics, logistics, transportation, computer science, databases, and other unique skill sets. Because we can't teach people these things – they need to know what to do when they come out of school."

"But I also believe that the best soup has a lot of ingredients," he said. "Too much pepper, and it doesn't work. So I like to mix up students we hire from different schools, and like seeing people from different backgrounds and genders. Otherwise, if you are too similar in recruiting, you get a certain way of thinking that leads to bias. And in most cases you need people from different places – someone from North Carolina, someone from Brazil, someone from Eastern Europe. Skill-building is something I love to do. I just brought in an Eastern European I met in one of the sites to be my director of the Pulse Center. I gave him the title Vice President of Real Time! Let's go meet him!"

We walked out into the drizzle of what was supposed to be sunny California. The Super Bowl stadium was in the distance.

2

LIVE! Transparency as a Core Operating Value

This is the world we live in. If you are not real time, collaborative, mobile and multi-enterprise, you can't survive.

—Mike McNamara, *CEO, Flex*

The idea behind the Pulse Center is to enable people to have the RIGHT information in REAL time. It is about having the right information, the right parts, and the right deliveries available at the right time. And not all information needs to be broadcast in real-time. It depends – on what it is you need to know!

—Marcin Fic, *Vice President of Real Time, Flex*

Nothing about the Flex Innovation Center in Milpitas looked out of the ordinary. A flat-topped building, constructed like many of the other high-tech companies along the Santa Clara–Milpitas–Mountain View sprawl we drove through along the way. Our host noted that a Mexican restaurant that had just celebrated its 25-year anniversary had been recently knocked down to make room for expansion of Google's headquarters – but that this was nothing new.

As we walked into the building, we were greeted by a group of young women, one of whom was our tour guide for the day. We were introduced to a tall, bespectacled fellow, Marcin Fic, Vice President, Supply Chain Solutions, but whose preferred title is "Vice President of Real-Time." Tom had recruited Marcin from an Eastern European Flex site. Marcin worked at Flex for 14 years, originally at a Flex factory in Poland as a planning manager and later as a material director. He moved into the supply chain systems sector, seeking to align its business processes with the tool set for Europe. "I got the offer from Tom to come on as a global lead for all supply chain solutions at Flex, and then he proposed that I come out to San Jose," Marcin said. "He told me he was getting ready to make some big strategic and organizational changes, and that I needed to be close to the action if I wanted to get in on it. And I did!"

The LIVING Supply Chain: The Evolving Imperative of Operating in Real Time, First Edition. Robert Handfield and Tom Linton.

Figure 2.1 Flex Pulse Center. *Source:* Courtesy of Flex

When we arrived at Flex's offices, we were immediately taken into the "theater" area. There we were inundated by a 360-degree movie about the world of Flex, and the number of different markets and projects they work in. The closest thing to this experience was a 360 theater I'd been in at Disney World. Not surprisingly, Michael Mendenhall, Flex's Chief Marketing Officer, spent 17 years at Disney and believes in making the customer visit a true experience, complete with the brightly decorated Disney-like buses that take visitors between buildings.

Our next stop was the Pulse Center™, shown in Figure 2.1. The center was a means to connect all the parties at Flex to a centralized nerve center, to keep everyone up to speed on what was happening across Flex's network of 120 factories worldwide. As we walked into the Pulse Center, we saw a line of laptops and desks facing a large oval room, half of which was covered with large HDTV screens that spanned about 100 feet end-to-end. On the screens were a multitude of maps, charts, graphs, and other indicators. But these weren't regular TV screens – *they were touch* TV screens. Our guide could use her finger to move pictures around, double tap on a graph to "drill down" into the data on the screen for a closer look, and swirl them around – much like I'd seen in the latest *Star Wars* or *Star Trek* movie. This was almost too much for me to take in!

"All the screens you see are also available on mobile devices. In fact, 90% of the viewers aren't looking at this information through the central Pulse Center, but on their mobile devices. The idea is for anyone who is impacted by any global event in the world at any time to be able to see what's happening, comment or add to the information, or even write about what they see when they see something that is worth noting."

The year before, Francois Barbier, Group President of Operations at Flex, required that all IT departments shift to a mobile platform where anyone anywhere can access and use solutions in app form, regardless of whether they were in a Pulse Center.

The Vice President of Real Time explained this further:

> Think about Henry Ford when he designed the Model T production line. His emphasis was that people needed to have the parts available on the line at the exact time they were needed. The same goes for information. It's not about having batch-based systems and intermittent downloads of information in large quantities that no one can use. What people need to make effective decisions is the RIGHT data at the RIGHT time .... not ALL the data ALL of the time! We needed to design a system that was transparent, and that showed what was happening not just in our facilities, but also in our supplier's facilities. That spans not just production, but social responsibility issues, and a real-time feed that allows us to continually adapt to what is happening in our ecosystem. The data needs to be filtered to eliminate noise, translated into information and prioritized; only then we achieve the ultimate goal of accelerating decisions that impact supply chain performance.

In one of the screens, one of the managers showed us video feed of workers busily working in a factory. "Ideally, we'd have video feeds on all manufacturing lines. This would be the epitome of transparency and confirm that our expectations for compliance with workforce policies are met throughout the supply chain. We might want (in addition to all emergency actions around planning & procurement) to monitor whether a critical production line is running smoothly. Another example would be the case of a natural disaster; when there was a flood in Chennai, affecting our Global Business Services center, we were able to monitor the situation in and around the building, and see how high the water was in the facility!"

"The Pulse Center^{TM} is about having multiple forms of the right data come together in an integrated fashion, but it is critical that we decide what is critical for us to monitor and watch. That is what makes us able to evolve. In fact, the LIVING supply chain implies an ability to be able to evolve and adapt – which is very organic and central to the way that our supply chain can operate. Supply chain networks are inherently organic creatures. They are constantly changing. Suppliers are being added or removed, transportation of material is constantly flowing, workers are active, coming and going, and machines are moving and functioning and breaking down. A healthy supply chain is one that continues to evolve. An unhealthy supply chain is one that stops adapting, and goes dormant and static. If you aren't constantly changing then you aren't healthy – and that is the end of your business and your life."

"The idea of 'real-time' and 'transparency' are not always heard in the same sentence – but they are here at Flex. Transparency refers to the ability to bi-laterally exchange both data and qualitative information, to provide an open view of issues, data, current state status quo conditions, and potential future predictions of upcoming events. This ability to provide a 'window into the future' is a predictive capability, that is not always part of transparency, but which can occur. The digitization and technological developments in the field allow us to ensure that transparency occurs in real time, or as close to it as you can achieve."

Later that day when I returned from my tour, Tom added:

What's stunning about Flex Pulse is that our CIO Gus Shahin was able to take a simple design which I sketched on a piece of paper, and in the space of three months build something beyond my expectations. The basic idea I brought to our CEO was for a circular room that reached into every dimension of supply chain. We ended up compromising to a semicircle but the essential idea was to have a place where data could be pulled up from wherever it resided, and through its visibility drive improvements. We wanted to have our hands on the pulse, in real time of what was happening or about to happen around the world. Our initial goal was to start with asset velocity to drive inventory improvements, but that expanded rapidly to include other areas of the supply chain and the business.

In using Flex Pulse we find we are entering into the supply chain in a somewhat visceral way. When you start to touch and manipulate data to simulate scenarios, you start heading down a path where concepts around predictive and cognitive supply chains become real, and data *comes to life* in ways not possible in a world of batch-based reporting or managing.

The Second Rule of the LIVING Supply Chain

There is more evidence than ever that the "old rules" of "strategic supply chain management" are fading in a time when transparency is the new law of the land and collective innovation of enterprises in the global network is the driver for growth. In a single-digit growth world, companies like Flex are an anomaly. The company's focus on the balance sheet, and not just the price of products, has enabled it to produce cash from its balance sheet and buy back stock. Contract manufacturing is by definition a low-margin business, but the company is attractive because of its ability to manage working capital. Jim Cramer, host of CNBC's "Mad Money," has raved about the company's ability to co-innovate, its move into the "Intelligence of Things™," as well as its ability to produce cash.[1] And the reason behind this is the focus on *velocity*.

Amazon and Flex are doing something that others have not yet mastered – the ability to think strategically in terms of the entire supply chain, including their partners, and to work closely with these partners to drive collective growth and profitability. This approach is equivalent to another law of the Serengeti desert.

Serengeti Rule 2: Some species mediate strong indirect effects through trophic cascades. That is, some members of food webs have disproportionately strong (top-down) effects that ripple through communities and indirectly affect species at lower trophic levels.

New Supply Chain Rule 2: Enterprises that mediate indirect effects downward (and upward) in the supply chain by considering system effects will thrive. Those that do not will slow down and become extinct. We propose that in a supply chain, some enterprises mediate strong direct and indirect effects in the supply chain, and those companies are proliferating an approach to transparency and rapid response to events in the supply chain. By promulgating the ability to rapidly adapt to uncertainty and change in their ecosystem, they will ensure that other enterprises (creatures) that they depend on, and which depend on them, will mutually benefit and thrive. Those that continue to operate in a silo, and fail to view the supply chain as an ecosystem, will slow down and not be able to adapt.

A number of examples exist of this rule. Walmart is the obvious counterexample, as many have argued that Walmart exerts an undue but negative influence on smaller companies, due to its volume of business (10% of US retail business) and its fierce emphasis on reducing prices. Walmart has been criticized for reducing margins by imposing fees for using distribution centers and stores, and delaying payments to suppliers. Walmart's approach to squeezing price discounts from suppliers for future purchases has worked for many years, but the company has lately experienced slower growth and signs of attrition.[2] In 2016, it closed 269 stores, 154 in the United States, due to slowing growth.

On the other hand, organizations that have adopted an approach focused on visibility, real-time response, and digitization have seen rapid growth. Amazon is a leader in the retail space, and has grown significantly, through their revolutionized markets and online marketplace. In fact, we find that WalMart is now seeking to mimic Amazon, in the hopes of returning to its once-vaulted position as the dominant keystone species. Others that are seeing growth and

---

1 http://finance.yahoo.com/video/cramer-believe-flex-231500797.html
2 http://www.bloomberg.com/news/articles/2015-09-11/wal-mart-sparks-battle-with-suppliers-over-margin-squeezing-fees

influence through digitization and visibility include Apple, which drive many different software platforms and app developers, as well as Facebook, which dominates much of social media and online advertising. Flex is also a firm that is seeing major growth through its approach to digitization and virtually integrated supply chains.

Coase and Williamson Wouldn't Like This One Bit!

If the concept of complete transparency as a corporate value is difficult for you to swallow, you're not alone. The transparency concept conflicts with many of the traditional theoretical foundations of inter-organizational behavior.

One of the pioneers of inter-organizational behavior theory was the economist Ronald Coase, who wrote *The Theory of the Firm* in 1937, while working on his doctorate at the London School of Economics. When he wrote the book, no one paid attention – economists were more interested in supply, demand, and the impact of prices in the market. After bouncing around England at several schools, he ended up in a presentation at the University of Chicago – presenting to none other than George Stigler and Milton Friedman. In 2 hours, he blew these gurus away with his insights!

Coase argues that firms make economic sense because they reduce or eliminate the "transaction" cost of going to market by doing things in-house. The assumption is that the external costs of doing business include negotiation, contracting, and transfer of information on what firms want from their suppliers. This argument made sense in 1937, when procurement was viewed primarily as a transactional activity. The only focus they had was to drive prices down – otherwise they kept their jobs in-house.

With the risk of outsourcing in the 1980s and 1990s, however, firms were trying to drive out as many business processes as possible. The number of activities that went out to global suppliers in India, China, Vietnam, Brazil, Mexico, and other "low-cost countries" was a function of lower costs – something that Coase couldn't have possibly imagined in 1937.

Even in a world of global outsourcing, however, digitization and the Internet have caused many of the old costs of procurement transactions to decrease. As firms move toward transparency, these transaction costs come close to disappearing altogether. Because transactions occur electronically, systems facilitate movements of funds and materials in a near-perfect vacuum. And as organizations seek to build collaborative relationships with a select group of suppliers, contractual-related complexities related to higher transaction costs fall by the wayside, to be replaced by exchange processes that are more efficient, giving rise to a new body of thinking around "social exchange theory" by sociologists like Peter Blau (1964). Economist Oliver Williamson introduced a second set of theoretical views with transaction cost analysis, which states that the risk of partner opportunism limits the effectiveness of relational governance in exchange relationships. This body of theory predicts that firms will exploit one another through opportunistic behavior if they get too close to one another through social exchanges.

Coase, however, was the first to drive the insourcing–outsourcing argument. Interestingly, Coase's final book, How China Became Capitalist (2012), notes that the Chinese economic model and its trajectory differs remarkably from the Western experience. Certainly an important difference here is the radically different role of social exchange in outsourced relationships in China, owing to the importance of both business and personal relationships that lie at the heart of China's Confucian culture. This concept, often referred to as "guanxi," is another subject altogether. Even shortly before his death in 2013, Coase was still wondering why firms behave the way they do.

The point here is that Oliver Williamson's traditional view of transaction cost economics positions many relationships between firms as driven by transaction costs. As visibility and digitization have disappeared, transaction costs have shrunk to zero, turning his theory upside down, something Williamson could never have imagined. The implications are significant: data can no longer be protected, but indeed must be shared to create the right insight and decision-rights in the supply chain-extended network outside the four walls of the company. We also will explore the fact that transparency is the "bridge of no return" – you can't go back once you've started down the path of transparency.

What Does Transparency Mean in Real Life?

The concept of transparency is one that every chief executive, CFO, chief risk officer, and chief supply chain officer will agree is a positive attribute. Transparency suggests that "you have nothing to hide," and that you have nothing but good news to share: "Here, see for yourself! We are completely open about how we run this company, and have nothing to hide!" Every Wall Street analyst loves to hear this, as the company can only be judged based on what it has in black and white in its SEC report. Companies that are "private" are not so transparent, and generally can operate under a shroud of secrecy – which can be a good and a bad thing.

But the transparency we are talking about in this book has nothing to do with financial reporting. It is much more about data, and how your organization and the people in it think about data. An implicit "psychology" is associated with sharing data in an open, collaborative supply chain. This is closely related to the development of a "culture" that welcomes transparency, and sees it as a core operating value not just for employees of a company, but for all parties in the extended supply chain. And that's when chief executives start to squirm and become more uncomfortable, as we will see.

Nader Mikhail, the 30-year-old CEO of Elementum, spoke to me on my visit to California, describing in a very forthright manner how transparency is challenging companies. Elementum was the company that built the platform that created transparency in the Pulse.

"Think about LinkedIn, one of the most popular social networks," Nader said. "You control your own LinkedIn profile, you control you own data in your profile, and you as an individual can choose who to share your profile with, as well as the level of sharing that you want to provide. We have adopted this model for our own platform, as we believe the LinkedIn model creates the right incentives across the enterprise. Only now, you have included factories and suppliers who control their own profile. So I can tell you if I pass my audits and my suppliers are conflict-mineral free, and I can also tell you what is helpful to you in understanding what is going on in my business. But by default, because this is now an open network that allows a high level of transparency, there is an implicit message sent if I choose NOT to tell you a few things about myself. And by definition, you know that if I am *not telling you something* you need to know to ascertain that your supply chain is operating appropriately, then your level of suspicion will go up and the level of trust will go down."

"This is creating a very interesting dynamic. People believe that large Fortune 500 companies are in control of supply chains. I believe the exact opposite is happening today. Suppliers who have been beaten down for a long time are finally coming into their own. The tide has changed, and has swung to creating more power for suppliers than the OEMs in the network. Suppliers are more agile, and OEMs are more dependent on them to deliver against the promises they are making to their customers."

"For instance, Jeff Bezos at Amazon is investing in his own transportation freight company, because FedEx would not commit to deliver against the promises Amazon was making to their customers! So if we are more dependent on our suppliers, then we need to make sure we have the right set of suppliers in our network. We need to think about how we create trust and share information, and develop relationships that foster the creation of open data sharing. We need suppliers who will share their LinkedIn profile with us. And in a sense, nobody 'owns' the data. Because everyone has their own data, and they can choose who they want to share it with – which is those partners with whom you have the right set of relationships. The implication of this type of network is very, very important, and people really struggle with it."

"Several dimensions of transparency as it relates to increasing velocity are worth exploring. These dimensions contrast with what 'standard' perceptions or definitions of transparency typically engender. These views will cause you to re-think whether your organization is prepared and willing to commit to transparency as a corporate value."

Tom added, "Transparency is a one-way bridge. When you cross it you have to blow up the bridge behind you. It's that significant a change in how you think and what you do. At Flex we have expanded it to be called 'Global Citizenship.' It's who we are – being transparent becomes your identity and it's a value driven by our CEO and embraced now by our entire company. Our Chief Human Resources Officer, Paul Baldessari, actually *owns* this for the company – in effect treating our supply chain with the same values that we expect of our company."

Sustainability in the supply chain is one of the most challenging issues at play in the workplace. The challenge occurs because it is so difficult to control what happens in these factories, which are hidden from the world.

In its Pulse Center, Flex is experimenting with cameras to supplement real-time data with real-time communications, leveraging state-of-the-art video networks.

Monitoring activity in a factory halfway around the world is much more difficult than it seems. Auditors can be brought in with a checklist of things to look for. They may look at financial and payroll records, interview workers, inspect the facilities, and conduct any number of activities related to due diligence. Such audits, however, do not guarantee that a supplier is meeting company expectations. And all it takes is a single employee who decides to "sabotage" the owner because they have a grudge, and issues a complaint to take down the stock price using a Twitter account. So the issue is – how can factory networks in apparel, electronics, and other areas effectively become aware of issues before they reach the mass media and are broadcast and possibly misinterpreted?

To become truly transparent requires that organizations also have living, breathing supplier networks that adopt a similar manifesto for data transparency. The implication is that organizations must strive to work with suppliers that have the same set of moral imperatives and integrity as employees within their organization. This also may mean that the lowest bid supplier is not always the best choice – a transparent supplier, on the other hand, may have a higher product price, but may have the lowest total cost when all other factors are considered. So how can organizations inspire transparency when it comes to sustainable outcomes in their supply base?

Tom Linton has some very strong ideas about transparency as sustainability.

"We have to be able to map the genome of our supply chain partners, just like we do with objects and material," he said. "Think of it – we have barcodes on everything. Every object now has or will have a part number and a country of origin on it that tells you where it came from, who made it, what countries it passed through on the way to getting to you, and all of the enterprises it passed through on the way to your location. You will also become part of that genome. We need to be able to do the same mapping for the labor issue."

He pointed to a bottle of water on his desk. "You need to have a source code that tells you where that bottle of water was bottled, the source of the water, the well it was drawn from and the place it came from. Why not? You can then go down to the chromosome level, and look at the mitochondria – and map out each element of glue, rubber, and source of the plastic. This is the organic analogy to supply chain management – it has to be that deep. The only way we can get our arms around this issue is to be able to have a problem in a factory flashed to us through the network, telling us we have an issue with a specific tier 3 supplier and a specific individual who has a problem at that factory. It is a warning indicator, like a tire pressure light, that something in a particular factory is out of alignment, and you get that message in real time. Perhaps the factory hasn't done adequate criminal background checks, or is using illegal migrant workers and working them 80 hours a week. Whatever the issue, there needs to be an indicator light. Until that level of transparency becomes available, you are subject to the random behaviors and events associated with supply chain disruption."

Transparency as a Corporate Value with Roots in Financial Accountability

Transparency is a concept that goes back not only to the laws of public accountability and generally accepted accounting principles (GAAP), but to the concept of shareholder accountability. Organizations that are open about their operational strengths and weaknesses are taking a stance that the markets can decide on the fair value of the company, but market perceptions have nothing to do with corporate integrity and leadership. In effect, transparency takes the stance that being an open book will always lead to the best outcome.

This is a tough proposition for many chief operating officers and chief risk officers to swallow. Nader Mikhail, the CEO of Elementum, states it this way:

> I speak to a lot of COOs and risk officers – and I always find it comical to compare their reactions between the first and the third meetings we have together. The first meeting inevitably involves conversations such as "this kind of transparency could get me in real trouble!" By the third meeting, however, the dialogue goes something like "Hey, this stuff is happening anyways! If I could know about it sooner, I might be able to minimize the damage."

Flex has undertaken its journey with Elementum to achieve its goal of becoming hyper-transparent. Flex's fundamental vision is to let everyone who needs to know what is going on – and that is a very wide net – have full-real-time visibility to this information. The opposite view, held by many companies today, is, "If anything bad comes up, we need to cover it up and fix it as quickly as possible, and hope that no one finds out about it!" But if we go about running a business pretending that bad things aren't happening, we will never make things better.

Nader offered a great example.

> The world is full of problems. Is there crime in the city of Pittsburgh? Yes, of course, just like in any major metropolitan area. Is there any city that doesn't have crime? No! Does that mean we should try to hide the fact that there is crime? Of course not! But if we actually have data that tracks the location and types of crime, and make the community aware of it, we can get all of the eyes and ears of people out there in the community more aware of what is going on, and they can become part of the solution.

> Similarly, Flex is an organization with 200,000 employees – a city smaller then the size of Pittsburgh. We start with the assumption that there will be crime – counterfeit, fraud, and so on (a topic covered in Chapter 6). But if we develop a capability to identify crime, deal with it, move quickly to respond to crime when it happens, conduct post-mortems to identify the source of crime and get ahead of it – then my city will always be tougher on crime and there will be less of it.

As Tom pointed out "It's not easy – our CEO had to call a meeting with the senior executives just to make sure everyone understands that this kind of transparency is not an option. It's not something you do one day and not the next or for one thing and not the other – it is everything. It is who and what we are."

The Transparent Supply Chain

Standard views of transparency in supply chains are often related to the concept of "inventory visibility" and "schedule visibility." In fact, most corporate planning and inventory systems operate off material requirement planning (MRP) systems, often encapsulated within broader enterprise resource planning (ERP) systems. These systems typically operate in a "batch" mode – they recalculate information based on feeds coming in from such sources as EDI transmissions, advanced ship notices, manual inventory counts, warehouse management systems, distribution planning systems, material planning systems, etc. Unfortunately, neither the quality of the data in these systems, nor the timeliness of the information, is reliable, and therefore, it is always suspected. I've spoken to people who maintain that they have to wait until the end of the month to know whether they've met their delivery and shipment and inventory targets, and whether they are on track. (Returning to the vehicle metaphor: Imagine if you got a report only once a month telling you how fast and how far you had driven that month.)

The Elementum platform was designed on the assumption that only real-time information is reliable and useful. Elementum has a mobile device app for each function. There is SOURCE for procurement, TRANSPORT for shipments, and INVENTORY for planning, as well as an EXECUTIVE APP that allows cross-functional visibility. Each function has its own culture and peculiarities when it comes to data form and type, and to how employees like to view it and act on it. But the source of the data comes from the same single source of truth.

An important component of the system is an organization's unique culture, and how people in the organization make decisions. For example, *centralized* organizations have a strong center of gravity, with decisions emanating from the core (usually senior executives). *Decentralized* organizations are the opposite, with a high degree of decision-making authority allocated to people in the field. *Center-led organizations* are in the middle, with some decisions relegated to centralized decision-makers who collect analytics, with governance allowing other decisions to be made by empowered field workers. There is no "right" organizational model, by the way – and these models often shift, based on a firm's "re-organization," especially those occurring when leadership changes.

Your firm's governance structure also should be designed with the organization model in mind. In a decentralized environment with five business units, each business unit is run separately, and the supply chain for each SBU may be run in an integrated fashion, but only within the business unit. So there is cross-functional data visibility, but only within each business unit. In a centralized structure, a common platform and approach spans all five units, and control over who sees and doesn't see the data may be delegated by specific user "admin rights" established in the system.

The designation of administrative rights is core to the concept and spirit of transparency. Some rules of thumb include:

1. People who are most directly impacted by information need to see it.
2. People who see or hear events that impact the supply chain (e.g., disruptive events, problems) are empowered to "create an issue."
3. Issues are normally reviewed and validated. All data input into the system must be validated before it is dispersed.
4. Data is typically shared within a business unit or functional group, unless it requires escalation to more senior levels.
5. Everyone empowered to see data can add insights, input, and other factors. This is important, as a piece of data may not mean much to a senior executive, but could be interpreted very differently by someone else in the field, requiring that data to be escalated in importance.
6. A user group called "executives" can have complete visibility. However, individual users who are creating users may not want the "noise" to go all the way up the chain – so data can be "abstracted" up to the executive level using a "permissions" model.

7. Every organization is unique; data transparency "toggles" need to be flipped based on the unique strategy and desired organizational communication model.

One element Elementum is developing relates to the TRANSPORT module which is focused on all movement of material in the supply chain. This is especially important for trans-ocean shipping, which traditionally has been considered the "black hole" of supply chain visibility. Think about it – once a shipment of products is put into a container, it is loaded onto a truck, taken to a port, and put on a ship. The ship leaves the harbor … and then what? Nobody knows where their stuff is until the ship, maybe, provides an update – but that could happen days later. And once the ship lands at a port … forget about it! We all know how non-automated port operations are, and a ship could be at port for days before it is even unloaded and put onto a truck for its next destination. Although some shipping companies are seeking to embed transmitting devices in their containers, products are still pretty much invisible when they are on a boat in the middle of the Pacific Ocean, where there are no Wi-Fi connections.

That is starting to change. Until recently, companies like Maersk, one of the largest shipping lines in America, were getting 12-hour updates on their location – which is still infrequent – a far cry from "real-time." Maersk is working with Elementum to explore ways not only to generate GPS satellite signals from the ship, but to discover ways to generate container signals and even product-level signals to provide greater transparency of shipment movements. And Maersk is also finding out that customers are willing to pay extra for this level of service.

One problem with traditional shipping lines is that they have focused on per unit cost savings, NOT on speed and flexibility. In today's challenging economy, which focuses on velocity and working capital reduction, this strategy is moving in the exact opposite direction of the competitive trends of transport customers. Airbus made a similar mistake in designing the A380, a massive passenger plane for long-haul trans-Pacific flights. While per passenger economics are good, this system requires that airlines fill the plane to the brim to derive benefit. This system thus limits the number of locations and flights available to passengers, as well as the size of the airports they can use. On the other hand, the 787, a much more fuel-efficient plane designed for smaller destinations, offers more flexibility for shorter routes and does not have to be full to derive value.

Recently a logistics company, Matson Logistics, began running a "fast boat" from Shanghai, China to Long Beach, California. The idea was to provide a premium, fast, and flexible service for priority shipments, targeted for customers who value velocity over cost. To speed up port operations, Matson invested in its own terminal at Long Beach, thus controlling delivery without being held hostage to local port operators. Matson's ocean services, company-operated warehouses on the East and West Coasts, and 53-foot intermodal containers create a network of asset-based services that support a supply chain from China to virtually any point in North America. The company also has developed strong relationships with rail and trucking providers to complete its broad menu of logistics services. This unique mix of resources allows the company to tailor specific solutions for a customer, and to remain agile as the customer's needs change. Matson's most important capability is that it provides *a guaranteed delivery time across the Pacific*. The combination of both velocity and consistency is a differentiated offering for which many global supply chain companies are willing to pay.

Management Principles for Executing Visibility Strategies

As organizations move toward visible, high-velocity, transparent supply chains, a number of fundamental but difficult questions arise:

- How do we extend concept visibility and control beyond our four walls to drive better execution in our supply chain?
- How do we get materials from suppliers to partners to customers – given that we rely primarily on spreadsheets and email to interact?
- How do we understand and limit the data we focus on for decision-making? The problem in most supply chains is not that there is "not enough data," because data is being created from machines, from people, from systems, and from external sources. No, the problem is too much data, not too little!
- What do I care about and therefore focus on? The primary factor that will hinder my ability to get products and services to customers. This means finding the right data, the right tools, and the exceptions, and rendering decisions based on the data excerpts available. No easy task.
- How do we identify problems that are hidden in the mass of unfiltered data we have today? Often the sources of information are hidden in piles of data that we don't think about. For example, Elementum identified the Tianjin explosion when someone took a photo of the explosion, tagged it, and posted it on Sina Weibo, the Chinese version of Twitter. Social media feeds are just one more form of intelligence that can be leveraged to deal with the flood of information. But the challenge is that although companies have all sorts of news and media monitoring, very little of it is actionable information.

The problem thus becomes contextualized into the following sets of questions:

- How do we translate information and data into the context of our company and our situation, and leverage this information into actionable insights?
- How will real-time intelligence help me any more than what I'm doing today?
- What impact does digitization (the Internet of Things, or IoT) have on my organization and my employees?
- Will digitization change the way we measure things and monitor metrics?

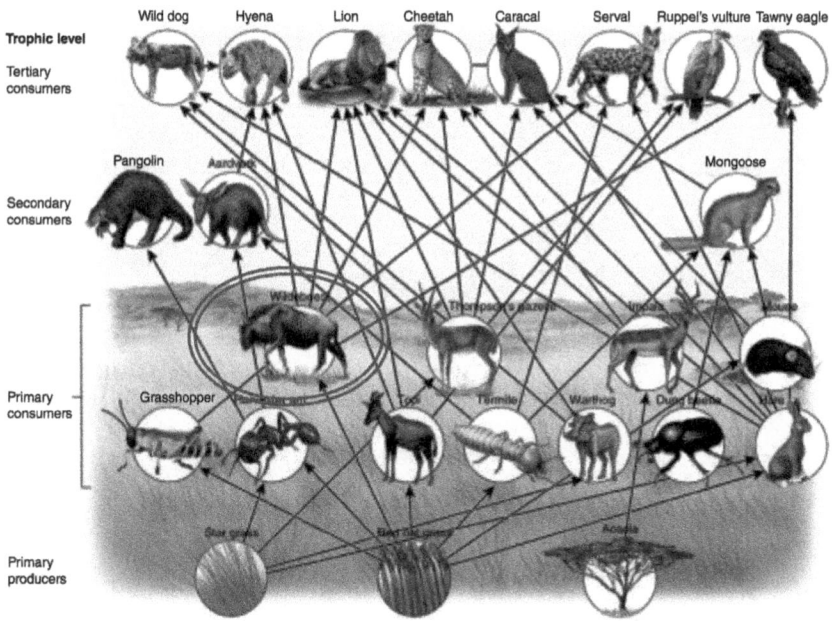

Figure 2.2 Wildebeest in the Serengeti Trophic Cascade. *Source:* Reproduced with permission of iStock

This brings up another rule that was observed in the Serengeti desert, based on the growth of the wildebeest population, and that also applies to digitized supply chains (see Figure 2.2).

It turns out that the wildebeest is a keystone species in the Serengeti ecosystem (see Figure 2.3). This wasn't immediately obvious, until a virus began killing the wildebeest hordes in the 1950s. This virus was eradicated in 1963, and disappeared entirely in wildebeest calves born after 1964. This resulted in a boom in the wildebeest population, which reduced the amount of grass, leading to fewer fires, more trees, and then more giraffes and other species.

The population of predators that fed off wildebeest (lions and jackals) also increased. This led to the third rule observed in the ecosystem.

Serengeti Rule 3: Some species compete for common resources. Species that compete for space, food, or habitat can regulate the abundance of other species. In the example above, the wildebeests' many direct and indirect effects on grasses, fire, trees, predators, giraffes, herbs, insects, and other grazers reveal that they have disproportionate impacts on the structure and regulation of communities. In effect, wildebeests dominate the Serengeti.

What makes this rule interesting is that there is a natural limit to the growth of some species, based on consumption of resources. If species are starved of

Figure 2.3 Wildebeest Herd. *Source:* Reproduced with permission of iStock

resources, their numbers decline. Therefore, it makes sense that species that operate using the optimal amount of resources will stay in balance, along with the entire network. Balance is the key to a healthy Serengeti desert, where all species balance each other out. If species are competing for common resources, then those that are able to either find alternative resources, or survive with fewer resources, will thrive. This leads to Supply Chain Rule 3a.

New Supply Chain Rule 3a: Enterprises operating at higher velocity consume fewer resources and will thrive. Some enterprises drive multiple supply chains and impact many industries, pulling in materials, intellectual capital, and talent. For example, Intel's invention of the microchip had a pervasive and massive impact on multiple industries beyond the personal computer. Similarly, Apple's invention of the iPhone created a massive demand for contract labor, which resulted in the explosion of firms like FoxConn, resulting in millions of jobs in China. But those companies that were able to do so using fewer resources, with less material and lower inventories, moved more nimbly in this environment. Outsourcing was only part of the solution here; even outsourcing requires a delicate balancing act to work across the network without decreasing customer satisfaction.

Organizations that operate with fewer resources are leaner, and are able to flow resources through their chain. Flow in this context refers to material flow, information flow, transactional flows, and flows of services, funds, resources, and capabilities. Indeed, multiple forms of flow go up and down the echelons of a supply chain. The problem of increasing flow has existed since the early days of Just-in-Time. However, the newest approaches stem from being able to employ cloud-based computing and real-time data in a way that has never been feasible before.

Elementum's Dana Martin's presentation at the 33rd Semi-Annual Supply Chain Resource Cooperative meeting at North Carolina State University on April 22, 2016 addressed the many challenges of the supply chain, and Elementum's journey to drive information flow across supply chains for their software clients to drive improved problem-solving.

> Dana (Head of Product Development) emphasized the need to think about the next generation of supply chains. "Vertical integration went away because we have moved in the direction of running virtual vertical integration," he said. "Brand owners are a key part of this. Companies like Flex are looking for ways to integrate vertically, not just on product manufacturing, but also in terms of how to collaborate better to drive more efficiency. This also implies the need to restructure contractual terms to be able to ensure that as problems arise – whether due to fluctuations in demand or other factors – managers can quickly adapt to these changes in the supply chain to drive the right outcome."

> "This ability to contextualize data into decision-making does not occur overnight. It is an evolution that occurs in stages. Today, we are mostly reactive, because we are so close to the problem. Though you may not realize it, executives aren't making many decisions, because there aren't many to make! Executives are forced down a path because they found out too late. But if we can begin to learn about problems earlier, we will have more options, and very often these options happen to have much lower costs."

Data Crosses Functional Silos

Dana emphasized that the shifts he described are happening as firms drive visibility into the supply chain. "The responsive piece is all about how to align teams not just internally, but across the organization," he said. "We are used to operating in functional silos that involve managing people and keeping them in buckets, and the data these people are exposed to reinforce these silos. And very often, the processes those functions have are within silos as well. A problem in procurement can impact manufacturing and logistics and planning, but often these dots are never connected, so there never emerges a cross-functional approach to working on them. But when we connect the dots linking a problem to other functions, we can create a coordinated and multidisciplinary team that together is able to solve the problem faster."

OK, great! We now know that cross-enterprise data can be automated and can tie people together. Big deal – people have been saying that for years. The real challenge is not only automating this process, but ensuring that only the *exceptions* are used to pull the functional silos together to solve problems. Let me emphasize that: *The exceptions govern. They bring the right team of people from silos together to solve a problem.* So what an enterprise needs is a mechanism that pulls exceptions and puts together in real time, a cross-functional team that operates across the end-to-end supply chain (including manufacturing sites, 3PL, 4PL, transportation, distribution sites, and suppliers). This mechanism must be driven not simply by external impacts, such as floods in Houston or explosions in Tianjin. It must work at a far more finite level to extract data showing events that impact the overall efficiency and throughput of our supply chains.

Monitoring Small Events, Not Black Swans

The mechanism for screening data is therefore not just about tracking black swan events, so-called because they are rare and difficult to predict. It doesn't make sense to optimize your supply chain in expectation of a black swan. The challenge is to filter out small issues and everyday events. Customers change the quantity they ship inside of lead times set by the supply base, and the quantities double. There is a quality problem in production and the schedule falls behind while the problem is being resolved. The server goes down for an hour and shuts down communication. Or there is a quantity shortage on a critical raw material at a sub-tier supplier that delays shipment by a day.

These types of small but important events require the attention of a cross-functional team, composed of individuals from multiple functions, including design, marketing, sales, order fulfillment, logistics, procurement, manufacturing, and suppliers. A demand fluctuation or a planning issue, if left unresolved, can quickly escalate into a bigger problem unless it is solved using the right team. The late delivery may be escalated if there is a contractual obligation with the customer. Small issues represent friction on the flow of the supply chain that drives up cost and impacts customer satisfaction. Addressing these issues requires a small team for the initial assessment, then building a larger team if the problem is bigger than anticipated. The speed at which teams are drafted and combined to solve problems is in direct proportion to the firm's ability to solve the problem quickly at a low cost and minimize this friction.

A problem in on-time customer delivery, say, really only becomes a major problem if it is not visible across a multi-carrier network route. A firm's ability to quickly become aware of the problem and solve it means having the right data pulled and put in front of decision-makers at the right place and the right time. Improved decision-making occurs when data is presented in a fashion that escalates specific information on an issue to decision-makers. This is also challenging if decision-makers are dispersed across Brazil, the UK, the US, and other locations. The worst-case scenario is that everyone believes everything is fine until the customer notices that they haven't received their stuff, and contacts the company to inquire about it. This is effectively the customer's first recognition that the delivery is late, but by that time, it will be too late to do anything about it. The late delivery has already occurred. So buyers are now in firefighting mode, trying to find the right data to explain where the shipment is and why it's late. No matter how this issue is resolved, the shipment is already late and the customer is upset.

Assumptions for Creating Transparency

The problem, of course, is that *information in the supply chain is never complete, and will always contain bad data*. Even as US-based companies worldwide invest in standard softwares such as SAP and Oracle, availability and consistency of data produced by these systems will never be 100% stable. And when a firm's supply chain expands to places like China, Vietnam, and Latin America, where emerging country customers are located, the variability in data standards and integrity only increases, as many individuals in these regions are still communicating with fax machines and phones.

The *de facto* position, therefore, should be that data is relatively easy to get, often contains errors and incomplete datasets, and is produced by a multitude of technologies. Any visibility system must be constructed with these tenets in mind. Elementum uses non-relational databases that have no set data schemas, allowing them to input any kind of data that will be stored and analyzed. Graphical interconnections between people, parts, and functions are constructed to enable a problem in one area to be immediately linked and related to another area, where the problems can be quickly scanned and potentially solved. This approach of linking data through non-traditional forms of relationships is the true "secret sauce" behind effective visibility systems in real-time supply chain systems. It is a characteristic that makes the approach powerful and actionable.

How are these connections identified, established, and hard-coded into the visibility system? Dana notes, "We want to understand your end-to-end supply chain, and begin by literally mapping the entire supply chain from supply distribution through to customers. We want to know where your subassemblies come from, at as granular a level as we possibly can, which is the level at which there is specific risk. We want to know how you are organized, where you have external dependencies, whether it is a location, a supplier, or something else, and how these elements are interconnected to your supply chain."

This simple mapping activity should be happening anyhow – but companies often overlook this tool, even though it can drive continuous improvement and visibility.

In one example, Elementum mapped out a client's supply chain and found that 93 sites in the network relied on a sole source. Of these sole sources, only 4% had a possible second source available. This was a current existing supply base. When these sites were mapped against revenue streams, it was discovered that 86% of the company's revenues were tied to suppliers in a small region of Malaysia. Any disasters in this region would shut down 86% of revenues! In this environment, the company was seeking to lower inventory and working capital, but was not tracking the risk impact of its supply chain design.

A recent study by the Center for Advanced Purchasing Studies also aligns with the concept of the "kill shot," by identifying what researchers call "nexus suppliers." A nexus supplier refers to a supplier that is critical to a buying firm's operations because of its structural position in the firm's supply network (i.e., how its business relationships are structured with other firms in the focal firm's extended supply network). Physically, a nexus supplier may be several tiers removed from the buying firm, and hence not directly noticeable. As a consequence, the challenge is identifying nexus suppliers so that a buying firm can proactively manage its suppliers, be better prepared to take advantage of potential benefits (e.g., innovation opportunities), and also mitigate the associated risks (e.g., materials flow disruption).

Nexus suppliers differ from strategic suppliers in two ways. First, nexus suppliers are critical because of their structurally embedded positions inside the supply network, while strategic suppliers are critical based on the characteristics of their products, services, or technologies. Second, nexus suppliers can be located anywhere in a supply network, while strategic suppliers are typically located in the first tier of the network. In other words, nexus suppliers might not be directly visible to a focal firm, while strategic suppliers will likely be visible.[3]

To give you an idea of what a typical supply chain looks like, CAPS (the Center for Advanced Purchasing Studies) examined the Honda of America supplier network. They found that of Honda's 10,832 suppliers, 245 are first-tier, 1643 are second-tier, 4605 are third-tier, and 4339 are fourth-tier. These 10,833 supplier companies span 83 countries and 66 industry sectors. The researchers also composed a "nexus supplier index" (NSI) and computed NSI scores for all suppliers in the second and third tiers of Honda's supply network. The NSI score indicates a supplier's overall structural importance in the network. In

---

3 Shao, B., Shi, Y., and Choi, T. Y., "Feasibility Study of a Nexus Supplier Index Identifying and Categorizing Nexus Suppliers through Business Analytics," Center for Advanced Purchasing Studies, 2016.

tiers two and three of Honda's supply network, the CAPS Study found major multinational companies (such as Siemens, SAP, Hewlett-Packard, and General Electric) as potential nexus suppliers across such diverse industry sectors as electronics, semiconductors, chemicals, software development, and the like. The study also identified companies of which Honda supply managers were unaware.

The importance of understanding what node in the supply chain can be disrupted and the cost of what happens when these areas of our supply chain are shut down, is at the core of the "kill shot" concept. Mapping and linking the supply chain structure creates these insights, and causes executives to rethink how they should rationalize their supply base, in a way that considers the many factors associated with risk. Executives also must consider how to establish leading indicators of suppliers to identify when a disruptive event occurs, and to find ways of working more proactively to mitigate that risk. This involves thinking through the types of data coming from different locations in the supply chain, and how to leverage this information correctly. This requires establishing a single data platform that collects incoming data, and then filters the data into an issues management system. A firm's challenge is to establish the criteria that will identify the exceptions, tie them to the problems created, and escalate the exceptions to the people who can solve these problems.

This is much easier said than done, of course. Consider the example of Gen. Stanley McChrystal and the "Team of Teams" he created in Iraq. (This was a foundation of the thinking that went into the Flex/Elementum platform). In Iraq, every intelligence agency had its own data platform, and its own intelligence in its own databases. No one was sharing data with anyone else in the service. This "siloed data" made getting actionable information to execute missions on a timely basis difficult. Once the teams began working independently yet in a unified fashion, and the entire operation's intelligence data resided in a single platform accessible to all, data became much more actionable and helpful to troops on the ground. The new system allowed the operations to ramp up from 6 to 300 missions a month, as better intelligence allowed the teams to connect the dots on what they were seeing.

The concept also applies to such supply chain problems as not getting deliveries to customers on time. Creating a data platform can allow individuals to more quickly and easily understand why problems are occurring, which in turn speeds up the velocity of decision-making. The goal, which ties back to our supply chain theory of everything, is simply to speed up the number of "wins" and slow down the occurrence of "losses."

Several key characteristics of creating supply chain visibility should be remembered here:

- The transformation is a journey – it doesn't happen overnight.
- End-to-end visibility is necessary not just for individual functions, but across the enterprise.

- Data freshness is critical. Instead of periodic roll-ups, data transmission needs to happen in real time.
- The supply chain context should move from internal to global, manual analysis to decision assistance, and shift functional silo's decisions to cross-organization, cross-enterprise problem resolution methods. Issue tracking via emails and phone calls should move toward enterprise issue management.

A Shipping Example

Many examples illustrate how quickly formed teams can focus on immediate problems when the right data is put in front of them. A typical example exists for companies importing goods into the United States from China, Vietnam, or India. Let's say a company has a product shipped from Asia to the port of Long Beach, then puts it on a truck to distribution centers and customers. Suddenly, the monitoring system picks up a Twitter feed from truckers at the port, one of whom notes, "We are seeing a slowdown in productivity at Long Beach, from 12- hour to 48-hour ship unloads." (By the way, this is not at all an uncommon event in the Long Beach Port). This may seem like an unimportant event, but the system also notes that the predicted ripple effect impact is that shipping times to customers will extend from 6 days to 12 days! To avoid late shipments to customer distribution centers, a team of transportation planners, analysts, and customer service representatives convene virtually and proactively devise options to avoid paying late-delivery fees. They might ask:

- Can we reship the product to another location?
- Can we repackage a similar product already in the distribution center's inventory and deliver that product to the customer on time?
- Can we expedite the product from the port once it gets through Customs?

In this manner, the team adjusts the dials on its supply chain so that a practical and feasible option is developed and executed. The customer gets a phone call about the situation and how the team has resolved it, and is immediately relieved to have dodged a bullet!

This example illustrates how real-time data, when structured in the right form and which is selective in nature, flows through the organization in such a way that it brings together key decision-makers across functions to solve real supply chain problems. Dana noted that the full implications of this approach are still being figured out, and that Elementum is working with its customers to explore how best to structure the flow of real-time data to drive the right level of cross-functional and cross-industry problem-solving. Information flow is key to reducing friction in the supply chain. Understanding information flows begins by understanding how work occurs, and the specific workflow that takes place when there are "exceptions" in the supply chain. As noted earlier, an "exception" is anything that slows flow: product disruptions, material problems, quality problems, lack of information, long cycle times, or any other headache that is part of a typical supply chain planners' everyday job.

The Old Way of Doing It

Today, exceptions are primarily managed by email. No analytics are involved – just an email that tells a planner that there is a problem, and somebody has to fix it. Typically, the planner will look at an Excel spreadsheet, comb through the data files, try to find the right contact person, and begin making phone calls. The planner is likely trying to find out which products are tied to the supply chain event, which suppliers are involved, which transportation providers are impacted, and most importantly, which customers will feel the impact and be irate at the end of the day. But since every planner does it differently, there isn't a document work flow process at all. So the initial problem results in the planner (or whoever gets the email) trying to get to the root of the problem.

In doing so, he or she will pull in 20 other people, both inside and outside the organization. The boss has been pulled into the problem, and everyone is involved in trying to understand what has happened. Too often, not all of the 20 people SHOULD be involved, as this is a problem over which they have no decision-making authority and which will not affect them. But they are pulled in anyway. As a result, all the strategic initiatives they are working on get pushed to the side, because it's "All hands on deck," and "We have an Emergency!" (Everybody hates an emergency case). The day-to-day issues have once again taken priority, so there is no time to work on driving down lead times, improving efficiencies, working capital reduction, initiating innovative projects, or other important strategic initiatives.

Defining Workflow for Unexpected Issues

However, optimizing the flow of information across the supply chain significantly curtails the number of people who get pulled into these emergencies. Because there is a workflow around how to deal with exceptions, and real-time data is broadcast to people's mobile devices, everyone knows the protocol. As a result, CxOs are only pulled into these problems once a month or once a quarter, when their level of insight is absolutely required. They can check their mobile devices to learn the status of a problem without getting involved, and can assess the magnitude of the issue, the history of the issue to date, and choose whether to get involved. These executives will feel the same level of control as before, are not taken by surprise by issues, and are kept informed on all updates and resolutions. They also are free to push the top-level strategic initiatives down into the organization when they see fit, and involve lower-level people who would otherwise spend their entire day on issue management.

To enable this capability, it is important to document which parties across functions should be the "owners" of an issue. Granted, this depends on the type of issue involved. In addition, a counterparty may be involved: a customer-facing brand owner, a logistics planner, a supplier, or others. It is imperative upfront to understand and define which parts of the organization need to be involved, and to ensure that these sectors are part of the real-time data flows when an issue is triggered in their domain of responsibility. This leads us to Supply Chain Rule 3b.

New Supply Chain Rule 3b: Static Supply Chain Risk Probabilities Aren't Predictive in Managing Supply Chain Disruptions.

Why Static Risk Probabilities Won't Work

Many supply chain risk management systems are predicated on being able to "predict" where the next major event and issue will occur. The theory is that by predicting the likelihood of an event, we can buffer against it by employing extra inventory, replicating capabilities, enlisting two supply sources, and other approaches. This is often known as "building a resilient supply chain."[4]

Tom Linton disagrees with this approach. Predicting where the next disruption will occur and creating redundancies is a way of creating extra waste in the supply chain. "Supply chain resiliency sounds *expensive!*" he said. "I don't want to build up a bunch of inventory and extra capabilities for something that I don't even know will occur. And how are people coming up with these probabilities? In most cases, it's a guess, using subjective factors. Resilience is about creating even more friction and slowing down your supply chain. It sounds bulky. Who wants to drive a tank down the street that can withstand anything? I'd much rather drive a Ferrari and get there that much quicker. Although the risk is there, I'm going to get there much faster."

Dana added, "The problem with static risk analysis is that it *doesn't consider what is actually happening today, at this exact moment*, at each of the nodes we deem as risky. We need to be aware of what's happening in real time. Realistically, how well can we guess that because something has certain attributes, it's riskier than something else? Is a new supplier in Afghanistan riskier than a supplier in Wisconsin? Absolutely. But a lot of the risk centers on how well they execute within your supply chain. We need to have real-time data that provides context on what is happening at that node. Once we have data, we can discuss how they tie in to other flows in the supply chain, the context, whether they are a sole source, how long will it take to qualify another supplier, and whether there

---

4 Sheffi, Y., *The Power of Resilience: How the Best Companies Manage the Unexpected*, MIT Press, Cambridge, 2015.

is an alternative. Does the supplier have a historical record of shipping on-time in-full? Does it have a good quality record and a track record for solving problems? These are all data that can drive the right level of discussion, which need to be pulled together quickly when an issue is discovered. If the data associated with a node are readily available, people can drill down into it virtually and see what options can be constructed. Because it's virtually impossible to predict where problems are likely to happen – a strike in Long Beach, an earthquake in Japan, or a flood in Thailand or Houston. So we need to find ways to be more agile and responsive to alerts of events when they occur."

Dana Martin is intimately familiar with risk. "I worked with the Department of Homeland Security after 9/11, and was tasked with ranking the biggest risks for every facility in the Federal Government infrastructure, and then fortifying the resilience of the riskiest facilities," he said. "So we found, for instance, that there was a building that was part of a critical infrastructure next to a river, so we'd build a jetty so that if there was a torrential rain, the building wouldn't be flooded. We spent billions of taxpayer dollars on these reinforcements. And after many years, all our investment was used in protection against a single disaster – but in this case, it still didn't fully mitigate the outcome of the disaster, so the same outcome occurred regardless."

Dana believes it is better instead to tie risk decisions to financial outcomes, and to focus on this dimension of performance. This approach involves creating new measures to gauge employee performance, and evaluating these measures on how fast they can solve problems in the supply chain. By definition, if employees know that speed of decision-making is key, they will tie themselves into monitoring demand fluctuations and events to achieve responsiveness.

"It's also important to monitor demand fluctuations, not demand spikes," Dana said. "By looking at fluctuations, you can reduce buffer stock significantly. For example, Elementum worked with a customer to monitor the standard deviation of shipping lane times from point A to point B. We found that the average was 30 days, the maximum was 80 days, and the 80th percentile was 50 days. Using this data, we planned for a 50-day route, and used a buffer stock equivalent to this time. We found that we had inventory planned for an 80-day period, which was highly unlikely, and we were keeping much more inventory then what we needed, which equated to millions of dollars of extra working capital that could be freed up. We took out a total of two days of working capital, which resulted in millions that could be invested in other initiatives. And because we had real-time, early warning detection capabilities, we had increased issue awareness, so if there was a slowdown in transit times, we would be notified well in advance of issues. Real-time data combined with reduced working capital is indeed possible. This occurs because of increased issue awareness, greater proactive efforts on the part of employees, early warning detection mechanisms, predictive logistics ETAs (estimated time of arrival), and cross-organization/cross-enterprise discipline. The company reduced inventory by over 10%, because they were holding the 'wrong inventory' for the wrong reasons."

Real-time visibility creates other important secondary and tertiary value components. For example, the qualitative factor of knowing what is happening because information is available drives improved workforce efficiency. How many more problems can they solve? How many more carriers, contract manufacturers, shippers, suppliers can they monitor? Today, companies have regional divisions doing all this work, and often employ shared services on top of this to supplement all the monitoring that needs to be done. Real-time visibility minimizes the number of people required to solve a problem, and increases the ability of these individuals to work with customers and focus on the things that make customers happy.

But there are challenges. It is important to ensure that data is kept within firewalls when extending it up and down the supply chain. If information about a supplier problem is surfaced to a customer, this may not please the customer. So it is important to evaluate a supplier within the context of the overall supply chain network design, and this has to be done on a global scale. Requirements for data feeds have to be negotiated into contractual discussions with both suppliers and customers independently; otherwise, risks can increase dramatically.

How do you get started on your journey toward creating a true data democracy, fueled by real-time data? Dana urges people to "Start out with a region and business, and understand your organization structure and the problems you're trying to solve. If you are in procurement or planning, you'll want to start with the business sponsors who see the most value in this tool. You want business sponsors out there promoting this concept in their organization and driving the change. The technology implementation is surprisingly quick: 2–3 months is needed to stand up a business unit and a whole company using a very flexible ingestion of data. The tough part, however, is figuring out how to fit this into your everyday life – and understanding how to purpose the system to enable everyone to become better at his or her job. We have to re-think how we as individuals interact with this new type of data, and the pyramid of information that it is based on. Issue management is the hook that gets people involved initially, and it is used typically to drive a weekly team operation meeting. This type of weekly meeting would be very different. The discussion would be along the lines of, 'What elements are in motion right now? and, 'Let's line up the 10 problems and line up actions to deal with them.' The software and tools and information become part of that day-to-day life, and that is a big change."

Elementum established a business model that is aligned with their concept of transparency, data democracy, and speed. "We made a couple of decisions to NOT charge by the user – or by the number of transactions, unlike many, we want it to be adopted by as many people as possible," he said. "We want an intelligence platform to bring everyone together. We recognize that everyone is so busy, and there are so many emails. This is a new form of interacting with digital information, and it will be a challenge."

The Bridge of No Return

To truly be open to change and to becoming transparent is a major shift in the way that organizations operate, and will require executives committed to this course of action. Because once you start on this journey, there is no going back. Customers and suppliers will expect that same level of visibility and transparency, and it will be seen as a core service that comes bundled with your products. In fact, it is fair to say that there is no such thing as a pure product or service – it is truly a bundled capability. It is impossible to become less transparent once you've opened yourself up.

3

INTERACTIVE! The Emergence of Federated Supply Chain Networks

Who wants to be the one to stand up and say 'I've found a problem!'? I've found someone who isn't working in a compliant manner in my factory, or I've found a violation of a supplier's working conditions, or product disposition regulations, or environmental waste water violations? Let's make a big deal out of it! Of course not. People, especially those in emerging countries, do not want to open themselves up to problems, and partners don't want to share issues they're having. So we have had to think hard about how we can create the right motivation in people to do so. The way we have thought of, and what we instill in our training, is that it is about "protecting revenue," and not just "revenue at risk."
—Nader Mikhail, *CEO, Elementum*

The Tianjin Explosion

On August 12, 2015, two massive explosions occurred at a container facility in the port of Tianjin in northern China. (An aerial photo is shown in Figure 3.1). The first two explosions occurred within 30 seconds of each other; the second one involved the detonation of about 800 tons of ammonium nitrate.[1] Fires caused by the explosions burned throughout the weekend, and the blast killed more than a hundred people, left hundreds more injured and devastated large areas of the city. The cause of the explosion was ultimately linked to an over-heated container of dry nitrocellulose.[2] According to the China Earthquake Networks Centre, the initial explosion had a power equivalent to 3 tons of

---

1 "China Blasts: Casualties as Tianjin Shipment Blows Up," *BBC News*, August 12, 2015.
2 Huang, P., and Zhang, J., "Facts Related to August 12, 2015 Explosion Accident in Tianjin, China," *Process Safety Progress*, vol. 34, no. 4, 2015, pp. 313–314.

Figure 3.1 The Tianjin Explosion. *Source:* Reproduced with permission of European Pressphoto Agency

TNT detonating, in this city of 15 million, and the second was the equivalent of 21 tons of dynamite.[3]

At the time, three of Flex's major product suppliers were in the immediate vicinity of the explosion, and multiple employees worked in the area. But unlike in many disasters, the Pulse Center provided an immediate alert and response to the emergency. Tom Linton recalls what happened. "When the explosion hit, I received an immediate alert on my mobile phone," he said. "The Elementum network monitors all Twitter feeds in the vicinity of all of our major facilities – and in this case, they were suddenly picking up a lot of Twitter traffic and police scanner reports in the airwaves around Tianjin. This was immediately communicated to all the managers and executives that had product, people, or activity related to that facility. The network had been preprogrammed to create the right level of alerts for these individuals based on their profile, and this ensured that all the people who needed to know were alerted immediately."

---

3 "Chinese Investigators Identify Cause of Tianjin Explosion," *Chemical & Engineering News*, February 8, 2016. The immediate cause of the accident was the spontaneous ignition of overly dry nitrocellulose stored in a container that overheated.

In this case, Flex had 3 suppliers located within 3 kilometers of the port. The system created alerts for all the part numbers associated with a possible disruption associated with those facilities. "This visibility increased the velocity with which we could react and take action to the issue," Tom recalled. "You can't move what you can't see! This is a universal truth that drives all our activity and decision-making; visibility and velocity decrease costs and increase revenues. But this can only occur when people have access to data, meaning that anyone who is able to see what is happening cannot only react to an issue, but also is empowered to 'raise' an issue. So if someone sees something that isn't right or which could impact the network, he is empowered to raise that issue and react to it."

Once again, the parallel to the military concept of "situational intelligence" took over. The first call from Flex's response team went to the supplier's themselves, to determine if there had been damage. Executives at the supplier's headquarters were taken aback: "What explosion? What do you mean?" "Haven't you heard? There was an explosion ... in fact, it's reported the windows have been blown out of your facility!"

Incredibly, Flex's response to the disaster was so rapid that the executives from the suppliers hadn't even gotten a word back from their own facility operators that an explosion had occurred. These executives called the facilities, determined that no one had been hurt and that production lines were intact, and reported on the conditions to the response team.

But it didn't end there. The HR team at Flex immediately took action after being notified through the Pulse Center to determine who among their personnel was on-site at supplier locations in Tianjin. They quickly determined that more than 60 employees needed to be evacuated. The system allowed Flex to quickly mine the data and contact these individuals with instructions on how to proceed. The team contacted its travel agency, which likewise was not yet aware of the explosion, and quickly was able to schedule buses from the site to the airport, reserve flight reservations and travel arrangements to evacuate Flex employees from the scene. HR's ability to act quickly ensured that everyone was able to get out safely in a timely and expeditious manner. The travel agency noted that none of the other global companies in the area contacted them with the speed and agility that Flex did in this situation.

The Tianjin explosion and Flex's ability to react quickly illustrates one of the many benefits of creating visibility and velocity in the global network through the combination of local insight and globalized actions. The Flex team was able to initiate action within 15 minutes of the explosion, based on tracking tweets and other signals in the network. Most organizations are unaware of the impact of natural disasters on their supply chains. In many cases, they are not even sure what the impact of such a disaster would be on their supply base, their logistics network, the products in the channel, and in the end, on their business revenue. So when they occur, they panic. But in a truly connected supply chain with real-time visibility, reacting to disasters and variability becomes a much more controlled and planned response.

The Psychology of Raising Issues in the Pulse

The Pulse Center's ability to create rapid insight is a combination of effective monitoring of "big data" (news feeds, Twitter accounts, police scanners, and multiple other data sources), combined with a structure that enables anyone in the Flex network to create an "issue." For instance, if someone in the network sees or hears a potential disruptor (or opportunity, for that matter), he or she is enabled to create an "issue" on their phone app. Similar to the idea of military servicemen observing enemy movement on the front lines and alerting others in the network, raising issues is encouraged, but has some established guidelines that govern how they are approved and escalated in the network.

A team of "issue monitors" at a third-party location in the Elementum structure assigned to the Flex account is able to validate the issue, and follow up to validate the claim that an issue has occurred. The systems assumes that the initial data coming in is not accurate, so a human curation team quickly takes steps to triangulate it with other data and validate it. This happens within seconds of the issue being raised. The analysis team may triangulate the information with other secondary data (tweets, social media, etc.) and establish whether it has evidence to support it. Much as an intelligence officer uses multiple sources of information to validate an insight (geospatial data, field observations, and secondary reports), validation is an integral part of the Pulse Center real-time capability.

Issue claims may be "closed" if there is not enough evidence, meaning that they are removed from the system. However, others in the network may "reopen" an issue if there is reason to believe that it has been incorrectly closed. This occurs frequently, because in some cases, the issue has meaning to someone close to the site, but may not seem to be important to an executive or to someone at a monitoring station who is not able to interpret the issue in the context of disruptions to the network.

When an issue is validated or closed and reopened, an established network of individuals on the notification list receive an alert on their mobile phones. The governance around this notification list may be aligned around geographies, product lines, functional groupings, or other factors that are organized and established around the individual company's corporate strategy and structure. In general, however, anybody is authorized to jump onto an issue, and empowered to say, "I can help," or, "Here's my insight on this issue." In this way, notes and comments are posted to an issue, providing an immediate forum for discussion and sharing of points of view. This occurs in real time, whereas many companies require days and even weeks of conference calls and meetings to fully understand what happened and how to resolve it.

A critical rule of disruption management is that as length of time to react to a reaction is reduced, so is the impact on operations and cost to resolve the issue. Because of the Pulse Center capability, the resolution time for Flex to address an issue has gone down by 30–40% since inception of the system. But the challenge isn't just about people in Flex's factories raising issues; suppliers themselves have to be willing to raise issues occurring in their own facilities!

The ability to adopt a unified approach to raising issues is a massive shift in supply chain thinking and culture. This is not simply a technology problem, but of a "people problem." The psychological shift and corporate culture associated with creating issues will undoubtedly be one of the biggest challenges to which companies who go down this path must adjust.

As noted in this chapter's opening quote, Elementum's CEO points out that problem discovery is key to transparency and requires federation of the parties in the supply chain to be able to act on data. In this case, revenue protection, not revenue risk, is the key. Companies need to think of their supply chain partners as those with the power to shut down supply chain networks, and who thus are the "guardians of revenue." Even the most minuscule of issues, which might be a minor violation, can quickly spin out of control, especially if it is captured by the press and embellished with innuendo and double meanings. And that causes a massive hit on product revenue. By the time it gets to decision-makers, every minor issue in the supply chain can become a multimillion dollar problem due to the length of the time required to escalate issues to senior executives who make decisions. Like the Vietnam-era soldier who suffered because of delays in decisions made at the HQ, those in the field need to create issues that have immediate visibility and can be acted upon quickly to address, contain, and resolve problems at their source.

The ability to rapidly assess the validity of an event requires highly intelligent machine capabilities, combined with intelligent analysts who can scan evidence and rapidly asses the gravity of a situation. The process is not perfect, but it combines automated data capture with human intelligence and decision-making. Just as farmers view satellite data to determine the changing color of their corn crops and estimate their growth pattern and timing, analysts need to use some level of judgment to enable decision-making in supply chains. But the power of "crowd-sourcing" is important here, as it is well known that the power of multiple observations and judgments highly exceeds those of a single individual, which is why others in the network can comment on the event. Flex's Pulse Center uses insights from supplier factories, IP address locations, satellite data, digital camera inputs, social media posts, and news feeds to quickly assess issues as they arise. This requires suppliers to share their data. One way of enhancing this capability is to provide suppliers with "free" software that not only allows them to better manage their shipments and inventory, but also provides data feeds on production levels, inventory, and issues. In many situations, changes in production levels can indicate issues and problems that may otherwise go undetected.

Many suppliers in low-cost countries are reluctant to provide the physical location of the factories where their products are produced. But if software exists that tracks IP addresses of production items, the data can be used to validate the point of origin of shipments, a capability that is becoming increasingly important. (For example, if the supplier says it has two factories as its risk mitigation plan, but they are across the street from one another, this isn't an effective plan!) If the production does not appear to be coming from the factory that was audited as part of the supplier qualification, then perhaps it is being illegally subcontracted from another location.

Information collected from the field is an integral component of the real-time, LIVING supply chain. Field teams are an integral part of the intelligence network, just as field agents inform intelligence analysts in the government. "Hope" is not a good strategy to rely on in today's global environment (e.g., "We HOPE our suppliers are doing the right thing! We HOPE a flood doesn't wipe out our inventory of hard drives!") The essential ingredient is not just technology, but reliance on people in the network who can be trusted to report something that isn't right, even if it is just a perception or a hunch. It also requires human curation and judgment to understand who is providing the intelligence, as well as the ability to understand what they are saying, map their insights to the parts of the network that are impacted, and determine how to solve the problem. But the key is to get the right people working in the supply base, because that's where it all starts.

The purpose of analysts/curators in the data centers is NOT to discover problems – that is the job of the people on the ground who are seeing first-hand what is happening. Analysts need to validate the issue, escalate it to the right people, and quickly coordinate the solution. Once the right individuals are presented with a problem, they can determine how to solve it. This change of mindset is a transformation that is going on today in the Flex network. This is where the acceleration in problem-solving has emerged as a key capability of its integrated global network.

But ultimately, culture trumps process. You can't always see the individual who is raising the issues in Pulse. But you can determine that person's reliability over time, and that is another factor included in the analytical dashboards. If one person is raising a lot of issues that are never validated, the analytics will show that as well. One can also see who is solving issues, which is another policing mechanism. Flex holds global issue management meetings to review the history of issues raised, and to determine who was responsible for raising, solving, and validating issues, and whether there is a problem with certain individuals. But to make it work, you have to have a core ingredient: trust.

Creating Federated Supply Chains

Trust is the currency of collaboration, in that it requires individuals to demonstrate that there is a visible effort to listen, understand, and be inclusive. It is up to senior executives and all leaders to invest in relationships with local leaders, to establish a culture that seeks to understand what is happening.

–Jeff Ge, Chief Supply Chain Officer, Steelcase

The need to create a new global culture and a new way of building an organization is fundamental to development of "real-time" supply chain capability. Jeff Ge, Chief Supply Chain Officer of Steelcase, shared with me his vision of the critical nature of becoming a data-driven, real-time organization that was bound by a common culture. Jeff emphasized that this change was less about building the right software platform, than with transforming culture. This was all the more important, he said, as we operate in a global world.

The idea of a "federated supply chain" is at the very core of this evolution. It is, as Tom points out, a realization that we are all in this together – no matter what tier of the supply chain you are in. One link fails and the chain breaks.

In a federated supply chain, the "customer-end" of the chain determines the behavior, requirements and norms expected of every participant in the chain from its earliest beginning to its end.

One element that is becoming increasingly apparent is that organizations that create supply chains that have a common purpose, a common objective, and an aligned set of cultural norms, seem to operate better than those who work in an adversarial, dog-eat-dog network. Once again, the natural laws of evolution provide a clue to this phenomenon.

Serengeti Rule 4: Body size affects the mode of regulation. Observers of animal behaviors in the Serengeti noted that creatures smaller than 120 kilograms tended to die from attacks by predators, while larger animals, who often were herbivores (giraffes, hippos, rhinos, and elephants) were often too big to be preyed on by lions and other predators. Thus, smaller animals are regulated by predators, but concurrently larger animals are regulated by food supply (bottom-up regulation).

A parallel rule exists in the global supply chain.

New Supply Chain Rule 4: Large firms dominate smaller firms through acquisition or "federation." New small firms sustain the growth of larger firms.

Or stated another way:

New Supply Chain Rule 4: Collaborative competition ensures that supply chains remain healthy.

This observation can be seen in the manner in which companies have acquired others in their ecosystem (Dow-Dupont, Dell-EMC, Medtronic-Covidien, Microsoft-LinkedIn). As firms grow, their influence on the supply chain expands, and they acquire competitors. This leads to increased size, which drives a continuous cycle of growth. However, as firms acquire smaller companies, they often find themselves less nimble, which is why smaller firms are often more agile and more innovative. This quality makes them a target for acquisition.

But is acquisition the only model of growth? An alternative to acquiring new firms is to work with firms through "federation." Federated supply chains presume that entities operate in a decentralized network, but that they are aligned based on a strong central entity, guided by a strong centralized purpose that is established by the dominant firm in the network. This dominant firm establishes the processes, industry standards, metrics, standards of ethical and sustainable behavior, and drives these cultural elements into organizations they work with. A lot of this occurs through collaborative means, suggesting that organic growth occurs when all the enterprises (living things) are in balance and operating on a common wavelength. But collaboration has to also be competitive – and only the healthiest animals will stay alive and grow. In the course of this, predators will integrate smaller prey into their network, but will provide sustenance to these smaller prey that will allow them to survive and remain healthy. The entire ecosystem of larger enterprises supporting smaller ones and vice versa keeps the supply chain healthy: natural competition is combined with collaboration.

The idea that large organizations can create a "federated" network by integrating smaller firms into their network, thereby dominating the network, is emerging as key to global competition. Federation implies common operating procedures and established standards, driving aligned supply chain processes and tacit understanding of how things work. The idea of federated supply chains has actually been around for a while, and Peter Drucker first described the idea.

> Any organization requires strong parts and a strong center. "The term decentralization is actually misleading – though far too common by now to be discarded. Federal decentralization requires strong guidance from the center through the setting of clear, meaningful and strong objectives for the whole. The objectives must demand both a high degree of business performance and a high standard of conduct throughout the enterprise."[4]

---

4 Drucker, P., *The Practice of Management*, Harper Business, New York, 1956, p. 214.

Suppliers who work for a larger company in a federated supply chain are happy. The suppliers I've interviewed at federated supply chains like Honda, John Deere, Intel, and Flex don't want to leave, as they feel they are treated as equals and assured a steady revenue. They also understand that they are in it for the long haul. Over time, suppliers' loyalty toward the dominant firm grows. That is one reason that companies like Honda have begun using the term "supplier for life," which suggests a strong, paternal relationship governed by high performance expectations, fair product price negotiations, and deep understanding of long-term technology and customer roadmaps.

So if "federated" supply chains implies a common purpose, standards, and approach – isn't this the same as "collaborative supply chains"? Not necessarily.

A cautionary note – In his book *The Serengeti Rules*, Carroll explains how the bottom affects the top in the chain of life. In the 1920s, wolves were effectively wiped out in the American West. This led to an explosion in the elk population, which caused a rapid decline in the aspen population, as elk eat aspen shoots. As the aspen was depleted, the elk struggled. The lesson? Success is in the balance, and even predators are an important component of the natural environment in maintaining this balance.

Beyond Collaboration and Integration: Federated Supply Chains Are the Next Frontier

The concept of collaboration has gotten a lot of grief lately. Recent articles in *Harvard Business Review* (HBR) and *The Economist* emphasize that collaboration has reached the point of "godliness" in modern business, and that as managers are overwhelmed with collaborative tools, they complain that multitasking through collaboration reduces the quality of work and takes too long. *HBR* estimates that 20–35% of value-added collaborations come from only 3–5% of employees. The cost of collaboration is also estimated to be severe; researchers at the University of Virginia estimate that knowledge workers spend 70–85% of their time attending meetings, dealing with e-mail, talking on the phone, or dealing with an avalanche of requests for input or advice. Such distractions are believed to make "deep work" difficult if not impossible. The authors suggest that distraction is the enemy and that we need to recognize that workers have a finite amount of time, and that small demands can quickly escalate into massive invasions into their ability to get work done.

While this perspective has some merit, real-time supply chain companies have found a way to manage the fine line between too much invasion into people's thinking time, and the ability to drive improved decision-making through a more process-driven form of collaboration, one that includes a level of governance and oversight that results in the right behavior. The Pulse Center at Flex has become a hub of activity, which drives collaborative behavior around data.

Access to real-time data leads naturally to *ad hoc* workshops, as people gather to review data, debate issues, and reach consensus on important decisions. But it is the data that creates the "place" that is Pulse. Data simultaneously provides a system, a place, and a natural magnet for collaboration. Real-time data is the glue that drives federated supply chains, as information leads to understanding and common action.

A supply chain executive at Steelcase, Jeff Ng, understands how global collaboration is key to a federated supply chain system.

> This need to understand many points of view is the central theme of collaboration. It requires that you be able to understand who people are, and what they do. It also requires that you understand how work happens today, and be willing to allow some variation in processes, up to a point.

Aligning people around data and a common process for decision-making is key to federation. Also, key is allowing some level of variation in how decisions are made. Organizations have always needed to establish standards of performance, embodied in policies and procedures. However, in a recent global study of logistics providers,[5] we discovered that top-performing organizations have designed a form of supply chain governance that builds in flexibility to adapt to local requirements. These organizations, for example, develop a global process for delivering an outcome in the form of a "maturity framework," one which allowed people in the global network to achieve the outcome in a manner appropriate to local cultural norms.

Many of the leading organizations we interviewed recognize that logistics requirements vary from region to region, and thus have moved to a regional logistics design governed by a centralized supply chain council. This governing council establishes overall guidelines and structures that allow regional work to operate at a world-class level. Typically, such councils' standards consist of three components: process, policy, and playbooks. First, the standards define the necessary processes (e.g., customer order promising, transportation planning, order fulfillment). Second, they define necessary policies (e.g., finalizing orders, allocation, scheduling). Finally, "playbooks" act as user guides on how employees should think through and achieve process requirements.

When major tradeoffs or conflicts occur between regional requirements, organizations have adopted a global sales and operations planning function to optimize global requirements across regional requirements, especially around global product lines. Once these plans are established, however, top executives realize that each region will interpret and act on them differently. The outcome – a federated supply chain – is the desired outcome for this approach.

---

5 Handfield, R., Straube, F., Pfohl, H.-C., and Wieland, A., *Trends and Strategies in Logistics and Supply Chain Management*, BVL International, Berlin, 2013.

Federation is based on the simple thesis that supply chain leaders cannot standardize the entire world, and need processes that solve issues in 80% of cases, allowing for local adoption in the remaining 20% of cases (so long as the outcome meets the process playbook). Federation thus requires a clearly defined organization, with clear roles and responsibilities, so that people may address the same processes using the same toolboxes. This ensures that all parties are "speaking the same language" and using comparable metrics and plans. At the same time, differences should be highlighted. Leaders should be aware of the challenges and successes of regions, what they struggle with, and what they are proud of. Leaders also should be prepared to accept different points of view on what is working locally and what is not, in order to adapt the process to fit local requirements. This requires interactive communication to ensure that everyone is kept informed of decisions. Interaction creates intelligence. Thus, a cyclical view of new ideas, feedback, and response that forms the interactivity drives new knowledge. Technology is the game changer that allows knowledge-building to happen more quickly. Trust, however, is the essential ingredient. It allows data to cross boundaries, and forms the glue for federation.

The idea of collaboration is also implicit in *Nonzero: The Logic of Human Destiny* by historian Robert Wright. This book explores the non-zero concept behind game theory, which suggests that over the course of history, zero-sum games are not as common as non-zero-sum games. In the latter case, non-zero-sum games involve collaboration between the parties in an ecosystem – whether they are cells from multicellular organisms, multi-village policies with centralized rules, or hunter–gatherer societies. When these parties work together, they tend to mutually benefit. Wright, who has a positive view of the world, suggests that positive correlations in non-zero-sum games produce two winners, and that this often occurs in economics. Wright does not deny the existence of exploitation, but is intrinsically upbeat, claiming that non-zero-sum games create more win–win than win–lose outcomes. This concept is fundamental to the LIVING supply chain. Unless organisms work together as a network with full information and trust, survival in a complex, constantly changing world is impossible.

So what does this mean for collaboration? It means that organizations need to create a culture that welcomes transparency, because, simply put, transparency leads to trust. In a culture of transparency and trust, collaboration becomes something that occurs naturally, and is not "forced" on people by apps, social media, or tools. The central theme is that people speak up when they need to, but that otherwise, guidelines that maximize flow and velocity drive the right balance of input. This concept goes beyond value chains, in which "control towers" pass down decisions from the top, toward collaboration, in which customer value is the primary objective. Collaboration works when it is an intrinsic part of the system, not added as an external tool. Similarly, nature is in balance through an intrinsic self-guiding collaborative environment, and falls out of balance when one or more forces are disrupted leading to disruption in the balance.

The guidelines below can help create the right balance of trust, collaboration, and flow that leads to federated supply chains. These guidelines, which apply to the extended enterprise, not just to the four walls of a company, are embedded in Flex's culture.

1. Multi-tier supplier management is a multicompany visibility imperative

Every individual in every supplier company has a responsibility and a commitment to raise issues and create a visible, transparent process. This is a massive commitment for many companies, and executives we met with emphasize that it is almost impossible in places such as Asia and the Middle East. The fact that these business cultures are averse to transparency is not an excuse. Visibility is a requirement for change. Creating visibility requires developing trust, which requires a "series of small promises kept" over time. When individuals perceive that their business partners' actions are well intentioned, change will come.

Legal and IP issues often hinder collaboration in the supply market. IACCM's Tim Cummins proposes that contracts, if developed properly, become vehicles that enhance collaboration. However, if all is well in the "ocean" of competition, then the shark–fish–shrimp–algae food chain should remain in balance. As discussed in "Serengeti Rule 4", larger predators keep the balance, and smaller animals and plants benefit. In the same way, supply chains stay healthy through balanced competition as dictated by "New Supply Chain Rule 4"; natural competition drives suppliers to continually improve performance, and enough customers exist to allow suppliers to switch from those that are not profitable enough to keep. Balanced competition implies a federated system in which larger companies ensure a large enough pool of suppliers to keep competition healthy, but not so many that relationship management becomes cumbersome. Flex calls this "managed supplier relationships" (MSR), which implies relationships that are practical, realistic, and healthy. And when transparency complements competition and healthy tension, a new dynamic is created that creates federated supply chains.

As another example, Honda, even though it believes in "suppliers for life," also always maintains healthy competition in its markets. Honda utilizes "cost models" that allowed them to pinpoint variables such as labor and material costs, appropriate levels of overhead for different industry sectors, and a healthy, but not over-the-top margin. In driving year-over-year cost reduction, Honda is continually seeking ways to remove cost from the variable and overhead segments of a supplier's cost, while ensuring a healthy margin. The company is however, always looking for new suppliers particularly as they expand to new global regions. However, new suppliers go through a rigorous set of audits and inspections, and must demonstrate that they are not only competitive on cost, but have the capability for delivery, quality service, and new technology development. New product introduction and ramp-up is a critical element of performance, and happens on an annual basis, with a 5-year rolling window. Procurement at Honda owns the "commercial" side of the relationship, while engineering works on the "technical" side, with the two groups working side by side to create effective competition and continuous performance improvement.

2. Technology can be applied to Create Supply Chain Transparency

The old tools of collaboration, whether they are email, LinkedIn, Facebook, social chatter, or Twitter are public, and have a very different purpose than the tools necessary to manage the real-time supply chain. New tools must be designed with the psychological understanding and intention to create visibility. These technologies must create greater transparency, the ultimate ingredient that leads to visibility in federated supply chains. The Elementum and Flex story provides a useful case study.

Nader Mikhail, founder and CEO of the software company Elementum, described how the firm got started.

> I was working for Flex, and was hired in to solve the problem of transparency. I looked at how the company was purchasing products and contracting services and working with suppliers, and thought about how we could solve the problem using third-party software. Eventually, I went to the board and told them I thought we could create this transparency network ourselves. Although we were "born from Flex," we had no software because nothing existed around our vision, so we had to build it from scratch. We hired the very top guys from Google and Netflix and Amazon and challenged them to address the problem. The premise upfront was that 90% of our transparency applications and usage would be on mobile devices.

Elementum is striving to build a culture of transparency across a number of global companies, using software that combines Big Data analytics, LinkedIn social media, and planning and control systems on steroids. Understanding how Elementum works is less about understanding the technology and more about understanding how technology drives transparency in a new, meaningful way. Transparency refers to upstream participants (suppliers) being transparent about what is going on in their factories. Visibility refers to the ability of downstream participants (the big animals) to see what is going on downwind in their supply chain. Multiple cultural issues get in the way of transparency and visibility, which is a key part of the federated supply chain concept. Nader explained:

> The reality, of course, is that "trust" is a very difficult word to get around in a highly litigious society. This is a very real cultural issue that companies need to give some thought to before they go down the road of transparency. If you are going to be transparent, you need to be prepared for the aftermath of what happens when all this information is out there in the network! The demands for transparency from suppliers and manufacturers are increasing rapidly. Governments now want to know whether conflict minerals are present in your products, and whether workers in factories all over the world are working in ILO-compliant working conditions. These same legal counsels are throwing a lot of money at these problems in the form of increased audits – but we all know an audit can only uncover so much, so they aren't having much success. And the key element to consider is that you can't sort out these kinds of problems on your own. You need to have a link with trusted partners in the network, to "design-in" a conflict mineral tracking process, for example, that spans multiple tiers of the supply chain, to include indicators that provide warnings that all is not right in third world factories. People are very excited about solving these types of problems – but fail to recognize the importance of the relationship that has to exist between companies in the supply chain network. You can't define software systems to measure these indicators automatically – they require that partners be certified, and have agreements to share information not just on their own internal operations, but those of their suppliers, meaning they will need to act as an intermediary. This is almost heresy when you start to look at cultures such as Asia, where no one wants to share information at all!

Driving this level of insight requires significant investments in new tools that meet the multicompany, multi-tier visibility, and transparency imperative.

3. Legal limits are needed to manage supply chain inter-company communication

While complete transparency is the ultimate objective, legal issues must be respected. Multicompany NDAs and memos of understanding are a start. However, ultimately, responsibility for behaviors comes down to mutual trust. Years ago, companies like Honda derived the term "supplier for life," which suggests that "unless you do something to break our bond of trust and mutual respect and improvement, you will continue to be a partner."

Elementum's leadership team encountered several big legal issues with clients. Whenever you start sharing information, lawyers start to get in the way. The first set of comments lawyers inevitably raise when confronted with a move toward information transparency and visibility are

- Who owns the data?
- Who can access the information?
- What is our risk exposure?
- We can't do this.

Lawyers are very good at saying "NO." I've also seen this in our work at our Supply Chain Resource Cooperative[6] at North Carolina State University. Our projects have focused on building collaborative platform for "should cost" models to track labor, material, overhead, and productivity rates for a standard set of manufacturing processes. Lawyers' first reaction to sharing data in any format, anonymous or not, is resistance. They often raise major concerns about intellectual privacy, or more often, making available information that could lead to litigation.

The second major legal hurdle is country borders. This issue is especially complicated in Europe. Not only has Brexit raised regulatory issues, but many European countries have regulations that basically state that "you have to make sure all data stays in Europe!" How can you keep data in Europe when by definition, you have a global supply chain with suppliers all over the world?! This causes a big hurdle: "I want transparency, but don't want my data to leave Europe!" We encountered the same issue in China, where the government restricts data from going outside the country.

The third legal problem occurs when companies want to start sharing information about planning across the enterprise. If you are a "secretive company" – and companies like Apple are very secretive, especially about their product releases – you don't want to share files and information with everyone in your supply chain. In the last year, rumors circulated from Apple's suppliers that their orders are lower than normal, leading to predictions about iPhone sales and Apple's lowering revenue projections. People want to hide information when they believe the markets – and competitors – will get wind of it. Imagine that your firm was hyper-transparent, so that everyone knew what was happening in the supply chain. This is enough to drive a typical general counsel absolutely nuts, as she or he can't control the message. Then the CFO gets concerned as well. Analysts who get hold of this information can start making all sorts of market trades that can careen the share price into volatile territory.

---

6 The Supply Chain Resource Cooperative (http://scm.ncsu.edu) is a university–industry partnership focused on thought leadership for the supply chain community.

Flex recognizes the importance of legal considerations in rolling out the LIVING Supply Chain. In fact, the company has helped to introduce what might be considered a new specialty in legal services by bringing on Ben Warner, (a 16-year veteran of Flex having served in both procurement and legal roles), who is now familiarly called the "VP of Future Time Information." Ben is requiring Flex's lawyers to become more integrated with the supply chain function, in order to understand the goals of the LIVING Supply Chain. Ben notes that "Running a legal services organization on Pulse and with the aid of the VP of Real Time Information helps us deliver more transparency and value to our customers."

The need to both be transparent about information as well as prevent leaks for customer can prove to be challenging. For example, an extreme amount of security surrounds new product events. Consider the following description of a new product roll-out for a major technology provider:

> Security is one of the most challenging components of a product roll-out, because the manufacturer wishes to be able to deploy a product roll-out simultaneously across the entire country, in California, New York, Chicago, Shanghai, and everywhere in the world. This makes it extremely challenging for logistics providers. Some companies emphasize the same "experience" for all of their products, and this was one of the toughest parts of meeting their logistics requirements on new products. This can be challenging as Customs clearance becomes critical to the success of the roll-out.

Does this mean that transparency compromises product roll-outs? Not at all. In this case, the availability of real-time data actually served to render the simultaneous, global roll-out of this product more secure and smoother than ever. This occurred because all parties in the supply chain were "federated," and aligned in a common goal: keeping the roll-out as secret as possible, and running it on time.

UPS is a third-party distributor that specializes in this type of activity. A UPS executive recently spoke in one of my classes on the importance of transparency and product tracking in the supply chain.

> One of the benefits of UPS is that we have our own people on customs, and we can get the material through much easier than a third party can. One of the biggest differentiators for us is that for demanding customers, every transfer point has to be electronic and real time – and there is a cost with the demands for the tracking and tracing of the shipment. Real-time commitment is critical. If you can't provide real-time tracking, you won't even be invited to bid. This is all done by real-time scanning with agreed-on scan points, including the transfer from their dock at the

plant, transport to the airport, turnover to the carrier, loading onto the plane, another transmission on wheels-up (showing whether the plane is behind), and the technology wrapped around all these scans and systems has a cost to be wrapped around that. Liability insurance is another issue. Will it be for each container, product in the container, or the entire aircraft? If the entire aircraft goes down, there is a cost to providing that insurance. If we don't use our own airline, we have to buy insurance. Once the plane lands, we move the product from the airport to the factory, and in some countries, need to worry about security of drivers and prevention of hijacking. The route has to be approved and in some parts of the world, chase vehicles provided with the trucks so there is no hijacking. This makes simultaneous product release at stores even more complicated.

Despite the complexity of product roll-outs, real-time data sharing is the key. That, and the alignment of people in a federated supply chain with a common purpose.

4. Collective, informed, individual decisions drive optimal outcomes

Is there a common governance structure that defines how observations are translated into issues, then monitored, validated, and translated into specific actions and responses? And, is there an approach that ensures that the data is treated appropriately, and that individuals are responsible for responding to it appropriately? This question drives scholars crazy. There is always a rationale for individual views of what is happening locally – but this can be counteracted when no centralized view of the "big picture" drives global thinking. The answer is that both are needed – a concept we call "collective individualism."

The essential ingredient driving LIVING federated supply chains to evolve and grow is interactions and relationships between individuals within the network of partners. Many recent views of supply chain technology emphasize the "control tower" thinking – an approach that also dominates supply chain scholarship. These scholars propose that centralized organizations are the core element in centralizing "big data" to drive and control what is happening around the world. In this view, only "experts" should have access to this data, as this is effectively what will drive the right level of control. Decisions should be passed down to the minions on the front lines, who take orders from their intellectual superiors.

This linear, "dictatorial" view of organizational operations has had very negative consequences over time. In fact, the problem was identified more than 50 years ago by economist Jay Forrester, who discovered the "bullwhip effect" of inventory, which promulgated the radical idea that massive inefficiencies exist in supply chains when decisions are made in a vacuum, based on individual perceptions of what is happening in the world.

The bullwhip effect (also known as the Forrester effect), was one of the first major theoretical advances in supply chain theory. (In fact, the term supply chain hadn't even been invented yet). Forrester based his theory on his observations of odd outcomes in a retail supply chain. He noted that an organization's orders to its suppliers displayed greater variation than the original source of demand for these orders.[7,8] This relationship was ascribed to behavioral (albeit rational) forms of decision-making associated with individuals' lack of visibility into supply chain demand forecasts. In the pre-integration age, suppliers' suppliers and customers' customers were kept at arms' length in terms of order visibility. When orders arrived, it was always considered a "surprise," and the external environment that produced these orders was considered a mystery. Order variability and volatility were considered business conditions that managers just have to live with, and so the natural response was to use large amount of buffer inventory to mitigate the risk of not "having enough" to meet this level of variability. This paradigm drove traditional supply chain thinking, as it enabled organizations to explain the underlying phenomena as part of the bullwhip effect.[9]

The central thesis of the bullwhip effect is that each individual's rational but limited view of their environment led to "local" thinking, which in turn created waste and sub-optimization in a multi-enterprise network. As managers were incentivized to "never run out of product," they bolstered inventory levels to create safety stock, knowing they would be penalized if they ran out. As a result, the further back one goes in the supply chain, the more the "extra" inventory increases. Consequently, inventory escalated to enormous proportions, while the level of transparency decreased.[10] The only way to counteract the bullwhip effect, according to many scholars, is full transparency of in-coming current orders, inventory, and forecasts across systems. A graphic of the bullwhip effect is shown in Figure 3.2. In addition, a real example from a medical products company showing the amount of days of inventory in the supply chain is shown in Figure 3.3.

Several recent books have also challenged the idea of a "centralized control tower" – notably in the military sector. One of these is the military, described in *Team of Teams*, a fascinating book by Gen. Stanley McChrystal. McChrystal

---

7 Forrester, J. W., *Industrial Dynamics*, Productivity Press, Portland, OR, 1961.

8 Lee, H. L., Padmanabhan, V., and Whang, S., "Information Distortion in a Supply Chain: The Bullwhip Effect," *Management Science*, vol. 43, no. 4, 1997, pp. 546–558.

9 Lee, H. L., "Taming the Bullwhip," *Journal of Supply Chain Management*, vol. 46, no. 1, 2010, pp. 7–10.

10 Forrester, *Industrial Dynamics*.

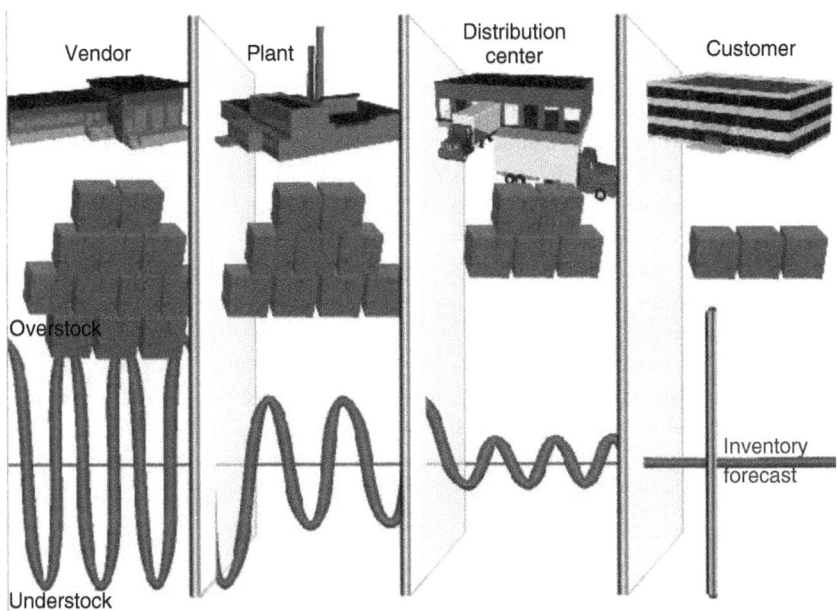

Figure 3.2   The Bullwhip Effect

notes that in the old "control tower" structure, his top-notch military team in Iraq felt they were superior in every respect to the enemy:

> We were exemplary in our discipline. Our superior resources had not bred complacency; we were pushing our assets harder than they had ever been pushed. ... But we also had to ask a deeper, more troubling question: If we were the best of the best, why were such attacks not disappearing, but in fact increasing? Why were we unable to defeat an under-resourced insurgency? *Why were we losing?*

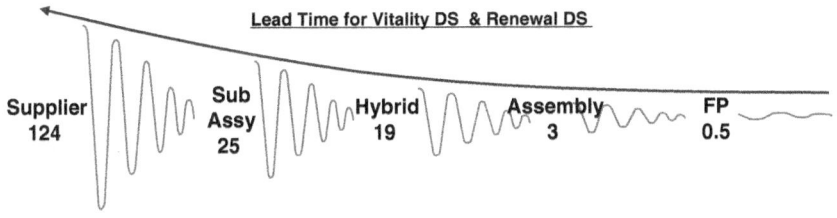

Figure 3.3   Lead Time for a Medical Product Supply Chain. *Source:* Ben Martin et al. Reproduced with permission of triz-journal.com

The answer came to the team when they began to understand that defeating Al Qaeda in Iraq (AQI) necessitated learning from them, and adopting AQI's approach to leveraging the digitally interconnected world of social media to their advantage. The enemy was connecting and developing battlefield intelligence at a much more rapid pace then the US forces, and were beating them consistently as a result. McChrystal notes that in so doing, they were able to combat Al Qaeda's battle style by adopting its norms and weapons[11]:

> In the course of this fight, we had to unlearn a great deal of what we thought we knew about how war – and the world worked ... Specifically, we restructured our force from the ground up on principles of extremely transparent information sharing (what we called "shared consciousness") and decentralized decision-making authority ("empowered execution"). We dissolved the barriers – the walls of our silos and the floors of our hierarchies – that had once made us efficient. ... We became what we called "a team of teams": a large command that captured at scale the traits of agility normally limited to small teams.

A foundation of the LIVING supply chain is based on disassembling the control tower structure, embracing instead decentralized decision-making and the "democratization of data," which utilizes a social-media-like technology to drive data into the hands of individuals through mobile devices. Again, the idea of collective individualism is important – in that people make decisions that drive collective benefits to the whole.

5. Speed in decision-making drives flow and drives out cost

Decentralized but informed data-based decision-making prevails in many other successful organizations. One also sees it in the so-called "flywheel effect," which John Rossman describes in his book *The Amazon Way*. Recall that the "bullwhip effect" proposes that rational decision-making based on limited human views of phenomena drives excess inventory in the chain. Amazon views independent decision-making as essential to its culture, and the phrase "Yes it is your job" implies ownership of decisions. The idea is that "Ownership means not only mastering your domain, but also being willing to go beyond the boundaries of your role whenever it's needed to improve customer experience or fix a problem."[12] Another concept – "invent and simplify" – also emphasizes that when employees are empowered to act independently, their ideas can simplify

---

11 McChrystal, G. S., Collins, T., Silverman, D., and Fussell, C., *Team of Teams: New Rules of Engagement for a Complex World*, Penguin, New York, 2015.

12 Rossman, J., *The Amazon Way: 14 Leadership Principles behind the World's Most Disruptive Company*, CreateSpace, North Charleston, SC, 2014, p. 28.

processes to drive out bureaucracy, solve problems, and find innovative ways of doing things that the rest of the company can adopt.

Rossman posits the flywheel effect as a core element in the rise of Amazon. He notes, "Allen Mandelbrot founded the field of fractal mathematics, which studies, among other phenomena, how patterns in nature have a tendency to repeat themselves at different scales – for example, the way spiral galaxies resemble whirling sea shells which in turn resemble tiny unfurling fern fronds. In a similar fractal fashion, the virtuous cycle is replicated throughout Amazon.com at macro and micro levels. It generates a set of self-reinforcing energies that continue to flow even when the energy source is discontinuous – much like a flywheel, which is the favorite metaphor to describe the cycle for success for Amazon."

This "flywheel" is a cycle that Internet pioneer Jeff Bezos initiated when he founded Amazon. Bezos was adamant about driving lower retail prices and free shipping to cultivate customer loyalty. Revenues were plowed back relentlessly into the "holy trinity" of lower prices, improved customer selection (as more sellers were attracted to the site), and availability of products, which led to greater traffic to the website. Greater traffic led to growth, which drove lower costs and lower prices, continually augmenting the customer experience.

Rossman points out that customers talking to each other produces a follow-on effect, and that the best customer service is no customer service. The best experience happens when the customer never has to ask for help at all. As a corollary, "The key to creating the most pleasant, frictionless customer experience possible was minimizing human involvement through process innovation and technology" (p. 8).

Allen Mandelbrot, who founded the field of fractal mathematics ("Mandelbrot sets"), noted that many natural phenomena produce patterns that resemble both whirling seashells and tiny unfurling fern fronds. The so-called "virtuous cycle" is similar to fractal patterns in that it is replicated throughout Amazon at macro and micro levels. This cycle generates a set of self-reinforcing energies that continue to flow even when the energy source is discontinuous – much like a flywheel. This phenomenon supports the idea of a living supply chain network which moves continuously, flowing information and materials at a faster and faster rate, keeping customers even more satisfied and driving funds and materials quickly through the supply chain.

The flywheel is the premise behind the Flex Pulse Center, which focuses on flow or speed over decision-making, and moves away from a control tower structure. A key underlying analogy is the idea of flow – an important premise in "lean," but which is not always well executed. Supply chains are like water, in that they will always flow to the point of least resistance. A Chinese proverb states that cost is like water: it will always flow to the lowest point if left to the market conditions. In the same way, supply chains will always find the fastest way, if the free flow of information enables managers to make natural and responsive decisions. Route maps have evolved into works of lean architecture where time is treated as waste, and waste is emblematic of higher cost. But by speeding up information flows, logistics networks can also be rescheduled and rerouted.

The "flywheel" concept of continuous cycles of improvement that drive cost structures down and improve customer experience is similar to the Flex Pulse Center because the center focuses on flow, visibility, and speed of decision-making (the "anti-control tower" phenomenon), which leads to lower working capital, which frees up cash, which improves share price, which allows Flex to grow, acquire more companies, or invest in new technology that delights customers and further drives down working capital.

Both the flywheel at Amazon and the Pulse Center at Flex drive supply chains to operate and flow to the point of least resistance. Both operational structures operate on organic principles, like water in the Chinese proverb. Supply chains flow because decisions are made rapidly and transparently, causing cost (like water), to flow to the lowest point.

Selfishness in Supply Chains Drives Non-zero Outcomes

Transparency is important between members of the same supply chain network. But trust and open data sharing between competitors in the supply chain has its limitations, especially when resource scarcity is an issue. Recall that in the Serengeti, survival is the most important daily activity for creatures. Likewise, competition in the global business ecosystem lurks around every corner, and competitive advantage is a daily activity. Supply chain executives in competing organizations are always willing to share information about how to avoid a major disruption before the disruption occurs. They will collaborate, share best practices, and provide insights to one another. But once a disruption happens, it is every man for himself. In the aftermath of a major supply chain disaster, or a major shortage of raw materials upstream, executives are much less likely to share information with competing companies. Why? Because then, they are fighting for limited resources, just like in the Serengeti! Whoever gets to those resources the quickest will feel the least pain and impact on their profit and competitiveness, will recover the quickest, will return most quickly to normal operations, and, critically, will have the least negative impact on customers.

The idea that selfishness drives healthy outcomes works both in the broad context of evolution and survival, and in the, "non-zero"[13] world view put forward by Robert Wright. Wright argues that "In zero-sum games, the fortunes of the players are inversely related," as in tennis, boxing, and chess. "In non-zero sum games, one player's gain needn't be bad news for the other" (p. 5). John

---

13 Wright, R., *Nonzero: The Logic of Human Destiny*, First Vintage Books, 2000.

Nash, the famous mathematician who discovered the field of game theory, also found that over the long run, equilibrium typically occurs when both parties work together toward a non-zero sum outcome.

Nash notes, "… if we want to see what drives the direction of both human history and organic evolution, we should apply this perspective more systematically. Interaction among individual genes, or cells, or animals, among interest groups or nations or corporations, can be viewed through the lenses of game theory."

Wright posits that, as technology evolves, newer and richer forms of non-zero-sum interaction are made possible, even as social complexity grows. He also notes:

> This isn't to say that non-zero-sum games always have win–win outcomes rather than lose–lose outcomes. Nor is it to say that the powerful and the treacherous never exploit the weak and the naive; parasitic behavior is often possible in non-zero-sum games, and history offers no shortage of examples. Still, on balance, over the long run, non-zero-sum situations produce more positive sums than negative sums, more mutual benefit than parasitism. As a result, people become embedded in larger and richer webs of interdependence.

This concept of non-zero-sum games directly supports the New Supply Chain Rule 4: Collaborative competition ensures supply chains remain healthy. In addition, the non-zero concept is also aligned with the healthy balance that occurs when larger predators are sustained by smaller creatures in the Serengeti ecosystem. Think of the parallel questions confronted by managers in supply chains. Does selfish behavior produce good outcomes in business? Does "looking after my enterprise first" after a major supply chain disruption produce the best outcome for the supply chain? Resolving the apparent disparate nature of acting selfishly (or on behalf of our enterprise) with the need to work collaboratively across the supply chain, is a question that confronts us in these situations. The non-zero view of the world appears to suggest that collaborative competition is the natural state of the system, so long as organizations operate efficiently and only consume what they need.

An example from *Nonzero* provides a good metaphor with which to illustrate the paradox of collaborative competition. Wright recounts the history of the coastal Tareumiut Eskimos, who rely on whale-hunting to survive. Each whaling boat is run by an umealiq – a boat owner – who recruits a crew which includes specialists such as a helmsman and a harpooner. Boat owners must band together to land a whale. And in a Tareumiut village, all boat owners have created a joint "insurance policy": "If any one owner has fallen on hard times, he and his crew can draw food from other owners, with the promise of future reciprocation. The Tareumiut say proudly, 'We don't let people starve,' and if one owner has had a banner whaling season, he invites boat owners from other villages to attend a feast in which he shares surplus blubber and meat. However, as Wright points out: "future reciprocation is *de rigueur*. Like insurance policyholders, the region's boat owners are playing a non-zero-sum game, finding in large numbers security against misfortune."

In effect, there are unspoken rules about the limits of trust. These people know that an implicit "debt" is created when they share their good fortune with others, and that if the same happens to them, others will help them. The same behavior seen in these hunter–gatherer communities occurs in the highly complex and sophisticated world of global supply chains.

Now, let's relate this to a supply chain example: in this case, the great floods that occurred in Bangkok, Thailand and severely disrupted the electronics sector in 2011. The majority of hard disk drives (HDDs)[14] and upstream componentry, including motor assemblies, head assemblies and components, are produced in Bangkok by Seagate and Western Digital (WD), the largest suppliers of hard disk drives. These two companies produce 90% of the world's supply of HDDs[15] at their Bangkok factories.

In October 2011, the unthinkable happened. A major flood hit Bangkok, and the major supply impacts hit all major PC manufacturers in the middle of November. (A picture of the damage caused by the floods, as well as the resulting price of Seagate and Western Digital stock is shown in Figure 3.4).

Seagate and Western Digital were essentially shut down. As a result, a number of major computer manufacturers, including Apple, IBM, Lenovo, HP, and Dell, witnessed massive shortages. Many companies use HDDs; they are installed in every computer and DVR. Western Digital assembles all of the HDD components into a final assemblies; when they shut down as a result of the floods, a massive worldwide HDD shortage resulted instantaneously. Because all of WD's customers relied on them to hold their inventory for them, there were no safety stocks to cover the shortfall. This had a multi-quarter impact on ALL upstream customers, who experienced massive component shortages and cost increases that they were forced to pass on to customers.

A senior executive from a major electronics company noted:

We first had to work through the realization of the impact and had to convince customers and ourselves it was a major issue. As we began to mobilize quickly we had to first of all convince ourselves and then convince others that this situation was WORSE than the Japanese tsunami in terms of impact to our business. People challenged us – how could it be worse? Floods happen all the time! We got through Japan so well – we can do the same here. ... The recognition of the severity of this disruption required us to mobilize and assess and get on the ground and

14 A hard disk drive (HDD) is a data storage device introduced by IBM in 1956 and is used for storing and retrieving digital information.
15 Chick, G., and Handfield, R., *The Procurement Value Proposition*, Kogan-Page, London, 2015.

Figure 3.4 Flooding in Thailand of Hard Disk Drive Manufacturers. *Source:* Reproduced with permission of WSJ Market Data Group

send people there. Suddenly, this became a very competitive situation for who would receive the highest global allocation of hard disk drives that remained after the flood.

We shifted immediately to a crisis management role and key supplier relationships and leadership became key to our recovery. We had to go in and establish knowledge of the situation, and establish communication with suppliers to truly understand the impact, bring it to a level of credibility, which allowed us to be able to describe to the business and to customers. This played out over several weeks – getting a handle on what was happening. During this time, WD and Seagate were also trying to figure out how to answer our questions and competitors' questions! Getting a handle on the facts and getting the business re-set was the second phase – and once we understood the supply impact, cost impact, and competitive response, we had to then determine the impact on our customers.

Given the limited allocation of HDDs that remained in Thailand, which customers ultimately received the best treatment from the HDD suppliers in this situation? The driver that determined which customers received the "best" allocation was ultimately determined by the strength of the relationships the major electronics manufacturers had with Seagate and WD. Those that had a reputation for "beating up suppliers based on price"... likely had a lower allocation than those that focused on long-term fair relationships. Although this was never formally documented, our inside sources revealed that relationships were key. In the end, a non-zero approach helped brand owners with supply allocation during a period of scarce resources.

Time and time again, companies that drive adversarial relationships with their partners have learned this lesson the hard way. But only a few companies truly understand non-zero behavior and practice it as a policy and a cultural artifact. Trust and collaboration are essential for tying together organizations in the interconnected supply chain, but a competitive element must underlie this trust. In our experience, supply chain executives acknowledge the axiom that "competition is essential for keeping the supply chain healthy while ensuring that suppliers are marking enough to reinvest in their business and survive in the ecosystem." In this sense, collaborative competition is key to building the healthiest supply chain possible.

Reacting to Disasters in Real Time

The roots of federated supply chains go back several decades, with companies such as Honda, Chrysler, Motorola, and others who internalized this approach. We cannot expect to see federated supply chains combined with the visibility provided by emerging technology in the next decade. Those companies who get this part of the equation right, stand to leapfrog their competitors, given the growing complexity of our global economy and the routine threat of natural and man-made disasters. Today, it is clear that the establishment of the Internet has led to the explosion of information and the subsequent procurement tools and applications that now harvest data. However, we believe the true potential of the interactive federated supply chain is only just beginning.

Traditional enterprise software systems accumulates silos of data. Managers call upon this data to make decisions. Data provides information in chunks or batches, which by definition is historical. In fact, almost all decisions in procurement today are based on information about past events. Can you imagine if your car speedometer told you how fast you were going yesterday? This is our current scenario. We know how much we quoted, sourced, contracted, and paid yesterday. What if we could make all our decisions in real time? What would happen to our performance if we had data in real time? Now, imagine that you have a federated supply chain with trusted partners, and that everyone has access to that data and is empowered to act on it, as in the Amazon and Flex models? This concept is extremely powerful, but we are only beginning to witness its adoption. But it is definitely happening, and in some instances, it is already here.

4

VELOCITY! Working Capital: The Overlooked Asset

Flex is a supply chain sketch to scale company, and basically everything we do is around supply chain. The Pulse Center is basically Flex digitizing, if you will, the supply chain globally.
—Gus Shahin, *Chief Information Officer, Flex*[1]

In seeking to improve Flex's earnings per share in 2016, Tom Linton was confident that working capital was the right pathway. He said so during his internal leadership summit, and estimated that Flex could take up to 5 days of inventory out of the supply chain. Each day of inventory represented roughly $60 million. This proposal made Flex's CFO, Chris Collier, sit up and take notice. Was this possible?

In many cases, inventory savings within an enterprise are absorbed into the business or shifted to another form of inventory or asset. Taking this inventory out of its pipeline would present Flex's CFO with a number of options. For example, inventory savings would free up cash to enable Flex to buy back more of its stock, sending its price up. This was something investors were acutely interested in. Alternatively, Flex could use the cash generated to acquire an emerging business, leading to further growth. Or it could pay dividends to stockholders and/or reduce its debt. Any way you looked at it, the outcome was good for investors. And a good reason to buy Flex stock. The ability to free up cash due to the asset velocity of materials provides real value to investors, something that is not always obvious to the public, or to internal senior executives.

Collier was excited about the idea of this way of generating free cash flow, but could Flex really *achieve* this outcome?

---

1 http://www.forbes.com/sites/peterhigh/2016/03/21/cio-gus-shahin-leads-flexs-digital-transformation/˝5f0b58fb3e65

The LIVING Supply Chain: The Evolving Imperative of Operating in Real Time, First Edition. Robert Handfield and Tom Linton.

Tom Linton recalled this moment with a grin.

> You have to remember the fact that companies are financial beasts. Most people don't want to hear the details about your supply chain improvement – they want to know what it means in terms of financial outcomes! And I'm in a position where we have the CFO's full attention, because I am intensely focused on both the income statement *and* the balance sheet of our company. Anything that produces cash from the balance sheet is going to make a CFO happy.

Balance sheet-related working capital is an asset that most companies don't consider very often. Instead, supply chain executives focus much of their time and effort on reducing cost, which is primarily a P&L-focused activity, explicitly reducing the cost of materials or labor. But the real value that remains unlocked in the supply chain is working capital.

Definition: *Working capital* is commonly defined as a measure of a company's liquidity, efficiency, and overall health. Because it includes cash, inventory, accounts receivable, accounts payable, the portion of debt due within 1 year, and other short-term accounts, a company's working capital reflects the results of a host of company activities, including inventory management, debt management, revenue collection, and payments to suppliers. One of the most significant uses of working capital is inventory. The longer inventory sits on the shelf or in the warehouse, the longer the company's working capital is tied up. When not managed carefully, businesses can grow themselves out of cash by needing more working capital to fulfill expansion plans than they can generate in their current state. As a result, working capital shortages cause many businesses to fail even though they may actually turn a profit.[2]

In a sense, working capital refers to the life cycle of cash, from suppliers to customers. Companies try to get cash as quickly as possible from customers when they sell them products or services, or offer them payment plans with interest that creates a future revenue stream. On the other end of the supply chain, CFOs love to extend payment terms to suppliers who provide them with the raw materials and services for the end products and services they sell to customers. A common strategy to extend the life cycle of cash is to extend payments to suppliers beyond 30 days. Companies may use 60-, 90-, or even 120-day payment terms with suppliers, which not only causes suppliers undue working capital problems, but also forces them to take terms to factor these

---

2 http://www.investinganswers.com/financial-dictionary/financial-statement-analysis/working-capital-869

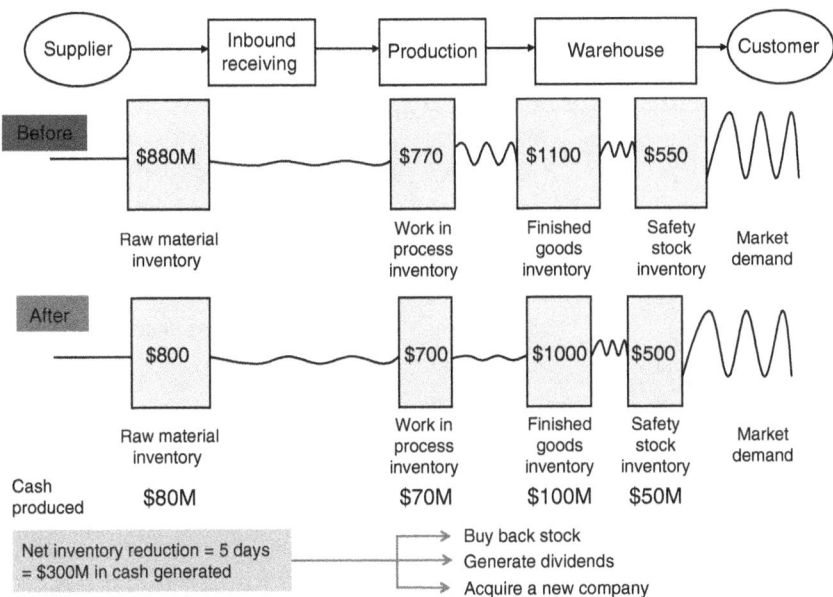

Figure 4.1 Working Capital Reduction Illustration

invoices that will often cut into their profit margins and reduce their ability to reinvest in their businesses.[3]

Figure 4.1 and Table 4.1 together demonstrate a fictional example of how working capital reduction can add value from a CFO's point of view. In the "BEFORE" situation shown here, inventory accumulates in the raw materials (plastic, printed circuit boards, etc.), work in process (semi-finished goods), finished goods (completed products), and safety stock (finished products used as a "buffer" against volatility in customer orders). One of the effects of increasing velocity is that material moves through the supply chain faster, and doesn't sit around as long in inventory. This happens because of increased visibility to material that isn't moving. Tom notes that in taking inventory out of Flex's supply chain, they discovered products in their "bone pile" that had been sitting there for years! In such cases, eliminating this inventory if it isn't needed may result in a short-term write-off, but will also eliminate all the working capital sitting around that isn't used to serve customers profitably. As shown in this fictional example, for a company that increases its velocity effort, inventory can

---

3 Factoring is a financial term meaning the supplier sells a business sells its accounts receivable (i.e., invoices) to a third party (typically a bank, called a factor) at a discount. The discount is typically 5–20% off the invoice amount.

Table 4.1 "Before and After" Impact of Velocity on Working Capital

Type of Inventory	BEFORE Inventory ($M)	AFTER Inventory ($M)
Raw material	$880,000	$800,000
WIP	$770,000	$700,000
Finished goods	$1,100,000	$1,000,000
Safety stock	$550,000	$500,000
	$3,300,000	$3,000,000
Annual revenue	**$21,600,000**	**$21,600,000**
One day of inventory	$60,000	$60,000
55 days of inventory	$3,300,000	
50 days of inventory		$3,000,000
Net cash generated		**$300,000**

be reduced by $300 million across all four areas of inventory. (Note that this is not Flex's data.)

Inventory is a monster that includes any material or product that ties up cash. Material has an economic life, a fact that many managers don't appreciate. Like fresh fish that sits in the refrigerator for more than 3 days, the value of inventory almost always shrinks over time, so it is not an investment into which a company wants to sink cash. Yet many companies don't think of inventory as an asset that shrinks in value over time. Cash sunk into inventory is an investment that is not working for you. It's like a bank account with zero interest and enormous monthly checking fees. Inventory embodies everything a company *doesn't need to satisfy a customer*. It is not necessary to make a customer happy. The customer doesn't care how much inventory you have. Customers want their product when they order it or make the purchase decision. Some would argue that "buffer stock" is required to fulfill customer satisfaction – but in the world of flow and velocity, buffer stock is a bad phrase. Companies need to think, not about stacking up inventory, but about asset velocity and flow – which means *not* having material sit in a warehouse, or on a shelf or receiving dock, but in a constant state of purposeful flow on its way to a customer.

As shown in this example, the real culprit of expanding working capital is inventory. As shown in Table 4.1, reducing inventory by 5 days in this example produced $300 million of cash! And what can you do with cash? Anything you like! You can buy back stock, which will increase your share price. You can provide dividends, which will attract new investors and keep current ones happy. Or you can go out and acquire new companies! The point is not what you do with the cash; the point is that in a flat economy, working capital becomes the next source of cash generation, and this occurs through improved velocity.

At Flex^{TM}, everything in its mission statement focuses on achieving flow and asset velocity. The key metric that is used to gauge flow is simple: days of supply. This refers to the number of days sales outstanding as represented by the value of inventory at the end of each quarter.[4]

Companies have traditionally employed systems such as "just in time" to produce materials only as often as needed. JIT often focuses on internal material flow, but doesn't always consider the life cycle of cash. For example, one standard practice is called "vendor-managed inventory," which requires a supplier to hold a company's assets, and deliver them when the company needs them and is used a great deal in the automotive sector. The problem with this method is that it pushes the material back onto the supplier – who then isn't very lean at all. The supplier is *fat* ... it's holding onto all the customer's inventory, then is threatened with high fines if it doesn't deliver exactly what is needed whenever the customer wants it. And if the lead-time on those parts is 28 days, then guess what – the supplier must hold that much inventory to be able to deliver whenever the customer wants it (typically within 24 hours).

This is not to say that "lean manufacturing" doesn't work. But the focus of lean is on reducing waste – not adding value. Lean is typically applied to manufacturing, and it does in fact improve manufacturing performance and efficiency. Lean doesn't necessarily improve the performance of the overall supply chain, and doesn't fit well with a Non-Zero view of the world. There is a difference between waste and value. A good example is if you want to create a faster car, you can reduce the weight, streamline the chassis, and boost up the engine. But if your car is now stuck in traffic, and doesn't have an intelligent system that can route it to your destination in a faster path, the end result is that you aren't really going faster at all! The goal needs to be to design a car that gets you to your destination faster, not one that is simply faster on an open road! Using the same analogy, if you really want to increase value produced by supply chain, the best idea would be to reduce lead times to produce and ship the parts, not making the equipment more efficient at set-up time reduction. Instead of a production time of 30 days of inventory, what if production lead time was 5 days? Then the entire planning cycle is shortened, there is lower inventory, and customers get their stuff even faster.

In the illustrative example shown in Figure 4.1 and Table 4.1, in March 2015, suppose that Flex had 55 days of inventory in its supply chain. Taking 5 days out of inventory across Flex's 12 businesses could generate excess cash from its

---

4 Inventory is typically measured in terms of days of sales outstanding. Thirty days of inventory means that the company holds an amount of inventory that is equivalent to 30 days of its typical annual sales volume, or 30/365 of its days sales outstanding.

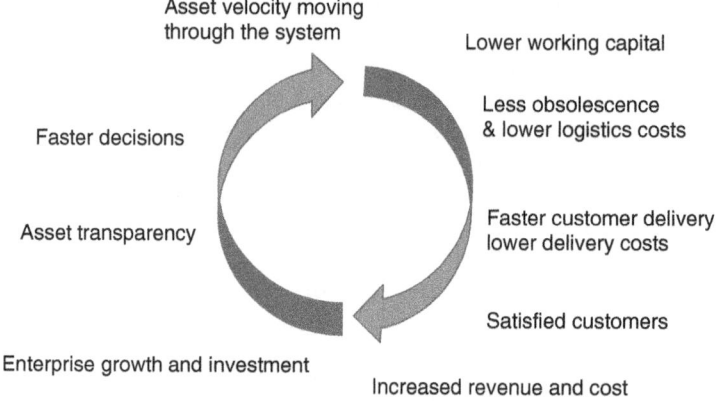

Figure 4.2 The Velocity Flywheel Effect

balance sheet, which would come out of its working capital. Note that the number of days of inventory will also depend on sales revenue. When sales revenues drop or increase, the same amount of inventory reduction may produce more or less inventory turns. But the point here is to generate *free cash flow across the supply chain.* The goal shouldn't be just on inventory turns, but on cash flow.

Tom recalled, "When I made the statement in front of our leadership team to attack days of inventory as a way of generating free cash flow beginning in December 2015, some people were a bit dubious. I knew we could do it, because we hadn't really focused on freeing up cash in this specific way. And we did. Our goal was to drive to this to five days of working capital reduction."

Taking out working capital and freeing cash flow is only part of the story associated with flow. The other "secret ingredient" is increased customer satisfaction and company revenue and growth. This is equivalent to the Flywheel Effect discussed at Amazon in Chapter 1.[5] In this case, we'll call it the Velocity Effect (see Figure 4.2). The faster you cycle your business throughput, the more likely you are to increase customer satisfaction. You will get your product to the customer faster, and as you "lean out" your supply chain, you are accelerating end-to-end supply chain processes. You will start to see logistics costs drop, because a slow supply chain results in a lot of unnecessary movement. As your inventory goes down, you will be able to expose excess, obsolete, and unneeded buffer inventory, and can write off or absorb this inventory. You won't be spending time, money, and effort on things that don't support customers' needs. And customers will be happier because they are getting their products when they

---

5 Rossman, J., *The Amazon Effect*, 2nd ed., CreateSpace Independent Publishing Platform, May 9, 2014.

want them. This is the secret ingredient of asset velocity and speeding movement through the supply chain. We have been so focused on the linkages that we have forgotten about the need to increase movement *through* the linkages in the supply chain.

It's About Time: Speed Is the Theory of Everything in Supply Chain

For many reasons, speeding up the supply chain (velocity) is at the root of everything that is good: improved revenue, reduced working capital, higher profitability, and less obsolete inventory. Conversely, slowing down the supply chain is at the root cause of everything that is bad: working capital write-offs, reduced profitability, and slowing revenues. Velocity can be used as the ROI driver for any type of improvement or re-engineering activity that is worth investing in. Take this example of planning a dinner. If you are planning a dinner for 10 people, and your lead time is 10 days to purchase food ahead of time, not only is the food going to be less fresh, but if two or three people cancel at the last minute (which always happens!), you have too much food and it goes to waste. But if you can purchase the food closer to the time of the dinner, say 2 days, you have more flexibility and order less food that reduces waste and reduces costs.

Traditional supply chain approaches focus on driving greater control over processes, and driving cost efficiency. But the goal of improving flow is not to put in process controls, but to put in fewer controls so that material flows more quickly. By imposing more audits and more controls on the process, you are slowing down speed, which slows down cash generation, as well as all the other benefits from free cash flow. This is not to say you can't have controls – only that they need to be minimized as much as possible in the interest of free cash flow. So understanding the flow of cost is more than just about improving profitability. It is also about revenue growth and working cash flow as well. Speed drives improvement in every aspect of the financial statement: revenue, profitability, and working capital. How so?

Think about the following example. Assume there are four quarters in a year, and the price of your products is dropping 2% every quarter. This is not an unreasonable assumption, as cost pressure, and price reductions are commonplace, especially in the technology sector. So if you buy something on January 1 and ship it 90 days later, on the day you ship it, a consumer can buy the same material or product for 2% less than the current price. In effect, profitability is a function of time. So it follows that the faster you move product from purchase to sales, you are not only reducing the time that your product is held as inventory (working capital), but your profitability is also higher. And because you get it to customers faster, they are more likely to buy your product over a competitor who takes longer to ship them what they want! If you can sell it one day faster than your competitor, on day 89 versus day 90, you will make 2% more profit. Supply chains that are faster also get products to market faster to capture market share. So in the end, focusing only on the lowest cost, at the expense of slower supply chains (as so many companies have done by outsourcing to overseas countries) is a big mistake that may be costing you more than you know!

Globalization Slows Asset Velocity

One of the biggest challenges in today's global supply chain is balancing the need to grow in new markets, which drives longer lead times as logistics routes expand, which in turn keeps more assets tied up longer. As the distance between entities in the supply chain grows, speed is impacted. A shipment from China to the United States can take 12 days, but for it to be unloaded and delivered to the East Coast can take up to 21 days. The entire time that material and products are on a ship or in transit, it is considered "working capital," as it is an asset that is tied up. Any asset that is not producing value is considered waste, and a fundamental of "lean thinking" is that inventory is waste, and time is money. And the idea was to put as much product into a container as possible, to boost the density of value of the shipment. This made sense for a long time, as China's extremely low labor costs were able to justify the money tied up in working capital, but this view has begun to change for all of the reasons we've discussed in this book. Many executives are now thinking more about proximity and velocity as key competitive dimensions. For this reason, the idea of moving nodes in the supply chain closer together is starting to make sense. The natural growth of global supply chains is linked to another of our "Serengeti Rules."

Serengeti Rule 5: Density: the regulation of some species depends on their density. Some animal populations are regulated by density-dependence factors that tend to stabilize population size. This rule is based on the observation that populations of wildebeest, elephants, and buffalo tend to increase, then decrease, then turn negative as their numbers shrink. Often, this occurs due to poor nutrition, as the amount of food available decreases during the dry season. The system's natural balance point has the same effect as a thermostat that triggers cooling when temperatures exceed a set point.

The notion of a self-regulating system is appealing for many reasons. Nature is constantly in a process of self-regulation, and animal populations expand and shrink as the availability of natural resources ebbs and wanes due to natural cycles and weather patterns. This pattern of self-regulation also occurs in LIVING supply chains.

New Supply Chain Rule 5: The growth of enterprises in a supply chain depends on their density, leading to globalization of markets, and expanding localization of the supply chain. As enterprises operate and absorb demand in a certain region, pricing pressure increases and growth levels peak, then turn negative as competitors enter the market. This leads many companies to seek global expansion as they pursue ongoing growth. As companies enter these new countries, they are finding that localization of the supplier and distribution network must also be developed. To succeed, companies that expand globally must develop supply chains that are proximate to their new ecosystems, meaning they need to develop relationships with new entities (suppliers and distributors) in the countries where they are expanding.

Now look at the corresponding example of a "Supply Chain" network in Figure 4.3. Notice the resemblance to the "trophic cascade" example that we showed earlier. The supply chain is essentially a trophic cascade that we showed back in Chapter 2. The only difference is that the "wildebeest" is the OEM manufacturer that supports the customers (lions and cheetahs, etc.) The Distributors are the animals that also benefit indirectly from the manufacturer (wildebeest), such as the aardvark and the mongoose. The Tier 1 Service Suppliers represent the different types of grass the wildebeest needs to survive, while the Tier 2 suppliers represent other specifics that are also part of the entire ecosystem (trees, hares, dung beetles, etc.) The point here is that all of these species

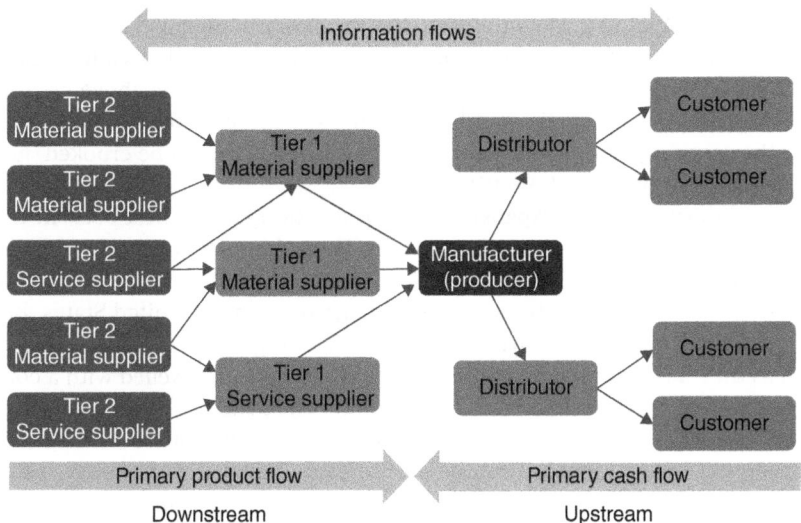

Figure 4.3 Supply Chain Trophic Cascade. *Source:* APICS, Supply Chain Management Fundamentals, Version 2.2, 2011 Ed., pp. 1–6

in the end-to-end supply chain either thrive together or die together, and the manufacturer in many ways is at the center of the entire trophic cascade.

Now think of what a typical "smart phone" supply chain looks like, and how complex it must be with all the different components. And think about what just happened with the Samsung Galaxy 7 being dropped from the market due to an exploding battery. How would you like to be one of the suppliers producing memory, or the processor, or the display and touchscreen for the Samsung 7? What about the foundries and component suppliers' business? What happens to these suppliers' business volumes when Samsung dropped their phone from the market? Your revenues and profitability are erased in a single announcement. And this is not due to anything wrong with your product – it is the impact on the trophic cascade by the wildebeest (Samsung Galaxy 7 in this case) dying off. This is a clear and troubling example of how dependent organizations in the supply chain are on one another.

The other reason why working capital is becoming more important is due to the globalization of the supply base. As companies outsourced to China, India, and other low-cost countries, all their shipments went by ocean – especially for bulk products like furniture. Ocean steaming can be very slow, and once a ship arrives at the port, products have to be unloaded, put on a trailer, shipped to a distribution center (DC), unpacked, broken down, and shipped to customers. This takes a lot of time! In the example shown in Figures 4.4 and 4.5, one can see what happened at a North Carolina furniture manufacturer as it outsourced production of its products to China from domestic sources. In this example, lead time went from 3 to 12 weeks, and safety stock went from 40% of a container to 2.74 containers. The inventory in the pipeline exploded, and subsequently, so did the inventory in the warehouse, which became packed with containers, causing massive chaos. The sawtooth graphs above assume that demand is linear, so the graphs form in a straight line. But of course that isn't the case – demand is variable, so the actual lines should be crooked, just like a heartbeat on a heart monitor.

This pattern of global expansion and localization can be best seen in the automotive industry. Fifty years ago, the Big Three dominated American roads. Today, every make of vehicle from every corner of the planet can be seen on the roads, and Toyota has the biggest market share of all in the United States. But American companies also have expanded to other regions in search of growth. And as they do so, they expand their footprint. In 2000, I travelled with a contingent of GM executives to Shanghai to meet with Shanghai Automotive executives. There I saw for myself, the rapid growth in that region as its joint venture partner was selling Lincoln Continentals built at Shanghai Automotive factories to a domestic customer base eager to drive large American vehicles.

But as global expansion occurred, assets stretched across longer channels, and inventories bloated as disruptions in the supply chain expanded inventory across the chain. To combat this effect, leading automotive companies such as Honda and Toyota worked to create a "localized" supply base. For example,

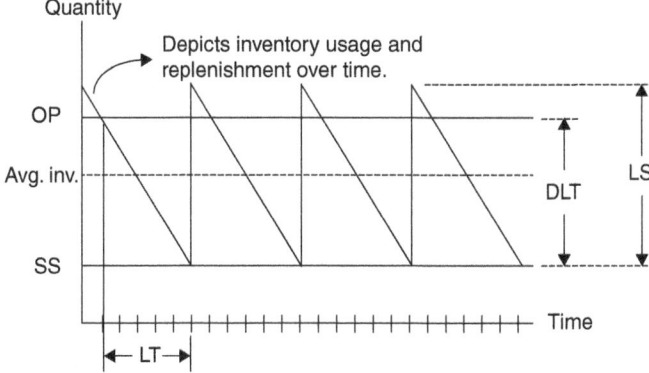

Quantity

Depicts inventory usage and replenishment over time.

OP

Avg. inv.

DLT

LS

SS

Time

LT

Definitions:

OP (order point): An established inventory level, which when reached, signals the need to issue a replenishment order.

SS (safety stock): A quantity of inventory planned to be on hand to protect against fluctuations in supply or demand.

LT (lead time): The time required to replenish inventory. This is normally measured as the number of days from when the order point is broken to receipt and putaway of the corresponding replenishment order.

LS (lot size): An established lot size, or order quantity, representing an agreed-upon amount of inventory in a replenishment orderd.

DLT (demand through lead time): The amount of inventory expected to be used during the replenishment lead time.

Formulas:

OP (Order Promise) = DLT + SS

DLT = Average daily usage (pieces/day) x LT (days) = X pieces

SS = percent of DLT. (Note: Numerous methodologies exist for determining safety stock levels: statistical, heuristic, and others. For simplicity in the following examples, we will assume SS is set by company policy at 10 percent of demand through lead time.) Average inventory = SS + 1/2 DLT

Figure 4.4 Inventory Sawtooth Effect

when Honda constructed its automotive facility in Ohio in the late 1980s, 95% of the components were initially built in Japan and shipped to the United States. Over time, Honda began to work to develop local suppliers, through partnerships, training, and joint ventures with some of their Japanese suppliers who also moved to the United States. This effort was known as "supplier development," and is a common approach to building and creating a competitive local supply base. Honda struggled at first. US suppliers had a different business culture than Japanese suppliers, and there were misunderstandings, language challenges, and many other difficulties. But over time they prevailed. Today, a vehicle built at Honda's Ohio facility (including the Odyssey, the Accord, and the Civic) are built using 95% manufactured parts from the United States, produced by local suppliers.[6]

6 Handfield, R., Krause, D., Scannell, T., and Monczka, R., "Avoid the Pitfalls in Supplier Development," *Sloan Management Review*, vol. 41, no. 2, Winter 2000, pp. 37–49.

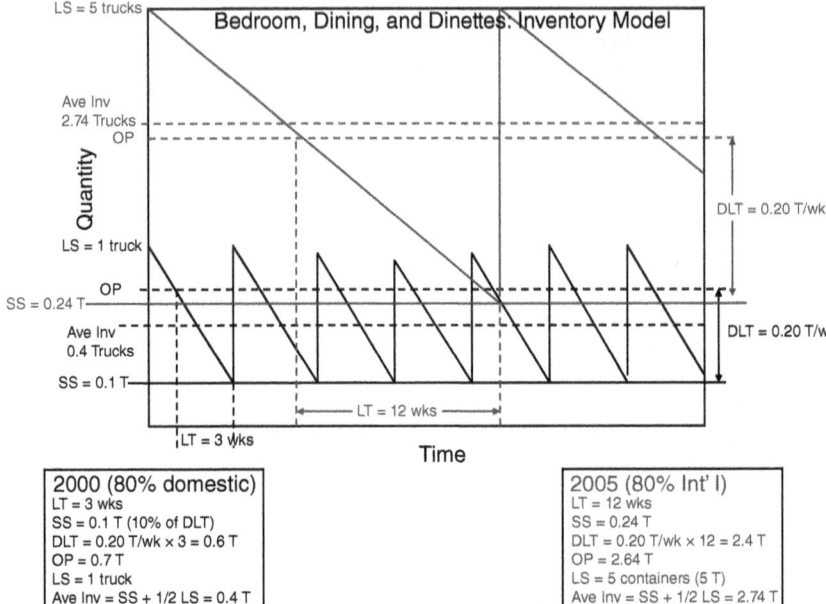

Figure 4.5 Global versus Local Inventory Effects

In fact, thinking about inventory as a heartbeat monitoring the health of the supply chain is a great comparison. For example, a runner's heartbeat pattern can be graphed as shown in Figure 4.6.

Notice that the runner's heartbeats per minute increases or decreases based on the stress on the system. As the runner goes faster, the heartbeat responds

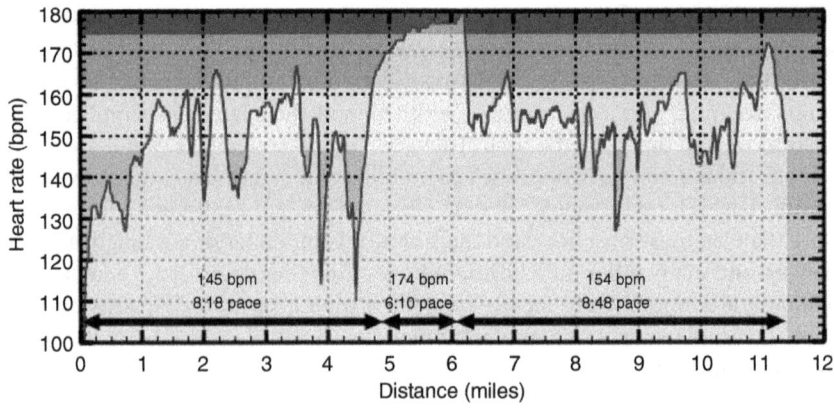

Figure 4.6 Runner's Heartbeat Pattern

and moves more quickly, in terms of beats per minute. Can't we do the same with inventory, the lifeblood of supply chains? A healthy heartbeat for a runner is one that increases in response to going faster, but which maintains a relatively low resting pulse. But how does this apply to working capital in a global supply chain?

Returning to our Honda example, when local suppliers are used, inventory can be reduced to a minimum. Because suppliers are located typically within a 12 or 24-hour drive from Honda's factories, they can deliver directly to the production line, with only a day's inventory.[7] Problems can be solved immediately in face-to-face meetings, instead of by Skype or conference calls in the middle of the night. And individuals build a stronger person-to-person relationship, as they see more of each other, and their trust in one another grows. They are more likely to share information and be more transparent with one another. And this is a healthier heartbeat than one that goes back and forth across oceans and time zones.

The "Three Vs" of Information: Velocity, Volume, and Variety

It is well known that the value of business data quickly fades with the passing of time.[8] In the Information Systems literature, data's age is characterized by a construct called *latency*, which is the interval between the time an event occurs and the time it is perceived by the user. High-latency data is old or "stale;" low-latency data is new or "fresh." Low-latency Big Data and high-latency traditional data are differentiated using three characteristics: volume, velocity, and variety known as the three Vs.[9] Volume refers to how much data there is to store, velocity refers to the speed with which this information is generated, and variety refers to the diversity of sources from which these facts are collected.

The velocity, volume, and variety of information that occurs in real time also drive the right set of activities and decisions more rapidly. Updates occur more frequently, and managers have fresh data that reflect the newest set of conditions. This enables rapid decision-making as close to the event as possible, resulting in improve responsiveness, more flexibility in decision-making, and quicker movement of dollars through the supply chain pipeline. As an example, consider Flex's material visibility system that spans its end to end supply chain.

---

7 Handfield, R., and Krause, D., "Think Globally, Source Locally," *Supply Chain Management Review*, Winter 1999, pp. 36–49.

8 Watson, H. J., Wixom, B. H., Hoffer, J. A., Lehman, R.-A., and Reynolds, A. M., "Real-Time Business Intelligence: Best Practices at Continental Airlines," *Information Systems Management*, vol. 23, no. 1, 2006, pp. 7–18.

9 Russom, P., "Big Data Analytics," The Data Warehouse Institute Research, 4th Quarter 2011.

The focus on velocity at Flex is largely driven by the times we live in. World GDP has slowed, and we are experiencing historically low levels of slow growth. Only a few companies are experiencing double digit growth. Many CFOs say they need to cut costs – but doing so has a whole set of negative effects, notably loss of people, one of a firm's most important resources. The real solution to a low-growth environment is to focus on free cash flow, to drive out slow-moving materials, and free up assets. Cash thrown off a balance sheet by reducing working capital can enable companies to do mergers and acquisitions, to integrate the cash to drive up return on invested capital, or to buy back stock and raise its stock price. CFOS are beginning to clue in on the secret of velocity and its impact on financial returns.

Transparency allows supply chain executives to drill down and identify the sources of slow-moving assets. It exposes long lead times for materials, customers, suppliers, production facilities – and slow-moving inventory.

Now let's go back to the heartbeat concept. Tom pulled out his smart phone, and showed me the pulse graph of inventory for one of Flex's major customers (Figure 4.7). The phone shows exactly what is going on with inventory in the entire end-to-end system, combining raw material, WIP, finished goods, and safety stock in the system. What is also unique about this level of detail is that it allows Tom to see the level of inventory in different segments of the supply chain system, in real time, based on whatever view he wants to see. He can look at the inventory pulse from several perspectives:

- Total inventory in the system
- Categorized by finished goods, work in process, or raw material
- Inventory for a specific customer
- Inventory at a specific facility
- Inventory in transit.

All this information can be viewed in real time – as well as historically. And to make this even more real-time Flex™ is working on a technology that will also track and locate any specific container or shipment anywhere in the world – without a track and trace barcode scan.[10] So if your shipment is sitting in a warehouse, in customs, or in a port, you can pinpoint its exact location.

The interesting part of an inventory pulse is that it truly reflects the life-like performance of the LIVING supply chain. As shown in Figure 4.7, when material is "above the line" (of $0) you have material coming in. When the pulse drops below the line, there is material going out. When inventory is at $0 for a brief time, there is no activity – and this occurs on Saturdays and Sundays. But the point is that this pulse is similar to a heartbeat – as blood comes in to the heart and then is pumped back out to the body, the extremities of the body

---

10 Patent pending, property of Flex™ International.

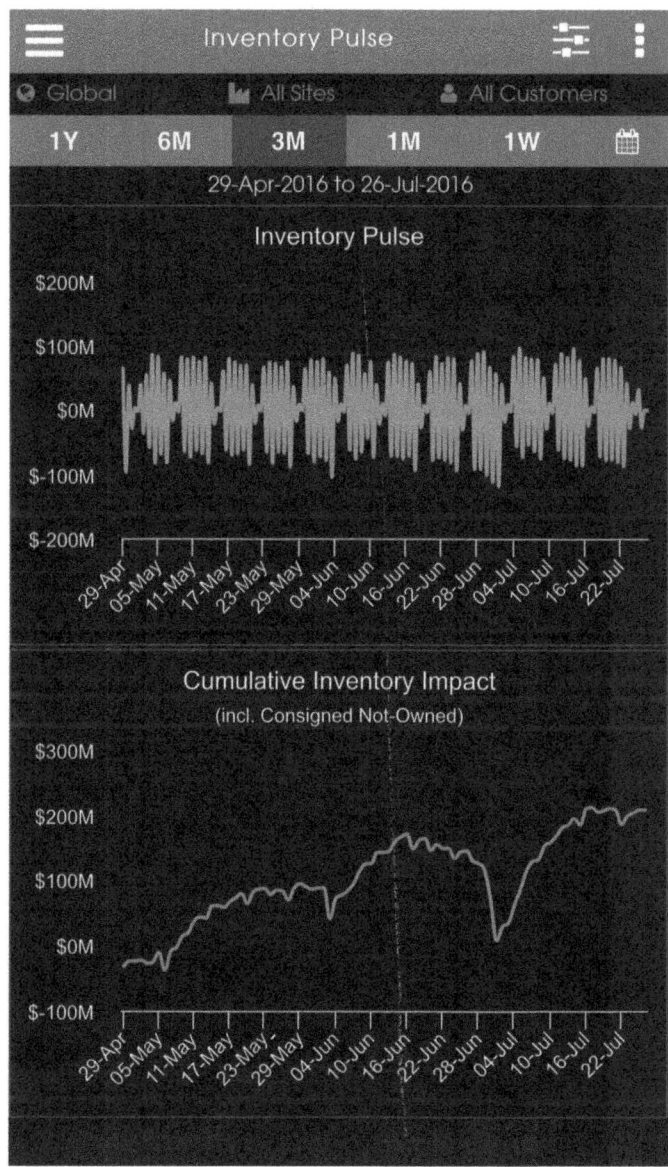

Figure 4.7 The Flex Inventory Pulse™ – Illustrated Example (Patent Pending). *Source:* Reproduced with permission of Flex™

receive blood that drives the entire system. *Inventory is in effect the life-blood of supply chains, and inventory turns are equivalent to the pulse of a heartbeat.* Leadership at Flex fully understands the role of inventory as the key to the LIVING supply chain's health. Francois Barbier, Group President of Operations at Flex, emphasizes, "Inventory is everything we don't need. The objective is to drive all our operations with that goal in mind." The inventory pulse is the key to understanding patterns related to a company's working capital and inventory (LIVING assets). For example, the pulse graph on Tom's mobile phone (Figure 4.7) showed that a major client's inventory levels were rapidly increasing. A quick check into trend revealed that this was a normal pattern for this customer at this time of the year, and the warning of a rapid increase was thus a "false alarm." The transparency of data creates visibility that allows companies to drive down space utilization, planned versus actual shipments, purchase execution, on-time delivery, and many other key business performance metrics. The future of business process innovation will be driven by transparency into key data and analytics everywhere in an organization's extended end-to-end supply chain. This also will merge into the area of predictive software that will no longer just tell us what is happening in real time, but will be able to reliably tell us what is going to happen tomorrow – or next week.

New concepts such as asset velocity will transform business balance and income statements as processes defragment and accelerate. A good example is dynamic pricing: with online shopping, prices can change in a second. Why can't businesses operate that way? As with online auctions, what if the entire economy operated like an online auction: live, with prices changing based upon the stock market? Brick-and-mortar stores would have to quickly reduce prices based on what online retailers were offering. This wave is emerging, but organizations are rapidly thinking through how this will jointly align financial planning and strategic supply chain planning. For example, a large fast food retailer has constructed an analytical total cost of ownership model that includes not just a package of fried chicken, but all of the chicken farming operations, including wages, feed, gasoline, energy costs, and transportation costs. But they haven't stopped there – analysts have extended their understanding to examine corn and feed costs, which constitute more than 30% of the cost of chicken. By hedging in these commodity feed markets, the company has essentially deconstructed the total cost of ownership for a bucket of chicken to a figure they have effectively hedged against for the next 2 years!

As we increase machine-to-machine communications, it is not unthinkable that the invisible hand of capitalism envisioned by Adam Smith will become increasingly automated. Buyers and sellers will not reach a price agreement over days or weeks but instantaneously. Data that forms a price derived from materials, demand, supply, labor, and location will form agreements. These agreements, or the meeting of the minds, could be reached quickly and efficiently. Business velocity will move more quickly, leading to increases in productivity and output. But to achieve true global integration, real-time visibility and transparency is a fundamental component ensuring that all parties are work-ing toward the same global outcome, based on local event updates and a single source of truth.

Speeding Up the Flow of Cash in the Pipeline: Procure-to-Pay Systems

Tom sees many of today's systems designed to deal with financial accountability as not only cumbersome, but often creating more complexity that in the end reduces transaction visibility and flow. This further muddies the waters and works against financial transparency and hence accountability. Purchase orders are one of the biggest elements of friction today.

"Purchasing is simply too transactional," Tom said. "The cycle of procure-ment requires a tedious process, beginning with a requisition, an approval, a purchase order, an invoice, and finally a payment. Organizations can't seem to conduct a commercial transaction without some kind of a purchase order every single time. But what has happened is that we have created a proliferation of purchase orders for every single order, and because the volume has escalated, organizations have once again used labor arbitrage to move their PO process-ing to China or India. And an entire industry has sprung up around processing POs, which is a non-value-added function!"

In a recent interview, an executive working in a major electronics company emphasized that its systems were creating massive problems for them – and driving the exact opposite effect of asset velocity. On the customer end, the company had millions of dollars of orders that had already been delivered to its customers in Brazil, but the ERP system they invested in was unable to gener-ate the invoices in a format that complied with Brazil's regulatory requirements. As a result, customers were unable to pay the company, as doing so would vio-late the law. The company had orders that had been delivered six months ear-lier, but had not yet been paid for, or even invoiced properly. On the supplier end, purchase order systems were so completely dysfunctional that several sup-pliers of common items like utilities, contract manufacturing, and other ser-vices had stopped performing against their contractual obligations until they were paid, thereby halting operations and further delaying deliveries to cus-tomers. What a nightmare! The company was effectively shrinking its assets, both on the customer and the supplier ends, due to a transactional systems issue.

In general, disparate ERP systems create friction, which in turn slows down the flow of material and information in the supply chain. Data transparency creates instantaneous knowledge and understanding of what is happening. As in the laws of thermodynamics, the fewer obstacles in the path of flow, the faster the flow. The new rules of supply chain advocate moving faster and this is accomplished by improving flow and reducing friction.

Another example of how typical supply chain processes can slow us down is the proliferation of just-in-time and kanban production systems. The original intention of these systems was to reduce inventory through multiple deliveries by suppliers in small quantities. This method worked well in places like Japan, where suppliers are located near the production facility. But in a country like the United States, or in global supply networks, it is doing enormous harm to the environment and is complicating transportation networks. There are more trucks, more deliveries, and more boxes. Many procurement engines are blasting out more POs per second than a machine gun, placing way too many orders, and generating too many shipments of small quantities. This is just gumming up the financial channels and causing a lot of needless effort.

To combat this problem, increase velocity and reduce system friction. Flex™ launched a project aimed at purchase order reduction, in an effort to enable commerce to flow more easily while maintaining the right financial controls. Tom describes the interesting outcome:

We recently went through a major part number / PO reduction, and took a third of POs out of the system. We found that every time someone wanted to order something, they had to cut a PO. In a lot of cases, they were cutting POs for 10 parts packaged in a box to be delivered. So we did a sensitivity analysis on the cost of inventory versus the cost of a PO. What we discovered is that PO engines are so drunk and disorderly that they are causing confusion in the context of trying to build efficiency using principles of just in time. And in the end, we were negatively impacting our profitability and our overall carbon footprint through more frequent deliveries. Contrary to what you might think, just in time is NOT an agile, responsive supply chain.

We took out a third of POs without increasing any inventory. But I also have a profitability requirement. I don't want to spend a lot of money flying around a lot of stuff that doesn't have some sensitivity analysis and which will impact my balance sheet. I believe that the whole focus on kanban and JIT has gotten out of hand. We need to stop, back up, and think about what it is we are trying to achieve. Purchasing has a lot of impact on the total cost of the supply chain, and I believe that JIT metrics have distorted the picture on what impacts end-to-end cost efficiencies.

It is also relevant to consider how purchasing is making decisions in the global supply chain. Labor costs have flattened out, so the only way to truly take out cost is to reduce either the amount of labor through productivity improvements, or the amount of material in the product, or to substitute material in the product. If volume won't grow in the "new normal" ecosystem, we have to be creative about how to take out cost.

An important development in the flow of financial transactions will be the "blockchain."[11] In a typical deterministic supply chain, it is imperative to strictly verify and audit the actions within the system as correct, including the inputs and outputs of the system such as automated bank transfers, orders of components from inventory, and shipment to locations. But this assumes that all information concerning all inputs and outputs must be provided. A blockchain is different, as each individual operation or interaction is perfectly recorded and archived using an agreed on business logic. Auditing is as simple as joining the blockchain network, as one can "replay" the operations of the past to build a correct model of the present. Blockchains are envisioned to be able to provide absolute guarantees of authenticity for every transaction in the supply chain, and this will dramatically change the financial supply chain of the future.

Note that it is easy for procurement executives to remain complacent when commodity costs are low. "Why worry? Prices are low and they will stay low!" is a common attitude. People have grown so confident in 2013–2017 about the cost of materials and oil. It is easy to get deluded into thinking that this is permanent, especially when 50 percent of COGS in manufacturing is in material commodities, and prices for copper, gold, cotton are all going down. It is also easy not to worry about transportation cost when oil is at \$30/bbl. Many executives agree that we are in a golden age of low materials and low oil prices. Material and oil prices will eventually go up. And then labor arbitrage will also be off the table. So where will your procurement and supply chain go in search of the next source of cost savings? Will you go to North Africa? Mexico? You will not reap a big gain, and it is certainly not worth it. So where do you go? To some extent, it depends on what you've done already – but if you've already explored all these strategies, you have limited options.

The Financial Sphere[12]: Oblong Is Better Than Round

A good way to think about the risks and costs in a supply chain is to think of them as a three-dimensional sphere populated with entities, much like the Earth, shown in Figure 4.8. The Earth's axis goes from the North Pole to the South Pole; its equator crosses the circumference of the globe at its midpoint. Think of the entire mass contained within the Earth as representing the supply chain costs associated with an enterprise such as Flex. The *vertical axis through the poles represents the elements of risk.* There are consumers of risk, and producers of risk, with your company at the very core of the sphere. As you travel toward the South Pole, you will encounter the *producers of risk.* These are those

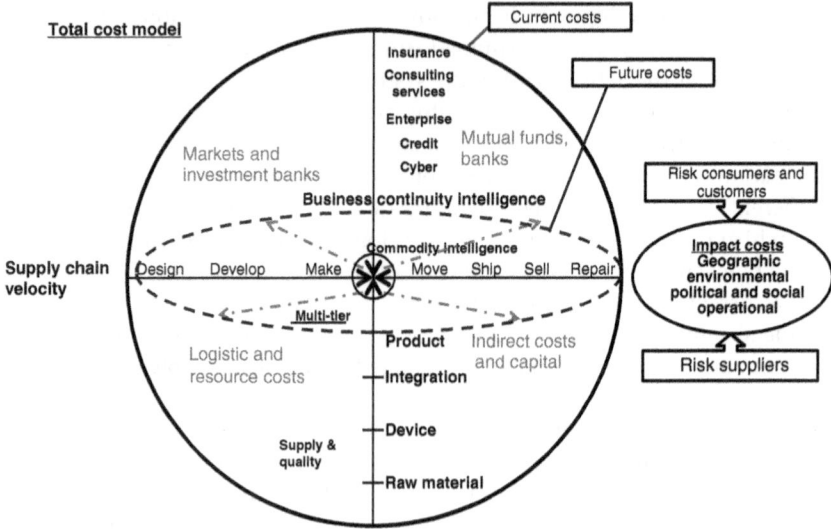

Figure 4.8 The Financial Sphere (Patent Pending)

companies that create events that produce risk, going back to supplier tiers 1, 2, 3. This would compromise the participants and integrators who assemble the product, logistics providers who ship the product, individual devices, circuit boards, and raw material manufacturers, all the way back to the silicon, resins, and oil that comprise the raw material for the final product. These parties are the producers of risk – the companies you have to worry about failing. If something goes wrong in the supply chain, massive disruption occurs, which is what the consumers of risk (the upper part of the globe) worry about.

The *consumers of risk* in the northern hemisphere include the banks, the insurance companies, shareholders – all the parties concerned about what is happening in the southern hemisphere, and which have to invest in, insure, or feel the impact of risk on their own operations. As you travel toward the North Pole, you move toward the commodity intelligence function, which seeks to understand commodity behaviors, the investors evaluating your risk, credit and banking institutions who trade your stock based on risk, insurance companies who evaluate your risk premiums, credit agencies like D&B, and others. These are the consumers of risk, who evaluate the riskiness of your supply chain. When there is a disruption, they will downgrade your stock or raise your insurance premiums. The deeper and longer the axis is, the longer your line through the tiers – tier 5 suppliers through insurance companies – and all these parties are impacted by supply chain performance.

There is a finite amount of risk in the universe. Like matter, risk cannot be made to go away. It is either passed on or absorbed by parties in the sphere. If a party absorbs risk, then it does so at its own cost. But the horizontal axis from equator to equator represents supply chain activities within the organization (in this case, Flex). If Flex is able to reduce the lead time to design, develop, make, move, sell, and repair products for customers, the equator shrinks, and the sphere becomes more oblong. This also can condense risk, making the entire sphere smaller. A smaller sphere has less mass, and thus lower cost.

Why is this? Well, if a company like Flex is able to "de-risk" its supply chain, then insurers may well believe there is less risk, and thus insurance premiums go down. Banks may believe the stock is worth more, which opens up lines of credit, and charge lower interest. Retailers may buy more product, which increases flow and drives economies of scale. Either way, as risk is reduced, somebody else in the ecosystem absorbs that risk – but Flex's costs go down, and the sphere shrinks.

Risk cannot be eliminated altogether, however. Let's take Taiwan Semiconductor Manufacturing Company (TSMC), a tier 3 or 4 supplier located in Taiwan. If there is ever an earthquake in Taiwan, and TSMC goes down, only 16 weeks of inventory are left for the global electronics industry. Why? Because TSMC produces 80% of the world's semiconductors. As Charles Fine wrote in his book *ClockSpeed*.[13] "Supply chain disruptions don't ripple – they roar!" The implication is that if something occurs at a tier 3 or 4 supplier, it goes ripping up through the supply chain and disrupts the entire sphere, including not just the producers of risk but the consumers as well.

Longer, multi-tier supply chains that extend all over the world thus tend to increase overall risk. This is one reason that companies are increasingly moving to localization of supply. Doing so eliminates risk, speeds up velocity, reduces cost (not the same thing as price), and simplifies planning because of shorter lead times. We see countless examples of situations where supply chains could have been better managed, but the design of the supply chain resulted in major disruptions. The Fukashima meltdown caused enormous risk for Japan and several large manufacturers, with ripple effects down the supply chain for automotive and electronics. The Boeing Dreamliner had multiple ripple effects because of delivery problems and quality problems. In each case, consumers, banks, and stakeholders also suffered.

The point of this analogy is that producers of risk make products, service products, manage quality, and ensure that logistics channels work. And those on the sidelines on the top half of the globe bet on whether the possible risks will actually happen or not. How much do the people at the top know about your risks? And how often do their predictions come true? The answer is – not

---

13 Charles, F., *Clockspeed: Winning Industry Control in the Age of Temporary Advantage*, Basic Books, 1999.

Figure 4.9 Changing the Shape of the Sphere

very often. Why? Because the consumers of risk know very little about what is happening in the world of risk producers.

There are clues, however. You can judge the health of a supply chain by the shape of the sphere, as shown in Figure 4.9. One with a wider equator (lower right) has long lead times, slow decision-making, and higher risk. A sphere which is also vertically stretched (upper right) with multiple tiers in the supply chain has higher risk, due to the difficulty of driving visibility into the supply chain. But as you increase transparency (up and down the sphere) and velocity (across the equator), what happens? Both dimensions get smaller, and the total amount of risk in the ecosystem shrinks, so the entire sphere shrinks, as do the costs. Thus organizations should strive to continue to not only shrink the size of the sphere, but increase the speed at which it spins. The optimal sphere is a small, round sphere that spins quickly. Any destabilization in the supply chain can cause it to wobble and not spin efficiently. But when all tiers are working together, the sphere is smaller and balanced and spins properly, driving the right velocity and health of the entire planet!

But increasing visibility and velocity at the same time is tricky. I want a deep view into my supply chain, but don't want to make it resilient and slow down decision-making. To return to the car analogy, I want visibility to my speed, and quick braking response, but don't want the brake on all the time. I also want it to be safe, but don't want safety features that slow me down. How do I make things move faster, while reducing costs and driving visibility and shareholder returns? How do we remove people from the process and let machines make decisions more quickly, but ensure that oversight and accurate data goes into decision-making? These are the questions we need to ask about the LIVING supply chain.

Shrinking the Sphere: Creating Transparency and Disintermediating Supply Chain Networks

Executives often wrongly assume that the relationships and enterprise design in their supply chains are immutable. We return to thinking about supply chains as ecosystems, which brings up Serengeti Rule 6 and our corresponding New Supply Chain Rule 6.

Serengeti Rule 6: Migration increases animal numbers. Migration increases animals' access to food (reducing bottom-up regulation) and decreases their susceptibility to predation (reducing top-down predation). For example, herds of wildebeest that migrate suffer only about one-fourth of deaths by predation, whereas those that remain year-round near stable sources of water suffer 87% of death by predation. Only 1% of migrating animals are taken by predators in a year, while up to 10% of non-migrating animals are taken. This is because non-migrating animals are easier for predators to locate and hunt. **New Supply Chain Rule 6: Enterprises that expand beyond their traditional place in the supply chain become more competitive and survive.** More specifically, as organizations expand beyond the traditional ways of working and roles in the supply chain, by exploiting the evolving digital ecosystem and employing analytics, they will expand and survive. Organizations that remain in their home markets, working in their traditional businesses, and fail to adapt will end up fighting for a shrinking market with less power as competitors expand into their market. Eventually these businesses will enter a death spiral as revenues shrink, profits dry up, attracting less investment and lowers their ability to recover and survive.

As globalization occurs, healthy organizations seek to move vertically into new markets, and also to expand into new industries, as we saw in Supply Chain Rule 5. But there is also another way that companies expand and migrate: in the direction of vertical expansion up and down the supply chain. Companies who begin to explore tier 2 suppliers and distributors begin to disintermediate many traditional boundaries. In this manner, they begin to change the balance of power, and define new ways of competing in the supply chain. Just as migrating animals have a better chance of surviving in the Serengeti, organizations that move and grow will reach the key leverage point in their supply chain.

One of the biggest and often overlooked traditional boundaries in supply chains is simple: *who owns the data on supply chain activities and processes?* A simple example will explain this principle in more detail.

A major source of angst for people in supply chains is logistics. People get paralyzed when logistics fail. That's why FedEx, UPS, and DHL allow you to track your package online. But who owns the data on the location of your package? They do! And in supply chains, the real gold is the data, not the physical activity. When FedEx or UPS lets you see a tracking number, they are essentially holding your data hostage. UPS tells you, "I will tell you when your package is coming." But they are the channel through which the data travels – from the package barcode on the truck through the scanner, through the Internet, to UPS's website to your email inbox, where you have to go through *their* systems to access information about *your* package!

Now imagine that you had a direct link to the box that contained your stuff. You don't need the layers of opaqueness between the box, the barcode reader, the driver, the truck, the distribution center, etc. You have direct access. In fact, these other elements in the channel are like clots in your supply chain data arteries – they just get in the way. Another way to think about this is through what we call the transparency principle, a variation of New Supply Chain Rule 6.

New Supply Chain Rule 6a (Transparency Principle): Direct ownership of and access to data on objects and activities in the supply chain create greater transparency and increased velocity, leading to quicker response and increased survival rates.

In effect, by focusing on barcodes transmitting data, we still rely on the wrapper, not the object itself. People will drop a box off and tell FedEx, "I want to get it to my location in 24 hours." This is the wrong approach. The approach should be to send a message that communicates, "I know where my box is in the channel, because I can monitor it, and the delivery company that gets it there quickest gets my business." In this scenario, the focus is on the data that tells you where it is.

A company's ability to disrupt traditional supply chain participants and get ownership of data in the extended supply chain is key to changing the dynamics of traditional supply chain management. A *Harvard Business Review* article on the electronics supply chain of LG Electronics (LGE), Qualcomm, and TSMC illustrates how this works.[14] Until recently, managers of large OEMs assumed they could save money by outsourcing the design and production of major supply subsystems. But when a company assigns considerable control over a product's bill of materials, the total costs of product ownership (including such things as transportation and inventory management) become opaque to the OEM. And, as some manufacturers found out the hard way during the

14 Linton, T., and Choi, T., "Don't Let Your Supply Chain Control Your Business," *Harvard Business Review*, December 2011, pp. 112–117.

2008 recession, that means the company has little leverage to reduce costs – especially if it has handed over an entire subsystem to a single supplier and can't quickly stage a competition or switch suppliers. Similarly, lower-tier suppliers can provide valuable information about the latest manufacturing advances and technological innovations. In consumer electronics, for example, direct access to the newest ideas of chip-design houses, which often are second- or third-tier suppliers, is critical. Such access has enabled companies like Apple and LGE to influence the development of emerging technologies, incorporate them into products before their rivals do, and secure supplies at an advantageous price. Conversely, companies that lack such access have found themselves reacting to competitors' innovations and struggling to match their features and prices.

By expanding vertically across multiple tiers in the supply chain, companies can gain control and also stay close to vendors that can provide early information on shifts in the economy. Firms with this capability, such as Taiwan Semiconductor Manufacturing Company (TSMC), tend to serve a wide range of industries. In January 2009, LGE bypassed top-tier supplier Qualcomm and established a direct tie with TSMC, one of the world's largest chip foundries. Concerns that Qualcomm wasn't passing on the savings or supply advantages from then-plunging chip prices and uncertainty about what would happen to the global economy that year prompted Tom Linton, then LGE's chief procurement officer, to take this step. In the first quarter, LGE learned that TSMC's orders from a large number of industries were picking up, that its capacity was tightening, and that lead times were increasing. These events all indicated that the global economy would rebound in 2009, sooner than many anticipated. In response, LGE rushed to negotiate deals with suppliers, and locked in cost savings before prices rose. Caught off guard, many of TSMC's competitors couldn't respond similarly.

The fact that Tom Linton and his CTO flew to Taiwan to meet in person with TSMC executives was a major disruption. Qualcomm, the intermediary, was very upset about what was seen as an aggressive action that disintermediated the supply chain. Up until this point, Qualcomm had controlled all information about wafer supply, wafer pricing, and volume negotiations with LGE, effectively telling LGE what wafers they would deliver and when. In effect, Qualcomm controlled a core part of the product they assembled for LGE, and thus was able "to set the terms for the deal." Executives at Qualcomm insisted that "TSMC is *our supplier*," and LGE should have no direct contact with TSMC. In a discussion with executives, however, Tom Linton made it clear that TSMC's wafers were in fact in *LGE's* product, as they were the end user. Qualcomm was merely an intermediary that integrated TSMC's material in the product it was selling to LGE. Tom's intervention with TSMC served to significantly distintermediate Qualcomm's control over supply, effectively disrupting the existing power triad. Afterward, LGE's relationship with Qualcomm was still strong, but it had changed. LGE no longer found itself on the defensive, as they had much better control over information on supply, demand, pricing, and other factors that directly impacted its revenue stream and product costs.

So what's the lesson here? Simply this: Controlling data and understanding what is happening in the supply chain is essential to visibility and transparency, which leads to velocity and effective decisions. This level of transparency must be used to drive competitive behavior that keeps the supply chain in balance. When there is imbalance, as discussed earlier, disruptions are sometimes necessary to restore order.

The "Uber" Effect of Supply Chain Disruption

Today "Uberization" is causing major disruptions in the supply chain. In effect, Uber took control of data channels in the service supply chain, creating a new industry. Before Uber, taxicab service in San Francisco was horrible. Uber disrupted taxicab companies, by connecting people who wanted point-to-point transportation service with individuals who had the time and the nice vehicles to provide that service. People no longer had to call taxi companies, wait for a driver to come by (if one was available), and pay the fare at the end of the ride. Instead, Uber customers could instantaneously get a price on their point-to-point transportation requirement, get a driver in a couple of minutes, be transported in a comfortable, clean vehicle, and communicate directly with the driver, who knew exactly where to find them.

This is upending the entire business. In fact, San Francisco's biggest Taxi Operator, Yellow Cab Cooperative, Inc., filed for bankruptcy protection in January 2016.[15] The yellow cabs face a steep decline in ridership, along with other financial difficulties stemming from lawsuits. This is happening across the country, with Chicago's Yellow Cab taxi service filing for bankruptcy in 2015. New York's yellow cab medallions needed to operate a cab plummeted from $1.3 million in 2013 to around $700 thousand last year. In effect, Uber (and its recent competitor, Lyft) have changed the landscape forever.

In a sense, the Uber success story follows the Serengeti rules, which codify the forces of nature. If one party in the chain becomes powerful, beyond its ability to provide service or to survive, forces of disruption will rebalance the ecosystem. If there are not enough wolves, the elk population will grow, trees will die, and the system will reboot. This is why many Native nations emphasize balance, killing only what they need to survive, and using "by-products" of their kill for other purposes.

---

15 http://www.wsj.com/articles/san-franciscos-biggest-taxi-operator-seeks-bankruptcy-protection-1453677177

GPS technology, cloud computing, and mobile applications are key driving forces in rapid supply chain disruption, and what is known as the "Uber Effect" will become much more prevalent in other industries as technology continues to drive disruption in the supply chain. For example, FedEx, DHL, and UPS spend hundreds of millions of dollars every year or so redesigning or developing logistics networks for their customers. Why? Because conditions have changed, customer issues have arisen, legislative issues have cropped up, demand volumes have changed – in fact, everything is constantly changing! Global Positioning Systems have created an entirely new form of real-time data, which is being exploited in novel ways. For example, in India, TVS, a third-party logistics provider, has installed GPS in most of its vehicles. Data is taken from the tracking system and processed in order to help customers help TVS continuously redesign customer routings. Virtually all information about total lead times, supplier wait and load times, driving times, and delays can be quickly downloaded and reviewed. This allows TVS to, say, identify troublesome roads or high-traffic roads, reroute drivers and change schedules. In countries like India, Brazil, and Vietnam, where urban traffic is notorious for holding up deliveries, this capability can provide a competitive advantage. TVS is developing and using optimization models that utilizes real-time GPS data to create real-time trucking solutions. They also can obtain information from warehouses to determine which parts are going out of stock or are aging.

A German fourth party logistics company, 4Flow, is also providing this capability to its customers. Information about the entire network, including inventory, shipments, advanced ship notices, vehicle routes, GPS tracking data, and others are uploaded in real time to its optimization algorithm. The algorithm is rerun at the end of each day, and the entire set of vehicle dispatches, schedules, and warehouse movements are reconfigured and deployed. This capability has created massive benefits for companies such as Volvo, which have used 4Flow as its primary logistics management firm.

Now let's think bigger: what happens when you expand this concept? Perhaps something that is going on in logistics now: a disruptive event that companies like FedEx and UPS are very much afraid of. Namely, the Uberization of logistics. Why couldn't Uber's approach work for freight as well? Well, it is – right in front of us. Premium freight service supply chains are evolving, and it won't be long before they will be "uberized." It won't be long before we have a "smart box" – a package with a chip on it that sends a signal stating, "I am in Portland, OR, and I need to be picked up and moved to Hong Kong." (This could happen anywhere in the world). What if this led to a bunch of boxes in a warehouse all sending signals to trains, planes, trucks, and an entire network of potential transportation providers? Some providers may even be automated, with no driver. And when a transportation provider picks up the signal that a delivery is needed and communicates with a network of other providers also in the chain, a truck could locate and load the shipment in less than a minute, take it to a port, and put it on a ship to Hong Kong, where it could be unloaded and trucked to its destination. This transportation system could be done not through a single premium service, but by any number of Uber-like trucking, shipping, and delivery services, responding to a chip emitting a GPS signal. The signal would also broadcast to the customer This could all be done not by a premium service, but through a chip with a GPS signal that will tell the customer exactly where their shipment is on its route at any time of day. Is this crazy? We think it's not as far off as you might think. Barcodes will be disrupted by GPS and Wi-Fi everywhere – and these supply chains will evolve, if not exactly in this way, but in some fashion. Why? Because supply chains always flow to the point of least resistance.

Real-Time Data Leads to Better Predictions

When decisions are made quickly, and people have access to real-time data, prediction becomes easier. This is because we are reacting to information that is more up to date. It is easier to estimate with reasonable certainty what is going to happen next and react in a more agile manner when we have real-time data, as opposed to data that is a week or a month old.

In May 2016, I met with Tom Choi from Arizona State University. Tom recalled two simple prediction rules, based on time-honored forecasting rules:

> In your forecasting classes, all you are really learning is a sophisticated way to create mathematical expressions to capture the past, and trying to extrapolate it into the future. And we always return to the two cardinal rules that deal with the accuracy of forecasting.

> The first rule is that aggregated forecasts are always better then product-specific forecasts. (Recently this has been made popular by the trend of "crowd sourcing.") The basic rule is that multiple points of view formed by individual experts and respondents act as a synthesizing mechanism to help us see what is going on at a macro level. They offer opinions and paint the future for us. If we can combine multiple insights, we can begin to get a reasonable view of the future. For example, predicting between whether the NFC or AFC will win the Super Bowl is easier than trying to predict which team will win the Super Bowl – and forecasting the trend for product *families* rather than individual products is likewise much easier.

> The second rule is that the longer you wait to develop forecasts, the more accurate it will be... That is because forecasts for tomorrow are better than forecasts for two months from now. We learn about accurate

response methods, and as you increase standardization and reduce lead time, you can get "first market data," which is the best predictor. Waiting to get the very latest (and earliest) market response to your product offering works best for product releases. So if you have a very flexible supply chain, you can afford to wait until that last moment and your forecast accuracy increases.

If you apply those ideas to the cognitive and analytics arenas, the implications are obvious. Access to real-time data occurring in the end-to-end supply chain is the next big power grab that can provide better predictive capabilities. More accurate prediction results in improved decisions, a better ability to exploit market swings, effective response to disruption, lower reliance on "guesses and estimates," and ultimately, lower costs and lower inventory. If you can combine data control, real-time access, cloud-based computer algorithms, mobile computing, and the right decision-making culture, you will have not only a very powerful predictive analytics capability, but also an organization with extreme velocity capabilities. You can afford to wait until the last minute to make a decision. You also can aggregate multiple sources of internal and external data from both internal and external, unstructured sources (using natural language processing). In the past, we made forecasts that were very linear and that attempted to extrapolate the future based on the past. But now, with real-time data, we are learning how to do this in smaller increments of time, using machines that also are learning faster and faster. We are using a high "alpha" value in our exponential smoothing models and weighting the most recent data the highest. This is driving greater velocity of decision-making.

Prediction is still a relatively emerging and new capability in the supply chain environment, but is increasing in importance, particularly in organizations that have already been through the cycle of spend analytics, supplier leveraging, segmentation, and consolidation. Predictive analytics requires a deep understanding of the technical and commercial attributes of the supply chain ecosystem, as well as advanced statistical and modeling capabilities. Prediction is based on identification of the true indicators for predicting revenue, disruption, opportunity, or whatever outcome is sought. It is often built on a strategic platform that provides data visibility and near real-time availability, as well as advanced data warehouses for collection of relevant third party datasets. Such insights also provide for visual representation of insights that provide a profound view into supply chain operational outcomes that are not easily apparent to executives in the business. Finally, prediction requires highly sophisticated levels of procurement analytical modeling capability. This represents an important opportunity for organizations – to harness the power of cognitive computing systems that enable the convergence of data pulled from machines, systems, and social media into a powerful real-time predictive system of the future.

For example, if you are trying to decide whether to buy precious metal from one location versus another, you can bring together data from both locations, and combine it with the location's record for production stability and market performance, and make a solid decision. Your decision can reflect events that occurred that very day. Regardless of how smart algorithms are, you are still doing forecasting. Nobody has a crystal ball – we are just getting a little more sophisticated in how we apply the two rules of forecasting, combined with recognizing on that owning the data is the magic ingredient that allows us to operate more effectively in our ecosystem. Ultimately, this capability is what we need to survive in today's global economy.

5

INTELLIGENT! Linking the Genomes of Products in Your Supply Chain

You can't fix what you can't see.

—Tom Linton

Developing a capability for real-time data streaming from thousands of points in the global supply chain is no easy task. Getting leadership at any company to buy in to a new idea is always a challenge. At Flex, however, the leadership team was open to investing in this new form of transparency from the outset. Leaders determine the culture of an organization, and culture has everything to do with the ability to adapt to the new rules of supply chain management described in earlier chapters.

Flex's culture is open to change for a number of reasons. First and foremost, CEO Mike McNamara is open to any good ideas, and his office door is always open. When Tom Linton proposed Flex Pulse ("literally on the back of a napkin"), his response was, "Let's do it!" Second, because Flex is in the business of operating supply chains for other people, its own supply chain boss has a pretty good soapbox to stand on when it comes to investing in new supply chain solutions. Tom notes, "I am the chief supply chain officer in a supply chain solutions company. That's like being a chef in a high-end restaurant. Everybody else is operating the cash register, buying the products, waiting on tables, but I'm responsible for the material and its movement. If the food isn't good, then the restaurant is out of business!" The final factor critical to Flex's success in launching this initiative is CIO Gus Shahin, who was key in "building and making it happen." In fact, Gus came up with both the idea of touch screens on a massive scale and the name "Pulse^{TM}." A close working relationship between the CIO and the CSCO is essential to driving your organization toward transparency and real-time operation. Finally, a clear vision of the end-state capabilities that are provided by the investments you are making in systems is essential to getting there quickly. That vision is driven by President of Operations Francois

The LIVING Supply Chain: The Evolving Imperative of Operating in Real Time, First Edition. Robert Handfield and Tom Linton. © 2017 John Wiley & Sons, Inc. Published 2017 by John Wiley & Sons, Inc.

Barbier, to whom the factories, the CIO, and CSCO report. This combination forms a dynamic environment with a bias toward action and innovation.

The Pulse Center™ required creating visibility to material in the end-to-end supply chain. The process to implement the Pulse Center™ took less than 6 months – but it required focus and top leadership support. Gus Shahin, the CIO, recalls that:

> [Tom] and I together basically put together the teams. IT provides all the back-end infrastructure, all the data capture, the KPIs and so on. They give us all the business requirements and what it is that they are looking for. It is true collaboration. If IT were to do this on our own, it would not have been successful. If Supply Chain tried to do it on their own, it would not be successful. What we did basically was co-locate a bunch of IT folks and a bunch of supply-chain folks and put them in a room together for several months to work this out. Then we had the market segment team, who give us a different perspective, a customer perspective. And then we had the procurement guys, who gave us the supply perspective. So, it took lots of collaboration for sure.[1]

As Flex began to build the Pulse, creating the right culture was especially important. It was key to think about what information people needed, and what information had to be in real time. Organizations need to think carefully about the design of real-time data visibility systems. They need to understand the key nodes, not just in their own production system, but in their suppliers' facilities, which collect data points. Not every supplier may welcome having their data broadcast to customers on the web! As noted in previous chapters, control over data in the supply chain is an essential advantage that can occur only when the supply chain is truly federated. Its participants must be aligned by a common purpose, such as social responsibility, and the ability to constantly adapt as an ecosystem, just as in the Serengeti desert. Desert animals depend on one another for survival. This delicate balance enables them all to thrive. As we noted in Supply Chain Rule 1 in the first chapter, enterprises in a supply chain ecosystem depend on one another for survival. This relates to the idea of federated supply chains.

> In a federated supply chain, the "customer-end" of the chain determines the behavior, requirements, and norms expected of every participant in the chain from its earliest beginning to its end of life.

In a federated supply chain, a firm looks to the customer end, focusing on how its actions will drive value and impact the customer. Think of a big, transparent

1 http://www.forbes.com/sites/peterhigh/2016/03/21/cio-gus-shahin-leads-flexs-digital-transformation/"5f0b58fb3e65

pipeline, where everyone can see what is upstream and downstream in the supply chain. This requires mapping supply chains and understanding which data should be broadcast in real time. This is a big challenge, and it occurs over time. Not all data will be elevated to an "issue," and classifying data as essential or nonessential through "noise cancellation" relies on human experience, not machines. A deep domain knowledge of the supply chain developed by tapping into subject matter experts who have worked in the field for years is an essential part of understanding the data control points that matter. These individuals know what categories of components and parts to monitor, what drives inventory, what the liability exposure factors are, what characteristics of demand patterns by commodity are considered normal …, the list goes on and on. All this knowledge is embedded between the ears of experts, derived from years of "tribal knowledge" – this is the true source of understanding that drives the right level of data "listening posts." Just as an intelligence officer understands who the reliable sources are, and who to talk to gather data, enterprise supply chain designers must understand their end-to-end supply chain and the key data listening posts. Once understood, these data points need to be collected in a format that can be rapidly aggregated, summarized, and visualized so that users can quickly scan and make sense of them.

The Pulse Center's goal is to bring together multiple forms of the right data in a singular visual format. In the Pulse's early stages of development, deciding what was critical to monitor was a massive task. But the task doesn't end – in fact, it needs to be continuous. This is because a LIVING supply chain implies an ability to evolve. Supply chain networks are inherently organic, constantly changing creatures. Suppliers are always being added or removed, material is constantly flowing, workers are coming and going, and machines are functioning and breaking down. An unhealthy supply chain goes dormant and static. If you aren't constantly changing, you aren't healthy – and that is the end of your business and your life.

Marcin Fic (Flex's Vice President of Real Time) and his team are a breed often referred to as "data scientists." This employee role is an emerging requirement for many organizations seeking to create a real-time analytic capability. A data scientist understands the two parts of the world: (1) the data world (databases, cloud servers, graphical user interfaces, algorithms, formulas, and all the programming that underlies the systems of representing information) and (2) the "real world" of complex, volatile supply chains and the needs of users. This dual knowledge allows data scientists to navigate between the real world and the data world to ensure that they are aligned and "jiving" with one another.

Research shows that in most companies, data scientists spend most of their time cleansing and organizing data, not really doing any analysis of the data. That has to change. While data governance is important, it is not essential that all data in the company be "cleansed." It is important rather to think about what data is needed to create value, and to focus on ensuring that critical data is cleansed, organized, and that a governance structure exists to manage that data.

Marcin leads a team of data scientists from around the world who specialize in applied mathematics and computer science. These fields, which involve working with large datasets to extract implied relationships and automating data collection and processing, are instrumental to the Pulse and to the capabilities that drive real-time transparency.

To be truly effective, however, data scientists not only need to understand how to work and derive insights from large datasets, but also have a "hunch" of what to look for. In fact, the single biggest misperception about "Big Data" is that you run massive searches, and the correlated variables fortuitously produce an answer that magically pops out of the analysis! But this isn't how it really works. In fact, data scientists need to develop hypotheses around where to look for data, what the relationships are among types of data. This process eventually leads to the right dashboard, visualization of data, and graphical interpretations that make the data useful. Therefore, a strong foundation of field experience obtained by working in the "trenches" is one of the best ways to prepare data scientists. They need to speak the "language" of supply chains, as well as the "language" of data analysis.

For example, prior to arriving at the Pulse, Marcin had strong field experience, working at a Flex factory in Poland for 14 years, moving from planning manager to material director. Marcin was then recruited into the IT world, supporting supply chain systems by connecting business processes in the factory to information system tool sets for decision-making. He proved to be so good at this that he was promoted to this function in the broader business group handling all of Europe, then to handling all of Flex's telecommunication customer value streams. On a visit to Europe, Tom Linton offered Marcin the opportunity to come to San Jose, California and take part in one of the biggest supply chain innovations in history: the Pulse Center. He became global lead for all solutions at Flex, with the title Vice President of Real Time. When I spoke to him in San Jose, he had been at Flex $2\frac{1}{2}$ years, and was responsible for systems support for the end-to-end set of Flex's global supply chain processes, from customer demand and order fulfillment through procurement, logistics, and warehousing.

To be sure, Tom Linton's responsibilities at Flex are unheard of in most supply chains. Holding a single individual accountable for the end-to-end supply chain is comparatively rare, as is hiring data scientists to work on an unproven system. As discussed in Chapter 1, most organizations employ one individual in each area: procurement, demand planning, logistics, manufacturing, etc. The traditional view is that each function is a separate discipline, with different performance metrics and approaches. But leading organizations recognize that an end-to-end view is critical to ensuring both the right alignment of performance metrics and that everyone is "on the same team" and pulling in the same direction. At Flex, Marcin supports all customer-facing solutions. Customers ask Flex for help with supply chain IT solutions, including ERP integration, process improvement, advanced planning solutions, and supply chain analytics.

Because Flex is moving toward being a total solution provider, it will provide a holistic solution that includes a configuration to leverage Flex's global data standards, including parts coding and configuration.

Marcin notes that the Pulse Center was (and still is) a massive undertaking. "When I arrived here I recognized that the first thing we needed to do was to create a set of standards that would help us to understand how to view data, keep it seamlessly synchronized across dozens of execution systems, and how to connect the business process with the data," he said. "You are never able to get your data 100% correct, and the challenge for analytics is to figure out the flows of data, and mend the integrity issues so they are synchronized, and people can trust the execution of the systems. The fact is that data integrity flows are part of our daily life."

This may seem like mumbo-jumbo, but is critical to understand when conceptualizing the role of analytics in the enterprise. All forms of data – whether performance metrics, inventory and material information, GPS location data, etc. – are visual representations of what is happening in the "real world." Individuals will observe or hear the information, which travels to their brains, triggering a decision or reaction. But what if the data that is being represented in the report, on the screen, or on the mobile device, does NOT represent what is happening in the world? What if it is outdated (a week old), or worse yet, claims to be real but contains multiple computation errors, or is somehow "mangled" when it is sucked up by the cloud system and broadcast to viewers? We tend to interpret everything that shows up on a computer screen as "true," but this is often not the case. A small data error can touch multiple other components of end-to-end supply chain systems, resulting in an escalation of errors that are all tied to a single error made in one data element!

A key control mechanism for data monitoring in the supply chain is knowledge, including knowledge tied to data. The assumption is that we need full and open transparency to everything happening in our network. For example, Salesforce (the software) has completely broken down the traditional realm of business relationships. It used to be that salesmen were successful based on who they knew in their client company, and the institutional knowledge they stored as a result of their business relationships. Salesforce blew that open, allowing all salespeople to understand who the decision-makers were in that organization. Execution and the ability to close a deal determine the success of salespeople, through fully democratized data.

Mapping the Genome of Products: The Life Blood of a Supply Chain

A major technological development now underway that will enable true connectedness among participants in the supply chain is the ability to map product genomes. Here again, a reference to the biological, natural world is in order.

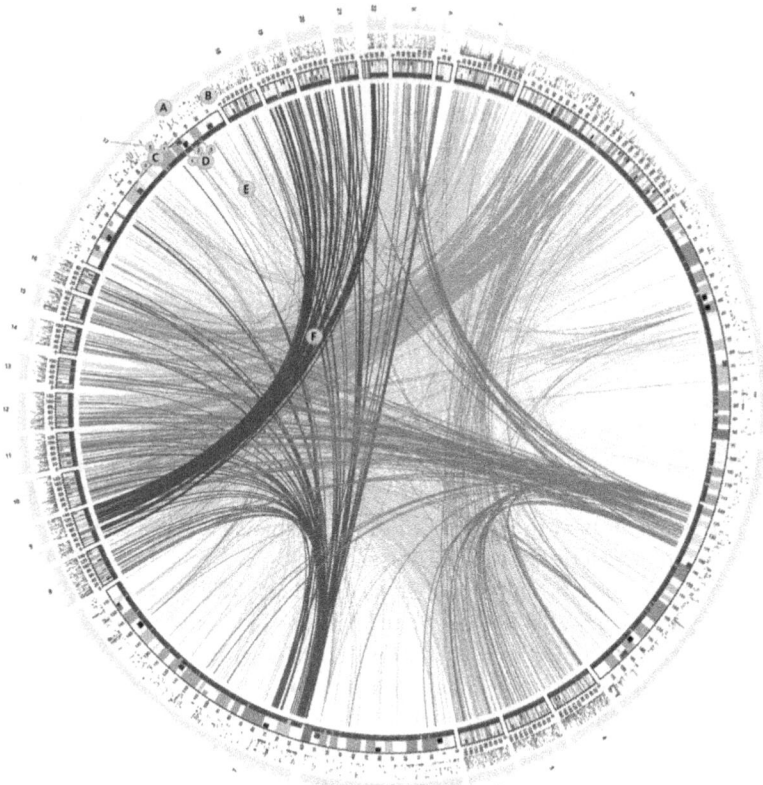

Figure 5.1 Mapping of a Genome. *Source:* Reproduced with permission of Circos

Product genomes are analogous to a living thing's genetic material. The genome includes the entire set of hereditary instructions for building, running, and maintaining an organism, and passing life on to the next generation.[2] In most living things, the genome is made of a chemical called DNA. The genome contains genes, which are packaged in chromosomes and which affect specific characteristics of the organism. A genome map helps scientists navigate around the genome. Like a road map, a genome map contains a set of landmarks that tells people where they are, and helps them get where they want to go. The "landmarks" on a genome map might include short DNA sequences, regulatory sites that turn genes on and off, and the genes themselves. Often, scientists use genome maps to help them find new genes. A genome map is shown in Figure 5.1 – they are truly beautiful images!

---

2 http://www.genomenewsnetwork.org/resources/whats a genome/Chp1 1 1.shtml"genome1

Genome mapping, which grew out of the biotech industry, is proliferating, largely due to the dropping cost of genome sequencing. In 2001, genome sequencing cost $100 million per sequence. By 2007, it cost $10 million; in 2016, $1000. By 2020, the cost of genome sequencing is expected to be one penny!

In a similar fashion, digitization is driving us to better map product genomes. Tracking products and pinpointing not only where they are today, but their entire history through the chain, is emerging as a key enabler of transparency and visibility in the supply chain.

Consider this: Can you connect the essential leverage points in your network through cloud, mobile, and other media that provide a platform for analytics? Can you track the DNA of your global supply chain at a part number level? Today, the answer to both these questions is no. Very soon, however, new technology will permit anyone, whether a consumer, a manager, or a supplier, to do this. As supply chains evolve, we need a structure for mapping their genome. This means establishing part number tracking and coding capabilities in the end-to-end supply chain. A big opportunity is to think about a vehicle for encoding the genome, to help us understand where products come from and where they go, a critical element for combating counterfeit and fraud. Supply chain scholars rarely discuss waste due to counterfeit and fraud, even though it is a large area of lost global profits and revenues. The importance of tracking and measuring all goods, including the possibility of counterfeit goods, must be estimated using data tracking. But unlike the calls for "Big Data," we must demystify the view that Big Data is the answer to improving supply chains. Big Data is static and useless by itself; *it's the questions you ask of the data that change supply chain outcomes.*

The digitization of products and things is a key technology development that will drive the ability of individuals in supply chains to track their LIVING supply chains. These digital signals are like our nerves, which transmit messages to our brains, driving us to react when we put our hands too close to a stove burner, or when we taste something delicious.

But we can't process everything at once in a supply chain. There is just too much data, which can lead to sensory overload: data is flying at us, and we can't process it all. At some point, we need to relinquish our cell phones and sleep – or play golf. So how is the digital LIVING supply chain going to work?

The key is to think about what data is *critical* at any given time. Human beings can only focus on a limited number of inputs, so we need to define ahead of time what we view as critical. If we need information on something that doesn't fall in that category, we also need to know where to look for it, and whether we have to do a "deep dive," which requires a system that allows a high level of granularity. But more than that, we need *useful* data. To be useful, data needs to be current – ideally, it needs to be in real time! And to process it quickly, we need *visual* data. That is, people understand pictures a whole lot better than tables or figures. So visualizing your data, and portraying it so it can be easily processed by any human being is key. That is what Steve Jobs understood immediately when he designed the Apple as an interactive, visual device with a human interface.

Flex's system allows people to pull up data to a large screen, and to drill down into it. Tom compares this to "defragging your hard drive on your computer." You can "pareto-ize" your data, and look at the buckets to see, for instance, how much inventory you have, where it is, and its age. In a workshop situation, everyone is looking at the same data, and grinding into it, and can start to see where the white space exists, what is causing high costs using the 80/20 rule, and where improvements should be made. The data will tell a story that everyone can agree on in a democratic, completely objective fashion. Using easy-to-visualize data leads people to make decisions more quickly, and to improve slow-moving inventory. This ability drives improved customer satisfaction: accessible data points everyone in the right direction.

A great example used by Tom is Waze, a traffic news crowd-sourcing application. Tom is a frequent commuter between San Francisco and San Jose, and a dedicated fan of Waze. Individuals contribute to Waze by reporting what is happening on the highway; participants' phone GPS digitally captures who is online, and users can see traffic bottlenecks, construction slowdowns – even speed traps! Sometimes Waze will take you down a side road for a mysterious reason. If you trust the data, and follow it, you will likely avoid a major traffic jam. This naturally increases your travel velocity.

Imagine using this type of real-time data, complemented by human insights, to guide management of the supply chain. Cloud-based real-time systems have enormous potential to coordinate unexpected events with human decision-making. If you can drive your supply chain and pareto-ize data in a visual format, and allow decision-makers to access this data and take action against it, working with one another in a federated manner, you will increase the velocity of your entire end-to-end supply chain network.

One of the biggest barriers today to real-time supply chains is reliance on "batch-based" systems, such as massive ERP systems. These systems allow us to see only what happened in the past – not in the future. Also, these systems often drive the wrong metrics, leading people to think only in terms of total landed cost. When we focus only on buying things cheaply, we overlook what customers require, so we may make the wrong decisions. If we can improve our demand planning, and understand what the customer wants, we can design what we need to support them. But we also may have to limit what customers may request. Salespeople often jump through whatever hoops are required without thinking about the cost. This can drive up inventory, which drives up the balance sheet, and makes the company unprofitable. Thus, there is a need to create better visibility of what is available and the costs to obtain it, and to map this against what the customer wants, managing this delicate balance using data.

Here's an analogy: If you are on a river delta, and all kinds of junk is coming down the river toward you – but not the stuff you want or what you ordered – you can't just stand there and gripe about it. You have to go upriver to see what is going on. Likewise, if you are upstream, you have to consider the impacts of what you are doing on the people downstream. And the most important metric of all is revenue and free cash flow. Because a lower total landed cost is no good if you have slower supply chain responsiveness.

What Data Do You Need? (Creating a Data Democracy)

One of the big problems associated with the massive amounts of data being generated by supply chain systems is the need to focus on the right kinds of data. This is more a people issue that a technological issue. People are tied to the idea of running a supply chain based on an ERP system, using a tactical picture that is downloaded into Excel and massaged into a form that can make sense. And this promotes a diversity of views, because every location does it differently, and you wind up with a list of big Excel files with lots of data which are viewed by individuals. This causes delays and drives everyone to look at different information – which is the *opposite* of the democratization of data!

Ideally, your data is visual, available to everyone, can be interpreted quickly, and will drive individuals to focus on decisions that matter. This is the idea behind a data democracy. People have a limited amount of time; their attention needs to be allocated to things that matter. The goal is to acquire data, plug data sources into a system that can make it real time, and visualize it so that teams and individuals can interpret it and make decisions. Everyone can buy into that concept. Selecting what data is important and who needs to look at what is no easy task. Wow! That's the problem! The real question becomes, what are the mechanisms for noise cancellation? What data can you ignore? What data should *not* be tracked?

Here again, self-selection and democracy come to the rescue. The data required is based on subject matter experts' domain knowledge. These experts, who work along the supply chain, have the "tribal knowledge" to know what categories of parts are key, what logistics channels need to be measured, what the critical nodes that determine performance are, etc. By tapping into these individual's knowledge bases, and peering into their Excel spreadsheets to see what they look at each day, we can begin to derive business knowledge in every domain, and begin to understand the ideal forms of visualization they require, and when data should be pulled up. These individuals know what drives inventory, what liability exposure factors are, and understand the characteristics of inventory within each category.

The people running the business know what they are looking for, but using current systems it takes them hours or days to accumulate this data. Flex seeks to provide the data they need – but not in an Excel file! This means understanding the firm's priorities and requires an innovative approach that requires tapping into their intellectual capital. This is the real innovation: prioritizing data using tribal knowledge. This is not a technology issue. Flex and Elementum are using commercially available systems. The real secret is how a firm connects its data points. In short, intelligently visualizing information into a manage-by-exception environment, for the right audience, and in real time, is the key to success in building a LIVING supply chain.

Data Integrity

One of the biggest challenges to creating such a system is data integrity. There are so many customers and entities with so many data nomenclatures, each with its own way of presenting a bill of materials, a product, a statement of work, etc. A flexible approach to defining the preferred nomenclature used to track material by different parties in the supply chain is essential for transparency.

This requires a data handbook which tracks the heritage and history of data management and which includes the right "translations" between nomenclatures, allowing the system to interpret them. This is not easy – indeed, it is one of the most challenging issues in SCM today. Data governance is important – but by no means does it have to be 100% clean.

There will always be data that are not 100% perfect, and there are procedures to deal with that. But the key is also to recognize which data do not have to be 100% clean to facilitate effective decision-making. Data integrity is required to run an ERP system – but not for a human being to make a rational decision. For example, Twitter feeds and news stories do not have structured standard data formats – but they can be extremely helpful in decision-making. A lot of information can still be used from structured ERP systems that are contaminated with mistakes and mismatches between products and customer bases. And data will always be a factor. The implication is that data managers should focus on finding the critical data that need to be cleansed and in synch (e.g., trusted) – and how to interpret data from other parts of the system that does not have a high level of integrity.

The Power of Product Genomes in Driving Transparency

Today, there has been a growing movement to track a product to its roots. In Western countries, people are now very cognizant of the sources of their food. They want to know where it was produced and under what conditions, how it was manufactured, and even whether genetically modified organisms were used. Toxin- and chemical-free organic food from certified producers is a huge industry. And when companies fail to track food origins or make food-handling errors (such as food poisoning incidents at Chipotle restaurants), consumers' negative reactions are quick and lethal. Even in China, people want better lives and better food. This return to organic roots and an interest in tracking the origins of our food and other products is very much part of the LIVING supply chain. In responding to customer demands like this, transparency is key. Recall what we said about transparency in New Supply Chain Rule 6 in Chapter 4.

New Supply Chain Rule 6a (Transparency Principle): Direct ownership and access to data on objects and activities in the supply chain creates greater transparency and increased velocity, leading to quicker response and increased survival rates.

Data transparency is a difficult rule for many people – particularly the Baby Boomer generation – to understand and buy into. For example, an executive at a major pharmaceutical company wanted to extract details on one of the company's suppliers. A 62-year-old manager asked the executive, "Why do you need to know that?" The simple answer was, "Because we want to know." In effect, this cultural shift requires that we change the way we think. We need to become more transparent because 25-year-old customers expect it. They want to know.

So now the question becomes, "How do we do that?" Today, every single object has a number. Pick up a water bottle – it has a bar code (Figure 5.2). That bar code may even tell you the source of the water itself. Country of origin laws

Figure 5.2 The Supply Chain Gene.
Source: Courtesy of Mendota Springs Water, Inc.

require this disclosure. We could think of bar codes as product genomes. And increasingly, organizations will need to track that information for purposes of labeling and marketing of products. That's the world we live in.

Transparency also helps drive financial accountability. Chief financial officers take a straightforward approach: they look at balance sheets and income statements. Supply chain executives are responsible for making improvements and positively impacting these numbers. Chief legal officers want to ensure that we are compliant, and chief human resource officers want to make sure that people are compensated fairly and rewarded, and that they have reasonable expectations. The challenge for supply chains, then, is to move the needle on the financial metrics *without* upsetting the CLO and CHRO, and to make sure people are paid on time. Supply chain executives have to turn their dials in the context of correct financial accountability. This also includes things I don't know about, but which I could nevertheless be held accountable for. If I violate a labor law or any other number of laws around Dodd–Frank, Sarbanes Oxley, OCEA, generally accepted accounting principles, or others, I may move the needle, but in a manner that conflicts with the agendas of the CFO, CLO, or CHRO.

Tom recalls that during his years at LG in Korea, there were no major corporate policies. There was a guideline called "Jingdo" – which literally translates as "do the right thing". At the corporate level, doing the right thing implies that because every situation is different, everyone is responsible for doing what is right in that context. There didn't need to be an industry coalition, a statement of corporate policy, etc. It was simply about simply acting ethically. Every company needs to take this to heart when they think about transparency. If something you did was reported in the *New York Times*, would you stand by it and state that it was the right thing to do? That is the litmus test. If companies are doing the right thing, transparency should come naturally, as there is nothing to hide.

Counterfeiting: The Opposite of Transparency

A significant problem facing many industries is the growing threat of illicit trade in the supply chain. Of these, one of the most onerous is the problem of counterfeiting. Counterfeiting is what the "bad guys" do to hide the true origin of the product genome from us. Counterfeiting has been taken on by the food industry and many others. Counterfeited goods or services appear to be same as the original goods or services but are often of inferior quality. These goods or services result in various losses for companies producing the original goods or services. Some of these risks include:

- **Compromised product quality:** Counterfeit goods in the market reflect poorly on the company that makes the "real" product.

- **Sales loss:** Since counterfeiters often sell their goods at a lower price than the original ones, industries lose product sales and revenue.
- **Reputation loss:** Industries suffer reputation loss because unsuspecting customers who have purchased the inferior goods think that they have purchased the original goods.
- **Consumer safety risk:** Counterfeit food or medicines may result in serious legal implications for the industry if they affect the health of consumers.
- **Dislocation of legitimate jobs:** The industries have to dislocate legitimate jobs because it becomes difficult to sustain employees owing to the counterfeiting losses specified above.

The high-profile examples below illustrate how problematic counterfeiting is.

- **Mobile phones:** When Argentine Customs (AFIP) seized 540,000 counterfeit mobile phones at Buenos Aires and Cordoba airports in February 2013, they discovered fake *BlackBerrys, Samsung models* including the *Galaxy S III, Nokia, Sony,* and *Motorola* handsets. They also found counterfeit *iPhone 5* handsets – a model that had been launched just 6 months ago, and which had sold 5 million units in the United States on the day of the launch alone. AFIP also seized mobile phone batteries, MP3 devices, and cameras. Altogether, AFIP estimated that, if the seized items were sold at the manufacturers' suggested retail price, their value would have been *UYU 450 million (USD 90 million)*.
- **International drug counterfeiting:** The US Food and Drug Administration commenced an investigation into the activities of Kevin Xu, a Chinese national who was suspected of counterfeiting and distributing counterfeit medicines to both the United Kingdom and the United States from China. Xu owned Pacific Orient International Ltd., based in China. US Immigration and Customs Enforcement (ICE), the largest investigative arm of the Department of Homeland Security, and the Food and Drug Administration Office of Criminal Investigations (FDA-OCI), launched an undercover operation. Xu discussed openly how he could supply 25 pharmaceutical drugs, including drugs produced by such major pharmaceutical companies as *Pfizer, Eli Lilly, Hoffman La Roche, AstraZeneca,* and *Sanofi-Aventis*. Chemical analysis revealed that although these drugs contained active ingredients, the ingredients were not present in the same quantities shown on the packaging. The drugs also contained unknown impurities. Investigators noticed that some of the lot numbers on the drugs supplied by Xu were identical to those that had been circulated by the United Kingdom's Medicines and Healthcare products Regulatory Agency (MHRA) in its recall notice – confirming for the first time that these counterfeit drugs were produced in China.

In a recent survey, we found that a significant *21%* of respondents estimated a loss of *1–5% of their total revenue due to counterfeiting. Thirteen percent* of respondents estimated a loss of *5–10% of their total revenue due to counterfeiting*, and *11% estimated a loss of 1% of their total revenue. More than 48% of respondents felt that their most popular product is at risk for counterfeiting*; suggesting that if your organization experiences a decline in sales, there is a strong possibility that at least part of this decline is due to counterfeiting or piracy.

Thinking Differently about Counterfeiting

Counterfeiting is a $1.77 trillion industry – which is equivalent to 5–7% of world trade. One avenue to combat this involves track and trace technology as a means to fight revenue loss due to counterfeits and gray market activities. Anti-counterfeit digital solutions are becoming very important in such scenarios as recalls, criminal investigations, returns, supply chain optimization, partner performance, and consumer insights. The United States alone loses about $300 billion of IP loss every year. One expert noted that "When I started down this road, I began checking out factories in China, and it became apparent to me that if you invested in bricks and mortar, you were immediately susceptible to a takedown. And I came to understand that China is employing hundreds of thousands of people in counterfeiting products, which are in key infrastructure industries like IT manufacturing products and routers."

"But it is very clever how it is done. It is a hub and spoke system, with a centralized person coordinating the activity. People are in different rooms, and are never together producing the final product. One person makes the PCB, the other the chassis, and a third the software, and they use a network of individual shippers that are often sent out one at a time. They are ordered, assembled, palletized and shipped to the US. In some regions, like Africa, up to 80 percentage of goods are imported and most are counterfeit. Africa doesn't have a lot of homegrown industries, and relies a lot on China and India for clothes, medicine, and formula, and most of these are counterfeit."

"The problem is that most large companies have no idea how much they are losing to counterfeit, because they don't track their product. Take for example a low-end product that costs $2000. It may use a stolen version of operating software, and suddenly it becomes a $20,000 telecom switch. The hack is tied to the upgrade, and that upgraded telecom switch may now be put into a hospital, a communications network, an air traffic controller station, or a team in Afghanistan. When the product failed, we go in and discover a counterfeit upgraded product, and there is nothing we can do. They just got ripped off. And there was no way to prosecute the people who did this."

"Other forms of fraud include service abuse, sending in fake products, counterfeiting cigarettes and not paying duty to bring them in, resulting in massive amounts of tax revenue being lost. You can count on at least 7 percent of iPhone sales going to counterfeiters. Java was losing 30 percent to counterfeiters, and their board was simply shocked. And this is very easy to do on trading platforms like Amazon and Alibaba. In China, people will even counterfeit hairy crabs, and will laser-etch their shells to make them look like the real thing!"

"Counterfeiters are very sophisticated. We ordered 10 products from a major international distributor, which consisted of 'controlled products' to sell to partners with full traceability. These were all cash transactions. However, buyers may choose to send it to Europe, as there is a stronger likelihood they will be caught in the US. But they also know the install base for those distributors in Germany, and can alter the serial number, and now that product can be sold as a product that is under warranty, and sold at a premium! They had changed the serial number and the upgrade was now a counterfeit!"

"Car parts are a big market. People will go to junk yards, pull brake pads from cars, and spray paint the rubber and package it differently. This is a huge issue in the automotive aftermarket, and many parts that are in legitimate distributors may be counterfeit."

A large telecom company spent $8 million on security labels, but they were stacked, so counterfeiters could peel on one and put on another. Next the team came up with the idea of a smart phone reader to authenticate the label, but it was not tied to the product in any meaningful way. Estimates were that the company was losing up to one billion dollars a year. But authentication codes, like a QR code, will not work, especially for medication and smaller products. And counterfeiters could send their codes to real phone numbers, which came back as authentic – because the system itself was faulty.

The problem at many companies is that nobody wants to admit there is a counterfeiting problem to begin with. The thinking is that if we come out with this in the markets, everyone will think we have a problem, and analysts will downgrade our stock! The problem is that everyone has a problem, and everyone is in the position of not wanting to admit the problem. Pharmaceutical companies have the same issue. Our expert noted that "I went to China and met with a counterfeiter, and asked them to make a pharmaceutical product. These were country farm boys doing this. I told them I wanted this product replicated, and they said they could make it with the same viscosity, but did it have to work? I told them no. They named a quantity and a price, and told me they'd have it in three days!"

But what about customs officials? Isn't it their job to stop counterfeit goods from coming into the country? Unfortunately, the only time customs will make a seizure is if they get a "tip." There are simply too many containers and shipments coming through the ports. And distributors and shipping partners can check on products, but again there is no real chain of custody on track and trace, and if any party loses visibility of a shipment on any point during its journey, someone can bribe someone else. So there needs to be a combination of chain of custody, track and trace, and authenticity, combined with a digital solution that determines the true path of a product in the supply chain.

Even in cases when companies destroy products, like printed circuit boards, counterfeiters figure out a solution. One company even took the measure of cutting the edge of the board, making it non-functional. A guy in China figured out how to put corners together so they would look whole, and even though they wouldn't function, he would resell them into the market! There are villages in the country that make a business out of scavenging old chips from old PCBs and scraping them off, cleaning the substrate, printing over it, and suddenly a 10-year-old chip looks brand new, and now it goes into a military installation!

Experts agree: counterfeiting can never be stopped. However, by building transparency and product genomes that allow us to map and assign specific, unique values to our products, we can create tools that will allow consumers to easily spot a fake. Counterfeiting will always happen, and the bad guys will always find a way to copy stuff, so the only solution is to empower consumers to make informed decisions. The idea is simply that companies have to empower people to authenticate end products if they choose to. It will also be important to have safe harbor for liability. If you cannot authenticate, and haven't given people the ability to ensure whether the product they purchased is authentic, there are grounds for a lawsuit. On the other hand, if you have put a legitimate solution in place and have given an end user the opportunity to verify authenticity, that provides a safe harbor.

"Is This What You See?" Authentication Technology

But what does an authentication solution look like? How do you create a "passport" for a product? People have tried holograms, mass spectrometers, soil samples for wines in Bordeaux, and many other solutions. People who haven't grown up in the world of counterfeiting will always have new, good products. Counterfeiting is a seedy, dangerous world, where investigators are attacked. But many inexperienced innovators aren't thinking about what counterfeiters will do to avoid detection.

The digital supply chain can leverage the power of mobile cloud software flexible and scaling, with a digital, real-time solution that allows analytics from data feeds coming from manufacturers to be authenticated in the field. The evolution of this technology is a combination of a QR code and a 1D barcode. Almost 90% of the infrastructure in distribution, channel partners, and warehouse facilities already consists of 1D barcodes. There is a transition from 1D to 2D but it is slow, and 9 out of 10 facilities have 1D barcode readers. A track and trace solution from contract manufacturing to channel partners to consumers should by definition use existing 1D infrastructure that can scan the product, is scalable, and can produce a flat file with a list of all scans at the end of each day.

Some solution providers are exploring printing complex labels with covert features – which makes sense, but only for certain types of industries, such as automobiles, aerospace, and defense. To truly authenticate (as opposed to being in the tag business), there needs to be a technology that can laser imprint on products in milliseconds, and which is also easy to pick up downstream at the customer. The QR code is unique, and has a DNA fingerprint – a unique binary code – which is a single product genome that the software can validate. Counterfeiters don't have the QR code initially, but will often try to alter the serial number. But they will not have the unique code, which is where they can be caught. If more than one QR code is authenticated in the field, this is a warning that the system has been breached. And the unique DNA of the QR code is very hard to replicate – which is not something counterfeiters are usually able to do.

Increasingly the information associated with the product, the shoe, the medicine, etc. will require engagement by the customer in some form to determine authenticity. But if the code does not match the product, additional questions occur: Where did you buy it? What was the price? These questions can be used to drive additional analytics that can help the manufacturer identify the leaks in its supply chain.

But this isn't enough. Combating counterfeiting is one of the biggest challenges facing participants in the LIVING supply chain ecosystem. The promise of combating counterfeit and other forms of fraud and criminal activity lies in the ability of organizations to align strategies and seek multi-echelon vertical and horizontal solutions that span multiple tiers in the supply chain. To truly create a means of driving out counterfeit, we have to go back to our federated supply chain. How do we get everyone in our supply chain to work together to combat counterfeiting, theft, and gray markets? This is the best weapon but remains elusive in many of the current supply chains we encounter.

6

NETWORKED! Co-evolution and Co-innovation in Federated Supply Chains

The species that survive are not those that are the most intelligent; nor are they those that are the strongest; the species that survive are those that are best able to adapt to change.

—Charles Darwin, 1859

Evolution, Not Revolution: Grolar Bears, Coyowolves, and MerLions

The ideas of federated networks presuppose that enterprises in the LIVING supply chain have several characteristics that are often tossed around lightly in conversation, but which in fact have very deep implications: words like trust, collaboration, shared information, transparency, and alignment. However, many people don't fully understand the meaning of these terms until they are reliant on others in the network, and there are risks present that would cause one or more parties to fail and fall into a perilous situation. Then the true meaning of these terms becomes real.

In September 22, 2014, the prime minister of Singapore invited Tom Linton to speak at the GIC Futures Forum. The GIC represents one of the largest investment banks in the world. As Singapore has done exceptionally well over the last few years, growing its cash surplus significantly, Tom was asked to speak about his investment strategies for the future of technology. Tom wasn't sure what he should talk about. Singapore had evolved quickly, and investors were wondering what the future held. The talk was attended by all of Singapore's top government officials, including the prime minister and his cabinet as well as senior bank and investment executives.

The primary theme of Tom's talk was to think about evolution, not revolution. Early in the presentation, he discussed the concept of non-zero as an important component of Singapore's history and as an important element of LIVING

The LIVING Supply Chain: The Evolving Imperative of Operating in Real Time, First Edition.
Robert Handfield and Tom Linton.
© 2017 John Wiley & Sons, Inc. Published 2017 by John Wiley & Sons, Inc.

supply chains. A core concept from the book *Non-Zero: The Logic of Human Destiny*[1] refers to *memes* as a way to think about Darwin's genetic changes. (Memes are referred to in the context of culture as "a unit of cultural transmission or a unit of imitation."[2])

Memes: Units of non-genetic cultural information transmitted from person to person; a word, a song, an attitude, a belief, a ritual, *an engineering concept.*

Wright, the author of *Nonzero*, discusses the idea of memes further:

> Don't think of songs, movies, ideologies as passive bodies of information that you, the active agent, choose. Think of them as competing for access to your brain, which they use to propagate themselves.

After speaking about memes, Tom next put up a quote from Jeff Bezos, founder and CEO of Amazon, in a 1997 letter to his shareholders written:

> Word of mouth remains the most powerful customer acquisition tool we have …

What do these quotes mean? What could they possibly have to do with investment strategies? The audience in Singapore looked puzzled, but continued listening. "Mr. Linton must know what he is talking about, as he is a famous executive," was the thought probably going through their heads. But what Tom put up next confused them even further: pictures of a bear and a wolf (shown in Figures 6.1 and 6.2).

"The bear on your left is called a Grolar bear. As you can see, the white and brown fur suggests that it is the product of mating between a grizzly and a polar bear. This bear happens to be stronger and larger than either grizzlies or polar bears, and is able to withstand a greater range of climates and feeding habitats. How did this happen? As the world became warmer, grizzlies started to travel up to the Arctic Circle, and began to mate with polar bears. A new species, the grolar bear, was born." (See Figure 6.1)

"The animal on the right is a coyote wolf (See Figure 6.2). Same story, different location. This animal is smarter than either species, and can survive in an urban environment. It is bigger and better able to survive. It also evolved in response to changes in its habitat that forced the two species to occupy the same landscape."

Next Tom showed a picture of the Singapore symbol, the MerLion, evoked in a statue of a hybrid between a mermaid and a lion (shown in Figure 6.3). "You too in Singapore have evolved, as you have shown in the mermaid and the lion coming together," he said. "Singapore has the beautiful sound and softness of a mermaid, as well as the strength and the courage of a lion. Your country has

1 Wright, R., *Nonzero: The Logic of Human Destiny*, First Vintage Books, 2000.
2 Dawkins, R., *The Selfish Gene*, 2nd ed., Oxford University Press, 1989, p. 192.

Figure 6.1 Grolar Bear. *Source:* Reproduced with permission of iStock

Figure 6.2 Coyote Wolf. *Source:* Reproduced with permission of Eastern Coyote Research

Figure 6.3 Singapore Merlion. *Source:* https://commons.wikimedia.org/wiki/File:Rear_
view_of_the_Merlion_statue_at_Merlion_Park,_Singapore,_with_Marina_Bay_Sands_in_
the_distance_-_20140307.jpg. Used under CC BY 2.0 https://creativecommons.org/licenses/
by/2.0/deed.en

grown and become successful not through a revolution, but because of your ability to EVOLVE, adapt to changes in your environment, and take on the best qualities of both the mermaid and the lion. You have moved through different phases of industrial growth, beginning in low-value manufacturing, then growing into pharmaceuticals and electronics, becoming an original design manufacturer in the gaming industry, building your resort industry (Universal Studios), and most recently becoming a tourist destination. So now you are wondering what is the next vector, and what comes next. I urge you to consider that things grow and are successful through *evolution*, NOT through *revolution!*" So how should you evolve?

This led to a story about the computer industry. "If you think about it, technology is constantly evolving. Although people say the 'smart phone' was a revolution, it really wasn't … it was more of an evolution."

"I used to work in Burlington, Vermont as a purchasing and transportation manager at IBM's manufacturing site, where we were assembling large mainframe computers. Eventually, computers were shrunk into something called the personal computer that could sit on a desk and have the same computing power. Apple created the Macintosh, which no one liked, but which used something called a mouse. Later, that desktop was shrunk into a laptop computer, and then an even smaller and thinner laptop computer. The laptop eventually became a tablet, and kept shrinking until it became a smart phone. So when people say the smart phone was revolutionary, in reality it was nothing more than a computer getting smaller and smaller. That happened over 20 years, and mobile devices are now becoming integrated into vehicles, clothing, and other forms of products. So if you want to understand what will happen in technology, think about how it will evolve, and what it will become in the next ten or 15 years, and then invest along that vector."

The point of Tom's story to Singapore officials is that LIVING supply chains can be seen as autonomous, evolving networks. They are like a circulation system that adapts, and are constantly evolving, shifting, and growing. They are the life blood of technology, the drivers behind globalization, the drivers to lower-cost consumer goods, and arguably a major factor in global GDP. If supply chains aren't evolving, then like the seals or any species, they will slowly die away. But in the right environment, supply chains can recover and flourish.

Federated supply chains are in our view the next form of an evolution that will distinguish the winners from the losers in the practice of supply chain management. Supply chain managers tend to be highly operational, often focused on data; their single biggest everyday tool is Excel. This isn't a bad thing, and these skills will continue to be important. But this book puts forth the idea that a new set of "supply chain rules" will shape how organizations work together. They will be federated and transparent, will share data in real time, and will be networked so that decisions will be made quickly with enhanced visibility of velocity and flow. As this occurs, machines will get smarter and smarter, will leverage the genomes of product structures, and will perform much of the operational work done by human beings on Excel spreadsheets today. Human beings will become curators, scanning information that is presented in real time in a visual format, and working with other individuals in the supply chain on ways to innovate, improve, and deal with issues and complexities as they arise. In short, human beings will become much more involved in the management of relationships and the alignment of corporate purpose within federated supply chains.

The Power of Technology to Create Federated Supply Chain Networks Driven by Shared Data

As human beings become more involved in creating and maintaining relationships, shared data will become the primary vehicle for consensus-building. Data that is real time, visible, and readily accessible in the Cloud will be the primary focal point for debate, discussion, problem-solving, and customer service improvement ideas. The idea of global intelligence gathering being rapidly

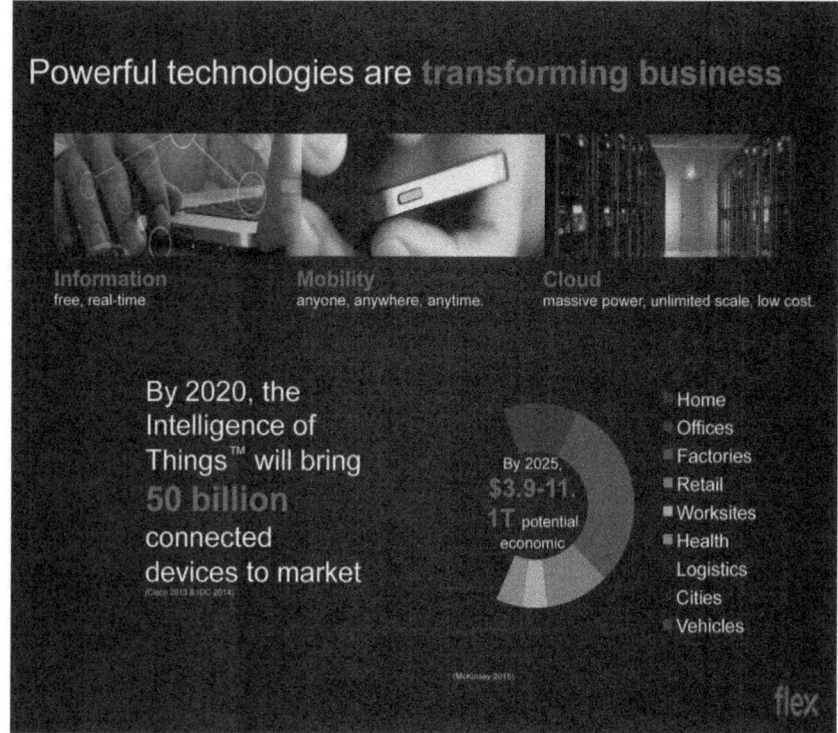

Figure 6.4 Supply Chain Evolution. *Source:* Reproduced with permission of Flex

communicated and translated into decision-making applies more than ever on the customer-facing side of the supply chain.

The biggest change in the last 3 years has been the rapid rise of technology as an enabler to create real-time interactive relationships. As shown in Figure 6.4, the "Intelligence of Things^{TM}" will evolve so that by 2020, more than 50 billion devices will be connected over the Internet, making the Internet the true utility for driving intelligence across networks. This will expand through real-time information that becomes available through open sharing across intercompany networks, the rise of mobile devices that allows anyone, anywhere, to share any information in open platforms, and the massive power of Cloud computing, which can perform simultaneous machine-based activities rapidly on servers that no one can see but which is pushed out to individuals as needed.

One of the core elements in the Flex model for the LIVING Supply Chain is the need for a virtual world in which individuals around the world are closely tied together to make collective decisions. Flex's future trajectory relies heavily on exploiting these changes, by embedding the technology vector of the Internet of Things to three specific goals:

✓ Building our entire company on mobility
✓ Distributive decision-making
✓ Real-time decision-making in the field

A networked supply chain is not difficult to imagine. Flex's platform, the Pulse™, is an interactive place and a mobile system that provides the focal point for collaborative discussions. The key issue driving this is the ability to engage in active tracking of issues, not batch processing, which delays the ability to be real time, but instead ensures that it is driven by data that is LIVING and alive. Throughout this book, we have alluded to the "natural" and "balanced" nature of supply chain relationships that must accompany the technological benefits of the Pulse Center and other systems currently under development. Evolution applies to supply chains, too.

The original thinker in this regard is of course Charles Darwin, the father of "evolutionary" thinking. Charles Darwin wrote about the general principles of evolutionary theory in a biological context in his book *The Origin of Species by Means of Natural Selection* (1859). The phrase that most people associate with this great work is "survival of the fittest" and, it turns out, this is not a bad metaphor to adapt in the realm of business. Before we explain how evolution applies in a business context, it is helpful to outline the basics of the biological story, because most readers will have some familiarity with it and we will be using it below to draw parallels.

The process of evolution is explained by reference to three building blocks:

• a source of variation
• a selection process
• a means of retaining variations that are selected

These building blocks, variety-selection-retention (VSR), are referred to collectively as "the evolutionary algorithm." The modern interpretation of the Darwinian account of natural selection (neo-Darwinism) explains the evolution of species as a result of blind random variations (mutations) in the genes of some members of the species. If a random genetic mutation gives rise to a characteristic that confers some advantage in the environment inhabited by the species, the mutants will have a higher probability of survival. Members of the species who do not possess the mutant gene will eventually diminish in number while the mutants will become more numerous and pass on their genes, and therefore their advantage, to their offspring. To illustrate some of the key features of the process, consider the following highly stylized story of the evolution of long-necked giraffes.

Assume that giraffes need to eat the leaves of trees in order to maintain their strength and to have sufficient energy to outrun lions (who like to eat giraffes).[3] Assume also that the most nutritious leaves can only be found at the tops of tall trees. Now assume that the members of a herd of giraffes in a specific geographical region have relatively short necks and are unable to reach the highly nutritious leaves. This means that competition or struggle for the leaves that grow at the lower level will be intense and, as a result, most giraffes in the herd will be malnourished and unable to outrun hungry lions. Now, if a mutant giraffe with an unusually long neck is born (thus providing the first building block of evolution), it will reach the nutritious leaves that are out of the reach of the other giraffes in the herd. As a result, the longer-necked mutant will not have to compete with the other giraffes and will become strong and healthy and be able to outrun the lions more easily than its malnourished short-necked cousins. This mutant giraffe fits the environment better than the other giraffes and, as a result, it has a much better chance of survival. It is important to note here that the mutant giraffe is relatively fit rather than optimally fit (i.e., the mutant only needs to run faster than the other members of the herd). This is a crucial point, for reasons that will become apparent.

The fact that the mutant fits the environment so well gives the impression that the environment has selected it for success (this is the second building block of evolution). Of course, the environment is not a thinking entity that exercises choices, so it has not deliberately selected the mutant giraffe at all; the giraffe has in fact been "naturally selected." If we assume now that the mutant giraffe gives birth to baby giraffes, then at least some of the babies should inherit the mutant gene and grow up to have advantages similar to their parent's, and eat leaves from the tops of trees. The parent will eventually die of old age; nevertheless, the long neck is retained in the herd because the gene that causes it has been replicated and passed on from parent to child (the third building block of evolution). In time, the offspring of the original mutant will give birth to their own offspring, to whom they will pass the mutant gene. As a result, the proportion of giraffes in this population who inherit long necks will increase. Note that what has actually been retained in this process is the information carried by the long-necked gene: in other words, the original long-necked giraffe no longer exists, but the genetic information that caused it to have a long neck does. Biological evolution is a story about how this "genotypical" information is retained in and diffused through a system.

The meaning of the phrase "survival of the fittest" should now be clear. When evolutionary theorists talk about "fitness," they are referring not to some abstract notion of good health and athletic ability, but to how well the

---

3 Example is drawn from a working paper: Cousins, P., and Handfield, R., "Evolutionary Economics and Supply Chain Management," Manchester Business School, Manchester, UK.

organism they are examining fits its environment and, in turn, how well the genotypical information it carries fits the environment. Thus, an organism cannot be declared "fit" without reference to its context, or environment. As time passes and the proportion of the herd enjoying the long-necked characteristic increases, what constitutes an adequate standard of fitness will increase also. Thus, "sustainable co-evolution with one's environment is a necessary condition for 'fitness' ... fitness [is] an emergent property ..."[4]

Darwin (1859) himself noted:

> The species that survive are not those that are the most intelligent; nor are they those that are the strongest; the species that survive are those that are best able to adapt to change.

The evolutionary comparison has been applied to the business community through a body of scholarly work known as complex systems theory. For too long, organizations have been managing based on transactional boundaries, using simple deterministic ways of thinking. However, the network of firms in the LIVING supply chain is more akin to the dynamics associated with complex systems. Complex systems theory grapples with how organizations adapt in the face of dynamic change over time, with those organizations best able to adapt ultimately surviving.[5] A further branch of thinking suggests that firms that survive essentially coevolve with those entities around them. This line of thought, sometimes called the "resource-based view," suggests that the changing relationship between a firm's activities and entities in its competitive environment creates whatever distinct capabilities it draws on for sustained competitive advantage.[6] In simpler terms, the organizational processes that occur with other entities in the value chain together provide the "emergent" strategies that shape how the organization survives.

As with Darwinian selectionist theory, which states that living things evolve as their parts (organs, biomolecules, or genes) mutate, organization theorists would suggest that organizations adapt as each of the supply chain competencies (representing microagents – the individual activities that make up the entire organization) influence selective advantage for the firm as a whole.[7] Again, translating this into operational thinking, organizations that drive

---

4 Epstein, J. M., and Axtell, R., *Growing Artificial Societies: Social Science from the Bottom Up*, MIT Press, Cambridge, MA, 1996, p. 63.

5 Aldrich, H., *Organizations and Environments*, Prentice Hall, Englewood Cliffs, NJ, 1979.

6 Many scholars have contributed to this line of thought. A good summary of these references is provided by McKelvey, B., "Avoiding Complexity Catastrophe in Coevolutionary Pockets: Strategies for Rugged Landscapes," *Organization Science*, vol. 10, no. 3, May/June 1999, pp. 294–231.

7 Kauffman, S. A., *The Origins of Order: Self-Organization and Selection in Evolution*, Oxford University Press, New York, 1993.

collaborative behavior with their key supply chain partners in their daily routines, contracting approaches, and relationships, coevolve to a higher level of performance that allows all entities in the chain not only to survive, but to adapt to the rapidly changing environment around it. More importantly, "... in co-evolutionary processes, the fitness of one organism or species depends on the characteristics of the other organisms or species with which it interacts, while all simultaneously adapt and change."[8] This evolution occurs even in an environment characterized by rapid change, regulatory pressure, new technology, and other major challenges. As Kauffman notes, "A critical difference between evolution on a fixed landscape and coevolution is that the former can be roughly characterized as if it were an adapt search on a 'potential surface' or 'fitness surface,' whose peaks are the positions sought. In coevolution, there may typically be no such potential surface, and the process is far more complex."[9]

The implication is that organizations must begin not only to consider their local environments in building their business strategies, but to extend these strategies to consider all the participants in the supply chain network. All organizations evolve based either on applying rules or on following a certain set of performance metrics that indicate progress toward those rules. The problem, of course, is that adherence to these rules may lead to evolution, but not all evolutions lead to successful adaptations to the environment![10] Many organizations may be following the wrong set of rules, or the wrong set of performance metrics to indicate whether adequate progress towards survival is being maintained! And even when progress is being made toward the right evolutionary outcome, if organizations are not fast enough to adapt, the competition within the ecosystem may extinguish them, meaning agility and velocity are key to survival.

Richard Dawkins, in his book *The Selfish Gene* went further, explaining how natural selection is driven to the gene level and invisible decisions drive who wins and who loses. In the same way, it is fair to assume that product supply chains evolve in their own selfish ways. Products that move faster to market, at lower costs, win. Slower, less adaptable products lose. The "invisible hand" (p. 572), first articulated by Adam Smith in *The Wealth of Nations* (1776), allows market forces to rule. The market in effect drives the evolution of supply chains so that the fittest survive and the weak are destined to fail.

The genetic code of all things identifies the DNA of materials in the LIVING supply chain. The most ubiquitous of these in our system is the simple bar code.

---

8 Kauffman, 1993, p. 33.
9 Kauffman, 1993, p. 33.
10 Morel, B., and Ramanujam, R., "Through the Looking Glass of Complexity: The Dynamics of Organizations as Adaptive and Evolving Systems," *Organization Science*, vol. 10, no. 3, May/June 1999.

This gene contains a wealth of information about the history and roots of the product – in the future, it will contain even more information.

If there is one corollary to the LIVING Supply Chain, it is that supply chains are selfish. The profit motive on each stakeholder or node in a supply chain focuses on winning – surviving by supplying faster and better alternatives. Why don't all our products go by air transport? They would if it were cheaper. Why did Panama announce a widening of the canal? So that bigger ships carrying more goods can arrive days faster than any other route. Why is near-shoring and regionalization gaining strength as labor costs climb in China? The total landed costs including the evolving need for mass customization and time to market are driving companies to shift.

Pretty heavy stuff. But what are the practical implications for the LIVING supply chain?

Co-evolution

Let's get back to the Flex tour. One of my stops was a trip to the Flex Innovation Center. We spent a good amount of time walking through a building, escorted by Natalia Pena and Alexandra Coltman, who took us through a series of rooms. One of the tour guides was a young man whose parents had emigrated from China and who had an engineering degree from Stanford. He was very excited about the work going on in these rooms. This was the world of "Co-."

"Co-" applies to the great many parts of the supply chain that involve making decisions in conjunction with others to drive the best outcomes. Elements in the world of "Co-" include:

Co-planning: Creating aligned supply and demand planning views that allow all parties in the chain to see the level of inventory, the level of demand, and the likely trajectory of possible shortages, capacity imbalances, and excess or slow-moving inventory. Averting problems due to mismatches between supply and demand is simply a fact of life. Organizations that discover the right way of working through these issues will drive increasing asset velocity.

Co-sourcing: Why does purchasing have the final say on which suppliers are likely to be awarded the business? "Because it is our right" is often the answer. But in a true co-sourcing world, the decision is made through an ongoing review of design objectives, cost objectives, technology roadmaps, stakeholder requirements, and ongoing projections, as well as a review of who has been the best partner. The latter element is often a function of nontraditional measurements. For example, perhaps suppliers who are the most honest about the lack of compliance or quality issues in their plants will be rewarded with the most business. Encouraging honesty and transparency as the ultimate basis for awarding business: this sounds like heresy in many purchasing circles, but reflects the need for a different model to drive the right level of trust in a virtual environment.

Co-logistics: We need partners who understand how to operate in different parts of the world – and know how to ensure that products can cross borders and countries with a minimum of hassle, extra taxes, and delays (all of which are forms of friction in the supply chain). The implication? We need logistics providers who know how to work with the government – who are now a critical part of your supply chain. And we need seamless communication that will allow people to reroute trucks, boats, airplanes, and ships mid-route, and track their product anywhere in the world. This is still not possible on most carriers, but will be a reality soon. Asset velocity will be a key driver of this activity.

Co-materials: As we continue to work on new and emerging materials that are more sustainable, we need to think about how to work with other partners in the chain to discover reusable, recyclable, and renewable materials that will perform better and at a lower cost than traditional products. For example, bio-based products are a promising area of growth, as these products use renewable raw materials such as biochemically derived molecules to replace traditional petrochemical-based products.

Co-innovation: This is perhaps one of the biggest opportunities – figuring out how to work with partners in the chain who have greater technical insight into our products. At Flex's Innovation Lab in Milpitas, start-up companies are encouraged to use the meeting space for engineering and design meetings with Flex. Flex helps these companies set up a small space for pilot runs, most of which use equipment for 100 pieces or less. These labs may go through up to 60 engineering changes per day on the products, and across all products the labs may oversee 15,000 engineering changes per year. Constant change is the rule of the day. But this fosters an approach for experimentation, technology development, and new products. Tom Linton notes, "We recognize that 80 percent of these projects will not work out. But for the ones that do, we will be ready to take their products, scale up the production from these labs, move it to one of our global factories, and begin commercializing these innovator's products. We know that the majority of innovations come from small companies and individuals, not from big companies."

As the nature of a company's relationships with other companies in its supply chain evolves, innovation in the form of new ways of collaborating will be one of the first elements that determine the strength of these relationships. Organizations that re-invent how they work with other companies in their supply chains will be at the forefront of this evolution. This is called business process innovation, and is about finding new ways to do business with others in the network.

Business Process Innovation Drives New Forms of Human–Machine–Data Interaction

Innovation is integral to the transformation to a LIVING supply chain. It naturally fits into an enterprise-wide culture around innovation, and is an inherent component of digitization of the supply chain and how companies work with and respond to changes in their ecosystems. This is of course happening in technology industries – but it's also happening in health care.

One key area of innovation focuses on how the "pulse" of the supply chain mimics the "pulse" monitoring of patients in health care. Healthcare technology allows a handful of nurses in a central area to monitor the heartbeat, oxygen, and blood pressure of patients in 30 hospital rooms. The monitoring systems make loud noises when a patient is experiencing an abnormal pulse. Maybe the patient's breathing is erratic, or their heartbeat is abnormal, resulting in a nurse rushing to the bedside to check on the patient and see if this is an emergency, in which case the nurse may call in others. We see this same type of "pulse" monitoring systems emerge in such industries as automotive, electronics, heavy equipment, oil and gas, and chemical facilities, where automated signals generate all sorts of events.

The world is becoming virtually vertically integrated. For years, large companies have lightened their asset loads by exiting the manufacturing business and integrating their supply chain. In the new ecosystem, companies that *cultivate* innovation from sources outside their walls will be the ones to prosper. Innovation won't "walk into your door" – but must be virtually cultivated and acquired. And supply chain executives may neglect to focus on business process innovation. Earlier concepts of open innovation are falling victim to intellectual property limits. How much can a company freely share? However, if the solution is a joint project and involves the collective joining of capabilities, a company's willingness to co-succeed is greater, and is consistent with natural laws of success.

Most of the interaction between business functions and IT information infrastructures is functional. IT is not closely linked to the rest of most businesses. At Flex, a team of people sits in the supply chain, working directly on the requirements of the business and with IT to build functionality – rather than having IT tell it what it needs. This is a fundamental change – having the business drive the technology requirements for the company, not the other way around! This change is fundamental to business process innovation. The litmus test should be, "Is the technology or tool I'm using giving me faster business speed? Is it moving assets through the business faster?" If not, it's not useful, and is a form of friction.

Tom spoke to executives at a Procurement Leaders Forum in San Francisco in June 2016 about the radical shifts in organizational culture that accompanied the roll-out of the Pulse. "When I first arrived, if I wanted information, I would send an email to a guy who would give me the information," Tom said. "That just didn't work for me. I drove the thinking that we all had to operate in real time, and change the way that data and human beings interact together."

"Look around. Everyone has a touch-based smart phone. The human–machine interaction is a natural evolution that is occurring all around us, whether we like it or not. We have to change our way of working to allow machines to work with us. Even Apple and SAP are working together to create apps that allow people to do transactions using a mobile app. We are moving to big environments that are mobile- and Cloud-based, to allow for the acquisition of data through mobile devices to allow people to act on information."

"The Flex Pulse Center creates a mobile platform for pulling information in a menu-driven format on material lead times, risk mitigation, and inventory," Tom said. He looked at his iPhone, and showed a picture of the inventory pulse. He was able to pull it down for any customer, for any facility, as the sum of raw material, WIP, and finished goods inventory. "The alert feature uses components of statistical process control to identify aberrations in the data that may lead to an alert," he said. "Different alert levels are established for different roles." Tom may see one set of alerts for the whole company, while a director may see alerts for a facility, and a buyer planner may see alerts for his category of spending or his group of suppliers. And it is all available on the phone, to create visibility.

"One of the key questions is what data needs to be in real-time and on alert. Not all information needs to be monitored, just as not all human functions are monitored electronically over time. But those elements that are brought into an alert setting can foster a 'workshop' environment – where everyone has access to the data. This is the opposite of a 'control tower environment.' Control implies decision-making: 'I want a flow tower that tells me when things are going wrong – not when they are going right!' I am 99 percent sure they are right – and I want to manage by exception. Alerts can tell me that. Flex Pulse, in the words of our CEO is actually an 'anti-control tower' as control slows things down. It's like tapping on the breaks when you are trying to go faster."

"As an example, last month someone placed a billion dollar purchase order. This came up as an alert on my mobile phone. Who did this? Turns out it was someone in Mexico who had 'fat fingers' and made an error. This could have quickly escalated into a major liability on the company – but the power of real time allowed us to get ahead of it, and defrag the problem."

"Many companies want to limit the number of IT vendors they work with, to standardize and control their environment. We need to implement change slowly, is the typical reason. We can't inundate people with too many new systems changes or we will shut down … this is the exact opposite of the strategy that Flex is using in deploying the Pulse Center capability."

Tom notes, "To create a true event-driven network, Flex is working with over 30+ applications across their supply chain, driven by the Elementum platform. They are all focused on creating mobile solutions that are enterprise-wide. All the innovations we work on must meet these two criteria. They can't just be functional. I am happy to work with as many vendors as needed to deploy new apps that make us more productive as quickly as possible. The more people we have involved, the faster we will get our business problems resolved, and the faster we can make these solutions more widely available across our supply chain network."

"We decided to move to a multivendor environment based on how people use apps on their smart phones. We don't live our everyday lives in a one-solution world, and one company can't do it all. Look at the Apple iPhone – everyone has multiple apps. Some people have 40, 50, or 60 apps they regularly use, until they run out of memory. My philosophy is that the rope is stronger if you have multiple forms of twine. The glue in the rope is the integration of platforms that keeps all the solutions working together using the same data. We need to become more comfortable with multiple business apps to deal with different types of problems, as we have so many issues on our plate."

The Challenge of Trusting Your Data

One of the big challenges of driving true collaboration in a federated supply chain is that people need to trust not only one another, but also the data they are sharing. If the data isn't trustworthy, people will always second-guess it. But can people really trust information produced from a system under high-stress, high-risk supply-chain-disruption situations?

This problem was indirectly explored by a group of researchers from NC State University's Laboratory for Analytic Science.[11] These researchers asked, what happens when human beings have to trust real-time data under the types of high-stress, high-pressure environments typical of major supply chain disruption events? Human beings tend to rely on available information while completing complex tasks. But what happens when information is presented by humans *and* automated sources? And what happens if those information sources conflict? This situation occurs more than you might think. For example, in 2002, a Russian passenger jet and cargo plane crashed mid-air. Automation told the two planes to change elevation in different directions, but so did an air traffic controller; these messages directly conflicted. One pilot listened to the automation

---

11 Boettcher, W. A., Mayer, R. C., Mayhorn, C. B., Simons-Rudolph, J. M., Streck, S. M., Pearson, C. J., and Welk, A. K., "In Automation We Trust? Identifying Factors that Influence Trust and Reliance in Automated and Human Decision Aids," Ph.D. Presentation made at LAS, March 23, 2016.

and the other pilot listened to an air traffic controller, and the planes collided. In the LAS study, a series of tests with undergraduate students was carried out, in which the students were presented with the following scenario:

"You will be performing as the leader of a vehicle convoy. Your mission is to deliver critical supplies to a nearby warehouse. *Your task will be to select a delivery route. Participants must select a route for their military convoy from three possible options.*

You will be shown a map displaying three delivery routes. The map will identify the location(s) of past IEDs (improvised explosive devices), as well as areas of insurgent activity. You will also receive information from a local intelligence officer who will provide you with additional data about the area.

Consider the three routes and select *one*. Make your decision as quickly as possible; you will have 60 seconds to complete this task."

In this scenario:

- An automated tool provides a map that contains information regarding past IED explosions and insurgent activity to illustrate one optimal route choice.
- The human being provides information that conflicts with the map and recommends a different route.

Under this simulation, the findings were very interesting:

- Presentation order did not significantly affect reliance/trust in humans and automated sources within risky decision-making tasks. In other words, there may be more critical design choices worth considering when designing systems to promote reliance for this type of scenario.
- When presented with conflicting information from automation and human sources in high-*workload* scenarios, operators may increase trust in human sources. In other words, increased workload negatively affected trust in automation.
- When presented with conflicting information from automation and human sources in high-*risk* scenarios, operators may decrease trust in automated sources. Increased risk positively affected trust in the human. This may be due to the added load of assessing automation's trustworthiness.

The implication of this research is that any real-time supply chain system must have the following characteristics to be successful:

- The system itself must produce trustworthy data. In other words, the data must represent reality.
- The information provided by the system must align with human perceptions of what is happening. This suggests that combining human observations with system data can augment the trust that others observing the information will have in the data.

- Under high-risk situations common in major disruptions, people will trust human beings over system-produced data. This is an obstacle that may need to be directly addressed.
- Under high workload stress, operators may trust more in human dialogue. This suggests an important need for human-to-human communication in these situations.

Because the emergence of real-time supply chain systems is so novel, many such cultural artifacts may need to be overcome, even if the systems issues are addressed.

Co-sourcing: Trusting Partners Based on Capability

Trusting partners to drive innovations is a big challenge today. So many issues come up regarding whether partners can be trusted to do what they promise, whether they will cheat you out of your IP, will follow through on agreements, etc. Yet partnering with suppliers is one of the most important ways in which large enterprises will be on the forefront of new technological innovation. And this may involve looking in places where most companies haven't looked before: Small companies in industries that no one has worked with in the past.

A great example of how driving innovation from unlikely sources was discussed in a great presentation I attended at the Sourcing Industry Group meeting in April 2016, where SIG's CEO Dawn Tiura had a "fireside chat" with John Sculley. Sculley was the legendary CEO of PepsiCo who was recruited to Apple by Steve Jobs. John served as Apple CEO for 10 years increasing sales more than 1000%. Under his leadership, the Macintosh became the largest-selling personal computer in the world in December 1992.

John recounted an interesting story from those days:

"It's 1978 and I'm CEO of Pepsi and we have been wildly successful in our marketing campaign. The Pepsi Challenge has allowed us to pass Coke in sales and market share. I was speaking at Harvard University, and at the end of the class, a student comes up to me, and says 'I created something knowing you were coming here that I want you to look at, that I developed specifically for you.' "

"So we go over to the other building and I see for the first time in my life – what looked like an Apple II personal computer. This was something this kid had put together – before Steve Jobs and Wozniak – and it has rows and columns on the screen."

"'What do you call it?' I asked him. 'I call it an interactive spreadsheet,' he said. The kid's name was Dan Bricklin and he joined with Bob Frankson to start a company called Visicorp that became Visicalc … and what he had just showed me was the first spreadsheet in the world, which eventually became the foundation for Excel, one of the most applied tools in the world."

"I was also there at the beginning of PowerPoint and HyperCard. I've watched small teams create tools that change the way we work – companies like People Ticker. We create tools that improve productivity that improve the workforce. These are tools that improve productivity. Slack went from 0 to $4B in sales in three years – because it is a great tool that improves productivity."

"I'm a huge fan of tools for people. The most important development is that we need to equip our workforce with better and better tools. Human beings still have judgment and they can do things that are repetitive and they can process things quickly. But if one provides people with the right tools, especially in contingent-skilled labor situations, they will double their productivity."

A question came from the audience:

> Fundamentally, procurement is measured on cost savings as the primary metric. But this can be destructive on the business. You set the requirements and set the solution that results from the requirements. Other metrics are whether you agree off purchasing agreements in the company, and some customer satisfaction metrics – like whether internal stakeholders are satisfied. If we are going to be truly strategic and not just drive toward cost mitigation – what are the things we should look for in terms of tools and sensory capabilities to help us evaluate more strategically what we are buying to drive customer retention and top line metrics? How do you see strategic sourcing leaders doing that?

Sculley replied with a very insightful comment:

"Here is how I think about it. I believe all technology commoditizes. What is unique and valuable today will become affordable at different price points tomorrow. The way I think about those various points I brought up – is you have to judge how you are recruiting talent in the context of domain expertise – and can't focus just on the costs in isolation of the domain expertise issue. Strategically, when you are looking to staff a project, almost all work will be done with project teams, inside of organizations and outside with contingent teams."

"Let's imagine we are back in 2007 – and Kodak was focused on a project which sought how to compete with Walmart in a single-use camera taking market share from their camera. They made a decision based on their expertise (and their business was film cameras) to double down and spend billions on additional vertical integration on film processing to compete on a cost basis better with Walmart. (And remember – Kodak was the one who *invented* the digital camera!)"

"At the same time, Steve Jobs introduced the iPod and began to make the connections around what was happening in the market around the development of digital components for consumer products. And he also understood that another domain, which was wireless operators, were moving from 2G (text sending) to emails and photos (3G). Apple understood that there were these other domains that would impact consumer electronics, in terms of how to take a photo from software to another mobile device. In 2007, Apple launched the iPhone. Three years later – Kodak files for bankruptcy."

"Strategically, when you look at recruiting talent, you need to look at domain expertise beyond the domains that you have in your company, and a wider scope of things you are looking at. We are all vulnerable and we have seen that in the last 15 years. And at the same time one can get into a new domain by procuring talent that may not already be in your organization."

Sculley made an important point: Innovation takes place on the fringes. We can draw a circle around domains and they are in motion – as they touch, they start to collide and change things. This means that procurement can adopt change to drive innovation and create new technologies by working on the edges of different technologies, where things touch. Innovation in supply chains has to be done in the context of different domains, which means developing talent in domains that you don't currently have and recruiting talent that is not on your full-time payroll. And in many cases, that domain involves working with suppliers that we haven't worked with before. This means working with more contingent labor as well, as the economy continues to shrink and more people are working on their own.[12]

Who Wants to Innovate with You?

A big issue in co-innovation is the sensitivity of supplier concerns when working with companies. Companies assume that suppliers are open to sharing their ideas, but this is certainly not always the case. In Chapter 7, we'll discuss details of the contentious relationship between a purchasing leader at General Motors (Jose Lopez) and his suppliers, which resulted in worsening relationships between the OEM and their manufacturing partners. I know for a fact (because I spoke to them) that tier-1 suppliers during the 1990s had no intention of sharing their innovations with GM, but were happy to do so with Chrysler during this period, as they knew they would get a return on their IP and that Chrysler would treat them fairly. The lesson is, it's hard to innovate with someone that you don't trust.

So what do suppliers look for in a customer they can innovate with? The big issue is indeed trust, but it goes beyond that. We've explored this question in direct engagements and interviews with suppliers involved in product

---

12 https://scm.ncsu.edu/blog/2016/04/20/a-fireside-chat-with-john-sculley-apples-former-ceo/

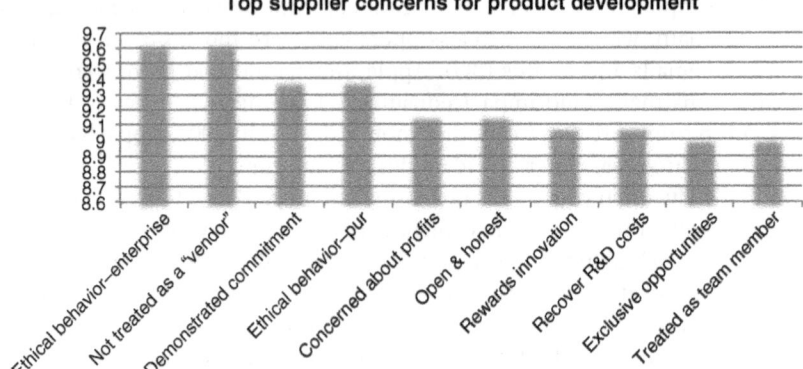

Figure 6.5 Supplier Concerns in Sharing IP with Buyers

development efforts with big OEM companies. In a large global manufacturer I interviewed, we interviewed a number of suppliers and identified their biggest concerns in working with the customer. The elements associated with the relationship that were the most important to suppliers are shown in Figure 6.5. These discussions produced insights that demonstrate the delicate and sensitive nature of the relationship between buyers and sellers that produce innovations. Suppliers are legitimately concerned about loss of IP and recovery of their investments, and buying companies must find ways to navigate these discussions in an open manner and with full disclosure upfront. As shown in Figure 6.5, they also are concerned with being treated as not just another "vendor," but as a true partner in seeking new technical solutions to customer problems. Suppliers are also looking for a demonstrated commitment to the relationship from the buying company. They are looking for ethical behavior, return on their innovation effort, an open and honest dialogue, and recovery of their R&D costs. Buyers need to find a way to address these concerns, if they are truly serious about co-innovation. Because suppliers are also good at figuring out if buyers are only giving them "lip-service" and not following up on their commitments and words.

Criteria to Consider when Co-innovating with Supply Chain Partners

Measuring innovation success is challenging at best, so it is important at this stage to derive measures that ensure that the project is progressing as planned, and that there are no major barriers to open dialogue. Exploring what both

Increasing levels of
commitment and
challenge!

Shared risk

Cost management

Informa on sharing, NPD,
governance

Strategic alignment, operational
integrity, fairness

Figure 6.6 Characteristics of Customers Considered "Partners"

parties can do to operate as a "customer of choice" and a "supplier of choice" is also critical. These discussions often can produce insights into what suppliers believe are the critical dimensions of performance. Interviews with suppliers from the aforementioned large OEM reveal that several dimensions of buyer behaviors are important to suppliers, including the following, also shown in Figure 6.6.

- **Strategic alignment:** Is the customer aligned with the supplier's targeted growth market, and is there alignment on the breadth of volume and team synergies?
- **Operational integrity:** Does the customer demonstrate ethical behavior at both the organization and team level? And does this inspire confidence that the supplier's design idea and IP will not be "shopped around"?
- **Fairness:** Does the customer demonstrate fair play when it comes to sharing commercial success and risks and rewards, and willingness to respect the supplier's innovation and IP?
- **Information sharing:** Does the customer provide consistent information, ongoing communication of changes to the business, and a demonstrated willingness to explore what is possible in cases when conflicts arise?
- **Product development process:** Is there a good project platform aligned with the supplier's product development process, as well as a forum for obtaining direct customer feedback on product ideas and innovations?
- **Strategic cost management:** Does the customer have a demonstrated record of not exploiting shared cost information? and is the customer legitimately concerned that the supplier will make a fair return on its investment?

- **Governance:** Is there a forum for joint decision-making and a demonstrated commitment to share risks and rewards over the longer term?
- **Shared risks:** Does the customer behave in an open and fair manner and demonstrate a willingness to consider the supplier for future exclusive opportunities under the right conditions?

These measures can be tracked using a third party, neutral consultant, or survey format, which guarantees anonymity.

Trust Goes Both Ways: How Do Suppliers Trust Big Companies?

A supplier that does not fully trust the purchasing company to be "fair" about rewarding them for their intellectual property (IP), is likely to hesitate and not fully commit to the project. Personal integrity is one factor, but the upside of working together needs to be emphasized so the supplier is fully aware of who they are working with and the potential opportunity that lies ahead.

One executive at a Cloud-based services provider discussed how trust was created, by not referring specifically to trust!

> I don't like to use the term "trust" – I prefer the term "Expectation." Trust comes and goes, and there is a lot of variation in the way trust evolves across cultures. In the United States, people will trust you early but be easily disappointed and not come back. In Europe, they may not trust you at all, and only much later begin to approach something like trust. In other cultures in Asia, trust may never really occur. By really understanding what it is you are buying, you are able to set the expectation of the supplier that drives the relationship. Trust is a function of people meeting expectations, which in turn builds the relationship, not the other way around. You can look back at buyer–supplier relationships and you trust those that met the expectation and the commitment.

In a large industrial manufacturer, we collected feedback from suppliers involved in product design and innovation activities on behalf of the manufacturer. We compared these suppliers' concerns to the assessment of a large manufacturer's performance relative to these factors to determine the biggest gaps. At the top of the list is a concern as to whether the supplier would recoup their innovation investment and profit over the life of the product. There also was concern as to whether the customer would reward the supplier for their innovation and technology, and whether they would be able to recover their engineering and R&D costs. And while suppliers were confident in the ethical behavior of purchasing, suppliers were less confident that the organization as a whole would operate ethically when it came time to valuing its intellectual property. As one supplier voiced:

> "They are raising expectations for suppliers every year. They can't keep raising challenges without rewarding suppliers with new business." Indeed.

In a "Nonzero" world, benefits have to flow both ways, and driving collaborative innovation is no different. But rewarding innovation appropriately is also part of being "Good": the final element in our LIVING supply chain evolutionary model, discussed in Chapter 7.

7

GOOD! The Ability to Build Balanced Supply Chains

Press Release: Flex Releases 2016 Global Citizenship Report

Flex (NASDAQ: FLEX), the Sketch-to-Scale™ solutions company that designs and builds intelligent products for a connected world, has released its 2016 Global Citizenship Report. This report summarizes Flex's worldwide social and environmental activities, performance, and results for the calendar year 2015, providing a look at how Flex employees contribute to a better world.

Key achievements cited in the report include:

- Reduced CO_2 emissions by 20%, exceeding the company's revenue-based goal
- Reduced injury and occupational disease incidents by 15%
- Reduced electrical use by more than 25,700 MWh/year by installing Flex-designed and built LED light fixtures in facilities in 12 countries
- Recycled 647,000 m^3 of water during 2015, equivalent to the annual water consumption of 1170 homes
- Named to Fortune magazine's "World's Most Admired Companies" list

"This past year we expanded our sustainability program to include global corporate citizenship in addition to social and environmental leadership," said Mike McNamara, Flex CEO. "In one sense, this serves to formalize some central elements of our culture – which we believe is key to the strength and resiliency of our organization – including our commitment to protect the environment, treat our people with respect and dignity and improve the communities where we live and work."

The 2016 report includes plans for global citizenship activities, aligned with the United Nations Sustainable Development Goals, and outlines Flex's commitment to 20 goals for 2020. Flex will report progress toward these goals twice per year on its external website.

The LIVING Supply Chain: The Evolving Imperative of Operating in Real Time, First Edition.
Robert Handfield and Tom Linton.
© 2017 John Wiley & Sons, Inc. Published 2017 by John Wiley & Sons, Inc.

Why Good?

Everyone acknowledges that we are in a global world – and that diversity is a common element that we need to build into how we operate globally. When we discussed the structure of this book, instead of focusing this chapter on a global supply chain, we landed instead on the need to discuss a *good supply chain*. (First, we needed something that started with a "G" ... but "good" just seemed like a better word than "sustainable," which I think is highly overused!)

Why "good"? Because good reflects on some of the most important – and sometimes implicit – elements that underlie how a supply chain should be operated with integrity that is the catalyst for building trust. One of the key elements of "good" is the supply chain network having a balanced structure that promotes diversity of competition, yet maintains harmony and balance among the constituents. We think of something as "good" if it agrees with us or aligns with our morals. Someone with integrity is a "good" person. Even a bar of soap from Whole Foods labeled "good" implies it will make you clean, make you feel good, and will provide some benefits (Figure 7.1). The soap also has "good," organic ingredients that will not irritate your skin. These are all admirable qualities.

Figure 7.1 "Good" Soap. *Source:* Whole Foods Market Inc.

But the concept of "good" also designates a current status that is stable ("How are you?" … "I'm good!"). To return to the Serengeti Rules: the dominant theme we have emphasized throughout our book is the need to establish balance in supply chain ecosystems. These rules apply outside the Serengeti Desert, and Carroll provides several illustrations of the importance of balance in many different ecosystems. For example, he discusses the wolves that were eliminated from Yellowstone in 1926. This national park, with the largest concentration of mammals in the 48 states, saved the population of bison and grizzly bears from extinction. When the wolves were all killed off in 1926, the elk population erupted, and the larger herds took a heavy toll on the system's trees and plants. By 1984, 10 years after 31 wolves were reintroduced into Yellowstone, the population had grown to 301. In the years that followed, not only was the elk population reduced by half, but elks' over-browsing of tree species, notably aspen, cottonwood, and willow, ended. The resulting increase in the tree population – known as a "trophic cascade" – also impacted the lives of beavers, which feed off willows. The reintroduced wolves also reduced the number of coyotes, which feed on young pronghorn antelope. Studies show that fawn survival rates of antelope are four times higher in sites with wolves than without them.[1]

The rationale behind the idea of good, balanced environments is one that everyone understands: Predators maintain balance in nature, and mankind needs to seriously consider letting the natural rules of evolution play out in their world as well. In the world of supply chains, the "natural rule" of evolution emphasizes open and free trade and open forces of competition, which drive naturally occurring outcomes. When wolf or elk populations are out of balance, bad things start to happen to the natural ecosystem. By the same token, supply chains should compete fairly within the guidelines of being "good." Unbalanced supply chains cause things to begin to go wrong.

What Are Characteristics of a Good Supply Chain?

Good supply chains balance performance, price, integrity, the environment, and social and political factors, allowing free and open trade while not transgressing the boundaries of integrity and human rights. This theme is most-often called sustainability. It is interesting that the original concept of sustainability also has ecological roots: *sustainability* is the property of biological systems to remain diverse and produce indefinitely.[2] Sustainability can also be defined as a socio-ecological process characterized by the pursuit of a common ideal.[3] Both concepts have an implicit reference to the idea of balance, endurance, and

1 Carroll, S., *The Serengeti Rules*, Princeton University Press, 2016, pp. 177–182.
2 https://en.wikipedia.org/wiki/Sustainability
3 Wandemberg, J. C., *Sustainable by Design*, Amazon, August 2015, p. 122. ISBN: 1516901789. Retrieved February 16, 2016.

diversity of life. And this leads again to the idea of the trophic cascade in the Serengeti Rules.

Perhaps the closest equivalent to a trophic cascade in the supply chain sphere is the economic concept laid out by one of the earliest visionaries of our time: Adam Smith.

Adam Smith, the Invisible Hand, and the Serengeti Rules

Adam Smith wrote one of the most important and enduring set of business tomes of all time, *The Theory of Moral Sentiments* (1759) and *The Wealth of Nations* (1776) over 240 years ago. Smith recognized that the "invisible hand" of the market would create the right balance and outcomes for society in the long run, if it were allowed to operate freely. He notes:

> The rich … are led by an invisible hand to make nearly the same distribution of the necessaries of life, which would have been made, had the earth been divided into equal portions among all its inhabitants, and thus without intending it, without knowing it, advance the interest of the society, and afford means to the multiplication of the species.[4]

In this manner, Smith makes a direct reference to the idea of diversity and balance in the natural order of civilization that maintains the sustainability of the system. The guidelines of the "invisible hand" apply here to the idea of natural competition in the supply chain. Open-source data and new cognitive technologies are enriching the invisible hand of the market and creating greater diversity of competition by the day. An emerging concept is that companies should go out and "mine" dark data, to "find" the market and the best suppliers, and in this manner explore markets to drive competition while establishing stronger relationships with the most competitive supply chain partners. Doing so makes the entire system healthier and more robust. Exploring vast quantities of market intelligence data on the Internet, the thinking goes, allows businesses to optimize cost and supply. This concept also prevails in the context of traditional "world-class procurement" principles, which dictate that one should reduce the supply base to the "optimal" few. The assumption in many cases is, "We have too many suppliers. We should pare our supply base to the qualified and critical few."

This marketplace is the essence of creating balance in the supply network. Balance is an organic concept, found in nature. In *The Serengeti Rules*, Sean B. Carroll documents how every living creature participates in and helps maintain

---

4 Smith, A., *The Theory of Moral Sentiments*, revised edition of the sixth edition published in 1790 (first published in 1759), Penguin, New York, 2009, pp. vii–xxix.

balance in the ecosystem, which helps the system to flourish. If human beings kill too many lions, the zebras starve. If there is not enough clean water, grass dies and zebras starve. But if there are too many lions, they kill off the zebras, the grass gets out of hand, and disease spreads. The point is a truly healthy system is a balanced system. According to *The Serengeti Rules*, a system is either in balance or out of balance; the same is true for a supply chain system.

The key to a "good" supply chain is balance among the following elements:

Integrity: Customers must believe a product's advertising and trust its label. They must be assured that no counterfeit elements or substitutions have been made.

Environmental health: At worst, a supply chain should do no net harm to natural or social systems while still producing a profit over an extended period of time; a truly sustainable supply chain could, customers willing, continue to do business forever.

Fair employee practices: Products are produced in safe environments with fair wages, overtime, fair working conditions, and adult labor, that acknowledge the rights of workers to form unions, and that do not bully, coach, or force employees to do anything that is not within the normal requirements for humane working conditions. (Note that this can cause conflicting issues in some countries; for instance, India just passed a law allowing 15- to 18-year olds to work in family businesses, in defiance of UN mandates).[5]

Politically and ethically sound policies: This includes appropriate governance over financial and social dealings, free of corruption, bribery, and fraud. Data is truthful, financial results are not overstated, and share price reflects the true value of the organization based on audited assessments of revenues and costs.

Good supply chains include all these characteristics. When they are all in balance, open and free competition flourishes, for all factors of labor, and all forms of free trade, allowing value to flow.

Open Competition Is "Good"

If open competition is good, it follows that one of the new rules of supply chain management is not to limit the number of suppliers in a market, but to *expand* the market to make it more competitive. We saw this in supply chain rules 4, 5, and 6. The more the suppliers (zebras) in a market, the healthier the buyers (lions) and the more balanced the system. Supply chains are very much like the

---

5 http://www.aljazeera.com/news/2016/07/indian-parliament-passes-contentious-child-labour-bill-160727073739213.html

Serengeti – by expanding the number of suppliers in a market, the more competition you have, the healthier the ecosystem is, and the healthier the supply chain is.

Similarly, continuing to work with a poorly performing supplier, and restricting competition in that market, affects the health of the supply chain. If FedEx and UPS cornered the delivery market, express delivery rates would no doubt increase and service would fall off. So the new rule of supply chain goes against traditional thinking – and instead suggests that companies should use systems and tools to expand the number of suppliers they choose to work with. The system will dictate through its internal dynamics and balancing mechanisms when there are too many suppliers. And the job of an effective supply chain manager is to ensure a healthy supply chain, and a healthy ecosystem.

What happens if supply chain health is restricted and suppliers are limited? Disease and hunger will follow in a system that is out of balance, according to the Serengeti rules. The same can be said of supply chains, based on our rules.

General Motors and Supply Relationship Pyramids

Creating effective relationships with other enterprises in the supply chain that are ethical and fair, but also competitive, is at the root of being "good." It also relates to federation in the supply chain. General Motors learned this the hard way. I visited General Motors in late 1999, when I was working with its senior automotive team prior to an education session I was helping them organize in China. At the time, I interviewed most of the major executives leading GM's supply chain. My arrival occurred just after the departure of the infamous Jose Lopez.

The purchasing revolution occurred at GM in the early 1990s with the appointment of Jack Smith as CEO, and Jose Ignacio Lopez as vice president of purchasing. Despite his bad reputation, Lopez should get credit for raising awareness around quality, service, and price (or QSP, a "mantra" at GM). By creating an internal culture focused on driving improved internal integration among purchasing, engineering, logistics, and operations, Lopez turned GM around when it was on the verge of bankruptcy. During his 2-year tenure at the head of GM's purchasing organization, he established a different mindset and raised the importance of purchasing and supply chain management as a core contributor to GM's competitive success. In his wake, he left many strained relationships with suppliers, who felt Lopez had betrayed them. He served as a true "shock" to the automotive system by instilling a level of competition that many suppliers had never seen before, and in the process, significantly improved the quality and the cost of GM vehicles. His methods were, however, unscrupulous and unethical, and caused many problems in the relationships that ensued. In short, Lopez ruined the balance of the ecosystem.

On my visit I also interviewed top-level purchasing executives at GM, including Harold Kutner, Tom Fabus, Bo Andersson, Woody Williams, Bob Burkhart, and John Calabrese, who described how they were working to "restore the balance" with suppliers. After leaving GM, Lopez was replaced by Harold Kutner. Kutner extended Lopez's concepts beyond the simple mantra of QSP, to include T: Technology. Kutner and Jack Smith realized that for GM to be truly successful, global integration across all of GM's product lines and platforms was required. To do so, they created a new purchasing organization, World Wide Purchasing (WWP). WWP was a matrix-based structure developed across product lines and commodity groups, which enabled vehicle platform teams to scan the globe for leading-edge technologies at the best quality, service, and price. A new measurement system for certifying and selecting suppliers along four dimensions (Quality, Service, Technology, and Price, or "QSTP") was instigated. Purchasing category managers and product platform managers worked hand-in-hand to manage supplier relationships. Every Friday morning, leading executives from all over the world would gather around a satellite camera for a global teleconference. Information shared included updates to product development efforts, changes in market conditions, pricing updates, and other developments. These meetings helped to ensure that on a weekly basis, all parties throughout the world were up-to-date and equally knowledgeable.

During our interview, Bo Andersson, one of GM's heads of procurement helped me understand GM's new perspective on supplier relationships. Bo drew a triangle for me (shown in Figure 7.2), explaining that its three sides represented three elements of supplier relationships: price, performance, and place. Performance related to the QSTP dimension, and price was obvious – but place referred to local relationships between suppliers and purchasing. Bo emphasized that all three dimensions needed to be in balance, but that at GM

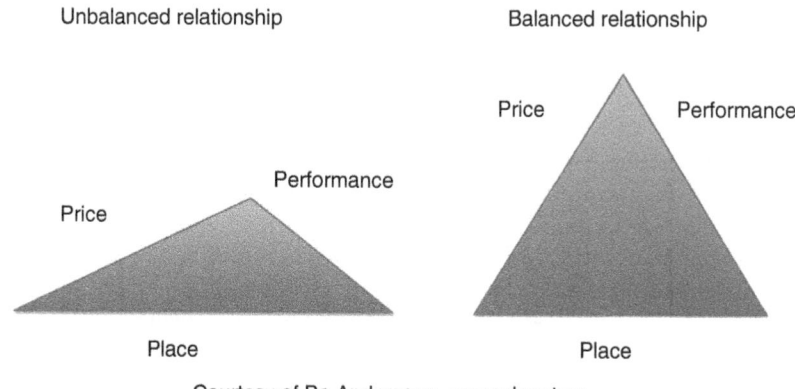

Unbalanced relationship   Balanced relationship

Courtesy of Bo Andersson, general motors

Figure 7.2 The Relationship Triad

the place dimension (e.g., the relationships between suppliers and purchasing) had gotten too important, resulting in a "squashed" triangle (shown on the right side of Figure 7.2). He emphasized that purchasing personnel often got too comfortable with their suppliers, and developed personal relationships with them that sometimes got in the way of price and performance.

"Competition is a good thing," Bo told me. "Lopez was able to shake up these relationships because we were getting too comfortable with our suppliers. They needed to know that global competition was present, and that we needed to be competitive in terms of cost and performance to succeed and grow."

What Bo was emphasizing, again, was balance in the supply chain. In this case, balance among price, performance, and place in the supply base was critical if GM was to survive. If any of these become too important in a supplier relationship, the whole relationship becomes skewed and dysfunctional. Perhaps the supplier grows too comfortable and doesn't make enough effort to drive down costs, and the price creeps up. Or the buyer awards too much business to local suppliers, who do not invest enough in remaining competitive, consequently falling behind in technology, delivery, capability, and so on. Or the buyer over-emphasizes price and chisels the supplier so that the supplier has no margin for reinvesting in its business and performance suffers. In any of these cases, an imbalance causes negative outcomes. The importance of maintaining both competition and collaboration is a delicate balance, but requires all parties to act in their best interest to survive while acting with integrity and purpose.

Fast-forward to 2016. A story in *The Wall Street Journal* announced that Bo Andersson, who had become the CEO of Russia's largest car maker, AvtoVAZ, planned to step down. The Renault–Nissan Alliance is the majority owner of the firm. According to the story, Andersson joined Renault in 2013 after he helped turn around Russian truck maker GAZ Group. He started at AvtoVAZ in early 2014 and slashed tens of thousands of jobs at its main Togliatti plant. He also renegotiated contracts with local suppliers in a bid to cut costs. When he arrived, the company was, in his words, "The biggest mess I've ever seen in my career." He encountered low morale, rampant corruption, theft of parts from the plant, a reputation for poor quality and a Soviet-style employee culture that rewarded seniority over job performance.

Things did not go over well, according to the story in the WSJ. " 'The cost-saving moves angered many in Togliatti, a one-industry city some 500 miles east of Moscow. Discontent trickled up to the highest echelons of Russia's political elite and prompted a warning shot last spring from an ally of President Vladimir Putin.' 'You're playing with fire,' Sergei Chemezov, a friend of Putin, recalls telling Mr. Andersson. Mr. Chemezov runs a state-owned defense and industrial company that holds a minority stake in the auto maker, OAO Avto-VAZ. Industry experts note that 'the Russian government wants it both ways – AvtoVAZ as a social project and a competitive business in the modern era. It's impossible.' "

Let's see – what did Andersson do that was so horrific that he deserved the wrath of Putin?

Well, he made the horrible mistake of laying off workers, even though the layoffs had been formally approved by the AvtoVAZ board. He then renegotiated contracts with suppliers to set a target of 5% cost reductions (a target that, by the way, is considered a year-over-year requirement for suppliers in the global automotive industry). Such targets are typically discovered through value analysis, productivity improvements, application of cost models, and material substitutions. Andersson also sought to improve quality. (AvtoVAZ vehicles are known for spending more time in the shop than on the road). He worked with Renault to invest another $448 million in new technology in the company. He even required the filthy facility toilets to be cleaned daily. In Bo's words, "The only way we'll become world-class is if we're clean – toilets and floors, too." In effect, he tried to create a competitive, "good" supply chain.

The point of these examples? We believe that allowing supply chains to operate through competitive forces is key, and that, under the invisible hand postulated by Adam Smith, will produce a much healthier system, assuming that price, place, and performance are balanced. The reason to have ethical, sustainable supply chains is not to replicate the smarmy, self-righteous assertions found on many sustainability web pages, but to create a healthy, competitive, balanced supply chain. The reason to have good, ethical, healthy supply chains that are environmentally and fiscally healthy is to allow the system to breath, to operate freely, and to allow all to profit. Those who try to cut corners, who say, "We don't need the safest meat or the strongest material for our products and customers," are destined to learn the hard way that this will come back to bite them in the long run.

But we need to rethink globalization – and to acknowledge that we can't overlook the implications of a "good" LIVING supply chain. Everyone now knows that our environment is global, which is a "given" for organizations that seek growth. The difference, however, is that organizations with a LIVING supply chain recognize that they must adapt to regional conditions and disparities, and learn to exploit the capabilities of each region to derive global competitiveness. Although the traditional view that "the world is flat," in that historical and geographical divisions are not relevant, there nevertheless exist regional disparities that must be accommodated and taken into account.

The focus on global process improvement across a global network by management teams began in the 1980s. However, with the birth of enterprise software, its expansion in the 1990s and with the establishment of Internet-based software, the process is about to be disrupted again. Business history is littered with disruption. Industrial revolutions dating back to the 17th century are full of examples in which one trigger started an avalanche of change: the printing press, cotton gin, telephone, automobile, airplane, and computer. But what they all have in common is that the trigger was often pulled decades before full-scale adoption took place.

Our view of global process but local deployment is based on the simple thesis that business leaders cannot standardize the entire world, and need processes that will solve problems in 80% of cases, allowing for local adoption for the remaining 20% of cases, (so long as the outcome meets the process playbook). This requires a clearly defined organization, with clear roles and responsibilities, so that people can speak to the same processes with the same toolboxes. This ensures that all parties are "speaking the same language" and are using comparable metrics and plans.

To understand this apparent paradox, let's examine some examples, starting with the military understanding of how to operate in Iraq.

A Team of Teams to Create Local Insights

We already have mentioned Gen. Hugh McChrystal's book *Team of Teams*, which explains how the military in Iraq had to learn how to deal with an enemy that was not organized, did not have an organized or regimented approach, and relied on guerilla tactics and suicide bombers to create havoc. McChrystal's team sought to use traditional military-style intelligence to understand the enemy, but learned that the information was also too little, too late. Eventually, they moved toward a structure in which true openness, trust, and transparency were not just important, but were the critical component in the battle against Al Qaeda in Iraq. Faced by an adaptable and networked enemy, the General and his team explored why traditional organizations aren't adaptable to change. The four fundamental elements that allowed McChrystal's "Team of Teams" concept included 1) transparency to ensure common understanding and awareness, 2) changing personal behaviors to establish trust and foster collaboration, 3) creation of a shared context to enable decentralization and empowerment of individuals to act, and 4) creating a broader environment of leadership instead of micromanaging. McChrystal points out that all organizations should adopt these approaches to ensure that they can survive in the years ahead. Sound familiar?

What distinguished McChrystal's new approach was that it empowered individuals closest to the front lines to act based on what they saw in front of them. The implication is that enterprises should drive decision-making based on ground-level intelligence – not just a centralized ("control-tower") view. The opposite of this approach was best described in a military context in the novel *Matterhorn* by Karl Marlantes. One of the key insights in this book (which covers such topics as leadership, diversity, strategy, politics, and military tactics) is the complete lack of ground-up intelligence present on the front lines in the Vietnam War. Indeed, at one point in the book, a front-line infantryman cries in desperation when he is told that what he sees in front of him on the front lines is incorrect, by a senior officer who is telling him this from a radio that is miles away in a secure zone!

The military has reversed this model since the Vietnam war to enable decision-making based on what is being seen on the ground. Today's military relies primarily on situation-specific decision-making, with generals and senior leaders there only to provide support, NOT to call the shots. There is even a term for it: situational intelligence. Situational intelligence combines traditional situational awareness (an individual's cognitive interpretation of what is happening around him/her) with the collective intelligence of those at the center of many global situations, resulting in a dynamic process in which data is gathered and interpreted and the information is shared.

I interviewed a former Marine who served in Iraq and who returned to take my supply chain MBA class. He described some of the activities he performed while serving in Iraq that emphasized the need for continuous communication, feedback, and intelligence-sharing in the field as the cornerstone of survival for Marines.

We are trained to report continuously what is going on. To begin with, we report the supplies we have on hand every day through a logistics status report. This included bandages, batteries, and all different classes of material. A war fighter on the ground at the company level sends up a report on the status of water, chow, ammunition on hand, etc. That report goes up to the battalion and up to a depot level. There is also a report that is produced that shows how many bullets during combat operations per Marine are required, versus the standard amount for each piece of equipment, and this is compared against the actual on-hand inventory. This goes up to regimental brigade and is briefed to the commander at every level. And every commander knows immediately when a company is within two days of being out of supplies. In a counter-insurgency environment, this allows a pipeline to be established in theater when supplies are hitting these units at different points in time. When disruptions occur, the battalion has plans to convoy materials at all times.

So how can organizations develop the same level of visibility and insight at the supply and customer level? Communicating and coordinating using forms of media besides planning systems is critical, and involves exploiting social media and other forums will become more important in the future.

Now project this to a global economic scale. People are making decisions in "control" towers to which data is transmitted in batches. People in mid-level operations or global sites are being told what to do from a centralized operation, by people who do not understand the local situation. This is particularly true in places like Nigeria, Indochina, and Angola, which is why some of the big oil and gas companies have been kicked out of these communities. However, when decision-makers can collect information such as on-the-scene photos, Twitter messages, weather alerts and recipient responses in real time, the quantity, quality, and speed of information available during a given event grows exponentially. This leads to better decision-making and more effective crisis communication before, during, and after an incident.

The PEOPLE Part of the LIVING Equation

One concept mentioned throughout this book is the mindshift of the people who work in the network. Real-time information that is live, interactive, virtual, intelligent, networked, and good fulfills a company's need to create the right mindset in people with the right skill set, enabled by a governance structure that allows, and even encourages, agile decision-making. As mentioned in Chapter 1, people need to believe that velocity is key, and that, armed with information, they may find ways to rapidly discover the HOV lane and move around the problem quickly.

Tom talked about how he is making this possible at Flex. "Many strategists debate whether supply chain should be centralized, decentralized, or center-led," he said. "I'm a big proponent of a center-led supply chain. Centralization allows aggregation of requirements and decision-making, but slows everything down because it's not possible to do this in real time. Decentralized organizations don't allow you to achieve the scale and alignment that is required to drive a unified approach to supply chain decisions. A center-led supply chain centralizes the major vectors of policy and procedure for the enterprise, but leaves the ability to make decisions on the ground to the people who are closest to the action … much like the "Team of Teams" concept. This is a critical component of the real-time LIVING supply chain, and companies often stumble in trying to implement this approach. Business history will tell you that center-led organizations are much more nimble, and that this is a much more flexible and faster way to operate." Tom notes the following:

> It is also a big change from my early days in the profession. I grew up working at IBM, a highly vertically integrated, centralized organization. I was a commodity manager, but by 1985 I was in charge of purchasing and transportation as part of my responsibility for that business. My responsibilities were clear: reduce cost and don't run out. But if you look at companies like Apple, Google, Microsoft, Amazon and Facebook – these companies have no manufacturing at all. They are 100 percent virtually vertically integrated, and operate very differently than large, centralized 'big iron' companies. They are asset-light and inventory-light on their balance sheets.

Companies are seeking a certain type of person that will flourish in the current supply chain environment. For example, one of my MBA students, who had an electrical engineering background, had eight interviews before he was hired by Apple. They wanted to make sure that he had the right mindset, analytical capability, and decision-making agility to operate in a rapidly changing ecosystem.

Tracking Data to Create Transparent Supply Chains

One of the major challenges relative to risk is sustainability. Many industry sectors that have "outsourced" their production networks to low-cost countries struggle with ensuring compliance to labor and human rights laws, as set forth by UN International Labor Organization (ILO) conventions. A program to audit suppliers across multiple tiers of the supply chain is an important first step. That process begins with a supplier code of conduct that provides a baseline for evaluating a supplier's basic labor and human rights policies. Based on this code of conduct, supplier audits are used to target tier 1 suppliers to ensure compliance with the code shown here. A scorecard can help quantify supplier performance on social impacts. Metrics related to safety standards, discrimination, labor conditions, child labor, and wages also can be part of every supplier assessment, as well as every business case. Countermeasures to react to unacceptable values of these metrics also can be implemented. This includes tier 2 suppliers, implying that the entire global supply chain from end-to-end is beholden to a single global code of conduct. This standard also applies to business ethics; increasingly, global consumer producers and retail companies are adopting a "one standard" view of the world.

This new focus on corporate sustainability often calls for companies to increase transparency in all aspects of their operations – and much more so in the supply chain. Apparel and electronics companies that source all their products from factories in emerging countries are especially targeted for allegedly hiring contractors that push the boundaries of human rights labor laws.

"Sustainability" is a word that became very fashionable about 15 years ago, and which everyone is now promoting as a facet of "the new normal." In fact, sustainability is about nothing more than "doing the right thing" – and most people would know what that means. If a 12-year old tells you that something "isn't right," this is a good measure for whether consumers will find it acceptable. Try running the statement, "We are using suppliers that we audit to ensure they are sustainable, but we can't help it if they pollute or don't pay a fair wage" by a 12-year old. The child's response is likely to be something like, "But that's still wrong. Everybody knows that." In short, focusing on what is naturally the right thing to do is a good indicator of sustainable behavior.

But what happens when you can't see what's going on in factories? Does that alleviate your responsibility, using the rationale that "We don't know what goes on in their factories because it isn't our business, and we tell them not to do it"? Nope. This rationale doesn't stand up anymore. Sustainability is less about multi-tier audits – it's more about knowing who you are buying from, and the implications of your behavior when you choose to purchase a product or service from someone. We need to know who and what we are buying. When you walk into Whole Foods, for example, you go to the meat counter and see a picture of the farmer who raised the cow that became your steak. Or you go to the produce counter and see a picture of the farmer who grew the tomatoes. Any consumer will "get" this. So why can't you also see the factory where your shirt was sewn, and be able to check and see what the factory looks like, what the bosses pay their workers, and what the working conditions are? Not only is this possible, it is happening today.

I recently spoke with a chief procurement officer, who recalled driving green manufacturing practices and labor conditions in the semiconductor industry.

"Years ago the electronics industry aligned on an Electronic Industry Code of Conduct," he said. "We would do a heat map around auditing suppliers, essentially a 'check-the-box' exercise, and then declare, 'We are sustainable! Well, we've gotten a bit better – we have people who do self-assessments in the supply base, and we still put out a heat map. We do a little more due diligence, so we tell ourselves this is the best we can do. But in my mind, it's not enough. It's the minimum acceptable level. Let's not pretend that we can't do better.'"

So what about if we base our sustainability on a label like "fair trade?" Isn't that visibility using a proven standard? With the introduction of labels, the fair trade movement has created a *de facto* standard for consumers to recognize that a product is "sustainable." But, as Andrew Pederson points out in a *Supply Chain Management Review* article we co-authored last year, the process used to certify producers in order to get such a label is often flawed.[6] That's not just Pederson's opinion. It was validated in a recent study by the Fair Trade, Employment and Poverty Reduction Project (FTEPR) team based at SOAS at the University of London. The study identified three major points of concern: First, wage employment in areas producing agricultural export commodities is widespread. Second, people who depend on access to wage employment in export commodity production are typically extremely poor. Third, in the areas studied, there is limited evidence that fair trade has made a positive difference to the wages and working conditions of workers producing certified fair trade commodities for export. In fact, researchers found that wage-earners

6 Pederson, A., Wieland, A., and Handfield, R., "Viewpoint: Ensuring Human Rights in the End-to-End Supply Chain," *Supply Chain Management Review*, November 2014, pp. 48–51.

in areas with businesses certified by Fairtrade International were paid significantly less than wage-earners producing the same commodities in areas without Fairtrade-certified businesses. Fairtrade International released a detailed rebuttal to these findings, noting that the results are generalized and do not adequately cover an appropriate sample.

This brings us back to the original issue. Being sustainable isn't enough. We have to be transparent to be clear about what is going on in our supply chains. This may mean acknowledging that there are problems in different parts of our multi-tier supply chain, because a global supply chain will always be full of problems. Is there crime in Pittsburgh? Yes, of course, just as there is in any major metropolitan area. Is there any city without crime? Highly unlikely! Does that mean we should try to hide the fact that there is crime in cities? Of course not! But if we have data that tracks the location and types of crime, and makes the community aware of it, we can get the eyes and ears of people in the community more aware of what is going on, and they can become part of the solution!

But audits aren't enough. As one executive I interviewed noted, "One of the biggest red flags we see is when a factory worker who is interviewed has clearly been 'coached.' Another red flag is when we ask to see their books, and we get comments such as 'Well we don't have those today,' or 'The accountant isn't in today.' These are indicators that something is wrong."

To augment audits, we must adopt technology to drive visibility, make real changes, and improve communication. Labor condition violations are most likely to happen in regions with poor infrastructure and with a limited ability to invest in appropriate technology and systems that enable visibility. However, as part of the investment in their supply chains, retailers can help suppliers establish IT systems that render supply chain processes more transparent. Although a conventional IT network may not be in place in emerging regions, mobile technologies are already prevalent in these markets. Those familiar devices can be coupled with software that can cope with "big data," combined with multiple data feed devices. Together, they can create tracking capability of products from raw materials to the final consumers. Large organizations should think about providing free software that will not only help improve low-cost supplier operations, but also can ensure transparency and access to potential malfeasance and fraud, as well as potential ILO convention violations.

This is a very, very tricky thing to manage, however. According to Dana Martin of Elementum, "We have to also tie execution metrics as another dimension to monitor malfeasance. Because in many cases, variability in delivery performance or line output can indicate supply risk, which is ultimately linked to other problems that exist in a factory." Again, this relates to "mapping the genome" of a product shipment. We have to think about compliance to auditing standards from a manufacturer's perspective, consider what they do to bypass compliance requirements, and construct ways that make it difficult for them to get around these requirements.

One pervasive issue in human rights in the supply chain is the "shadow factory." This means that one factory is set up as the "show factory" for audits. Bills of lading show this factory as the point of origin for all shipments. In fact, other, "shadow factories" which are either subcontractors or which are supplier-owned but not compliant, but which produce lower-cost products, and are hence more profitable for the supplier. So you might receive a shipment of 10,000 units, but only 6000 units come from the "show" factory and 4000 from a non-compliant factory. However, if you created digital tracking that married production line output to shipment information data as it is received, those 4000 non-compliant units would be much easier to spot.

An important element in ensuring compliance to fair working conditions in supply chains is to "trust but verify," until your relationship with the supplier moves from its early stages to a fully trusting relationship. Even then, performance measures and monitoring are required, if only to ensure that performance is not compromised or achieved through unacceptable routes. Manipulating line or machine data is very, very difficult, particularly if line-level scans of all inputs and outputs that pass through a factory are captured in data flows. Also, continuous audits are very expensive. Ultimately, what's most important is to capture difficult-to-manipulate data.

Here's an example: An executive from a large service-based company noted that he would often monitor variance of on-time delivery data, where variance was defined as the degree to which a delivery referred to the number of days before or after the scheduled delivery date. Both early and late delivery were considered sources of variance. Delivery promptness was monitored in a chart, and the trend (up or down) was tracked. If the variance level went outside of the 3-standard-deviation limit, a call to the factory was merited. "Nine times out of ten, when I called the factory after seeing an upward or downward trend of three points in a row, or a point outside of the upper or lower control limits, I would learn that something was going wrong in the factory," the executive explained. "The data was a clear indicator that something was amiss!"

Through ongoing monitoring of performance and production data, collected through "free" software embedded in supplier factories, variance can be detected and performance can be improved. The critical element of this cultural change is to promote the philosophy, "We *expect* that deviations will occur, and you will not be punished for discovery of these deviations. It is more important to be open and transparent with your problems than to have minor problems and try to hide them." This emphasis on total transparency in the supply chain will result in more business being awarded to open and honest suppliers, as opposed to those with strong records who hide problems from their buying partners. Implementing a system this transparent is a massive cultural change, especially in low-cost countries where the attitude of "You don't need to know what happens behind closed doors" prevails in many business relationships.

So how do we begin to apply visibility principles to identify what is going on in our supply chains? Two examples come to mind. The first is a project realized by NagerIT, a German organization aimed at producing a fair trade computer mouse. NagerIT understood that a product can only be sustainable if the end-to-end supply chain is managed sustainably. A map of the mouse's supply chain is available on NagerIT's webpage. However, even an organization like NagerIT has to admit that when assessing raw materials and components from conventional production, they cannot say anything about the labor conditions during production. In other words, due to the lack of available data about such components, today, it often still seems to be impossible for companies to create a fair product. The solution? Centrally managed databases, provided to consumers by producers and retailers to track sustainability are needed. Consumers may access the data using various technological devices.

It's time to start thinking about how to harness the strength of social media, smart devices, and Web-enabled analytics to provide consumers with the power to make their own decisions. This brings us to our second example. Switcher, a Swiss company, manufactures T-shirts with an individual "Respect Code" included (see www.respect-code.org) that enables consumers to view the entire supply chain associated with the product they are buying. Visualization of the supply chain, as shown in Figure 7.3 provides data to all supply chain tiers, and others on the number of employees, dates of audits, and certificates. This case shows that, contrary to statements by major brands, tracking the entire supply chain is indeed possible. This relates to the product genomes we covered in Chapter 5, which allow anyone to see the entire history of a product. Ultimately,

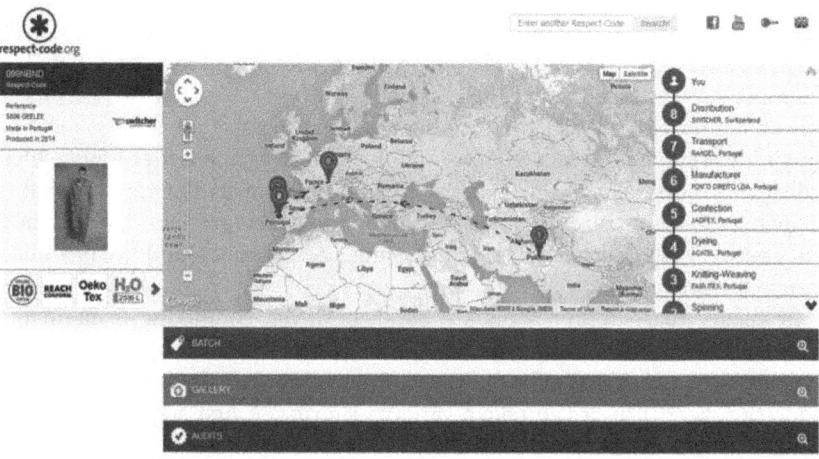

Figure 7.3 Switcher's "Respect Code". *Source:* Reproduced with permission of Respect-Code

Figure 7.4 Nike manufacturingmap.com. *Source:* Used under manufacturingmap.nikeinc .com/

transparency, "being good," and product genomes are starting to merge in this digitized world.

The simple fact is, NGOs like WRC, Sedex, and others are always going to poke around in factories looking for flaws. This is the new normal, which is ultra-sensitive to worker rights (and rightfully so). Companies like Nike, Adidas, and Under Armour need to address this reality head-on, and strive for complete transparency. Nike's approach is to open up its global manufacturing network and be as transparent as possible. The company even created an open website, manufacturingmapnike.com, which allows the public to see where all of its products are produced, and even provides worker demographics (females, migrants, etc.) in each factory (Figure 7.4).

Even countries such as China are being forced to drive toward sustainability. Chinese citizens already are calling for better lives and better food, which indicates a movement toward a more organic and transparent view of what is happening to our environment, to our food, and to the products we purchase and use every day, from vehicles, to medicine, to electronics, and to a healthier, sustainable way of life.

To ensure that supply chains are good, however, competing firms in the same industry must collaborate. Very few companies can manage a socially responsible supply chain in low-cost regions on their own. For that reason, collaboration is critical. It can take a variety of forms. A first step is to commit to joint standards. One such standard relates to fair trade. For example, the Fair Wear Foundation, a European nonprofit, aims at improving labor conditions and provides rules for its member companies. The foundation ensures that member companies comply. Another example is Nike's sustainability index,

which eventually became the Higg Index, adopted by the entire apparel industry. Corporate social responsibility isn't easy – no one said it would be.

Are you able to connect the essential leverage points in your network through
Cloud, mobile, and other media that provide a platform for analytics? Can you
track the DNA of your supply chain at a part number level, globally? These are
the big questions to consider when we think about how supply chains evolve.
We need a structure for mapping the genome of our supply chains. This means
establishing part number tracking and coding for the end-to-end supply chain.
One of the biggest opportunities is to create a mechanism for encoding the
genome, to help managers understand where products go and where they come
from; this information is critical to combating counterfeit and fraud. Counterfeit and fraud waste, though rarely discussed by supply chain scholars, remains
one of the biggest and most overlooked areas of lost profits and revenues in
the world. Thus, companies must not only track and measure all goods, but
also estimate the possibility of counterfeit goods. Executives would be wise to
demythologize Big Data as the answer for supply chain improvements. Big Data
is static and useless; *it's the questions you ask of the data that change supply
chain outcomes.*

The Trans-Pacific Partnership: Another Reason to be "Good"

Another important reason that executives need to pay more attention to being
"good" is the risk and unfortunate decline of the Trans-Pacific Partnership
(TPP). The TPP was a regional trade agreement (RTA) between 12 membership countries around the Pacific Rim. Those countries are (clock-wise
geographically): Canada, the United States, Mexico, Peru, Chile, New Zealand,
Australia, Brunei, Singapore, Malaysia, Vietnam, and Japan.[7] More interesting
are the countries excluded from the TPP: China, South Korea, and India are
just a few. Excluded countries may join at a later date if they wish, and if the 12
membership countries agree.

After 7 years of negotiation, the TPP was signed on February 4, 2016 in Auck-
land, New Zealand. The next step for each member nation was to ratify the TPP
so it can come into force.

---

7 These 12 countries have a population of around 800 million people with an average GDP per
capita of $34,761. The TPP has 30 chapters covering areas from trade of physical goods (agri-
culture, IT systems, textiles and apparel, etc.), cross-border trade in services (financial services,
cloud-based computer services, logistics, engineering, etc.), telecommunications, electronic
commerce, government procurement, intellectual property, state-owned enterprises, labor,
environment, and regulatory coherence. It also covers how partnership countries handle transparency and anticorruption issues, disputes, technical barriers to trade, and sanitary and phy-
tosanitary uniform measurements. Thanks to Tim Barnes for these comments.

Following the US election in November 2016, President Donald Trump announced that the United States would not support membership in the TPP. This is despite the fact that if it had passed, the TPP would drive organizations to focus even more on establishing and maintaining "good" supply chains, if they want to be able to engage in global trade. This is because the TPP has specific mandates that require participating enterprises to comply with human rights, better working conditions, environmental regulations, and other factors that will essentially "level the playing field." Some of these elements are described next. Although it is unlikely that the TPP will be reconsidered in the United States, the following issues will still need to be addressed in future political cross-border trade negotiations and agreements to foster a "good" supply chain in global trade.

Environmental Health

As the world's business focus shifts to social responsibility, and specifically, to environmental health, a number of newly minted free trade agreements have been established. The TPP dedicated a whole chapter (Chapter 20) to the environment. Its focus is to ensure that all member countries agree and adhere to policies related to wildlife trafficking, illegal logging, illegal fishing, and marine pollution, all of which threaten human health, habitat, and biodiversity. The chapter also establishes enforceable commitments, and allows for cooperation among countries to ensure that environmental crimes are policed, both within member countries and in countries and companies who do business with TPP countries. These rules meant that companies would have had to ensure a focus on environmental health when evaluating their global supply chains. World trade shifts resulting from incentives provided by trade agreements, duly enforces compliance to first-world environmental manufacturing practices. As countries grow and evolve, and as free trade molds key supply chain decisions, adherence to environmentally sound practices is an absolute necessity.

Social Responsibility

Unfortunately, as a result of decades of business supply chain decisions made on cost alone, numerous manufacturing and other aspects of the supply chain have been mixed with undesirable labor practices in countries with very weak or nonexistent human rights and labor safety laws. As a result, all recent US-led free trade agreements, weather bilateral or regional, include language stipulating labor protections for all parties. The TPP devotes a chapter (Chapter 19) that mandates that all 12 member countries adopt and maintain laws and practices that comply with fundamental labor rights as recognized by the International Labor Organization (ILO). These include freedom of association and the right to collective bargaining, elimination of forced labor, abolition of child labor, and elimination of employment discrimination. These laws ensure that all TPP countries practice socially responsibility. In conjunction with zero tariff incentives, the laws provide further incentives for companies to take advantage of the TPP and similar global free trade agreements.

Political, social, and business ethics: To ensure that global trade and business is conducted without the interference of corruption, bribery and fraud, countries with histories of political and ethical corruption need incentives and opportunities to eradicate corrosive practices. As a result, the TPP requires the current 12 and any future members to adhere to agreed-upon rules and policies, and to provide enforceable laws in each country. Chapter 26 of the TPP, "Transparency and Anti-Corruption," addresses the effects of bribery and corruption on trade, and delineates investment and government policies designed to regulate trade and investment. It commits TPP parties to pass and enforce anti-bribery laws, and promotes rules against conflicts of interest in government. This is an add-on to previously created US-instigated policies, such as the OECD's Anti-Bribery Convention in 1997 and its broadening at the UN in 2005. In order to maintain a clean, reliable, and cost-effective supply chain, political and ethical policies are critical going forward, and the focus of trade agreements like the TPP are a major step in providing incentives for countries to adopt sound and ethical rules and policies.

The authors hope that these issues will be integrated and become part of future international trade deals in the future.

8

The Future of Supply Chains

In writing this book, we hoped not only to get people energized about the important developments converging in digitization, technology, collaboration, trust, and co-development, but also to alert our readers to the art of the possible. We sought to connect the natural balance of ecosystems to balance supply chains. Other analogous ideas include evolutionary supply chains, complex adaptive networks, "non-zero" anthropological behaviors of human beings through history, genome mapping, military intelligence, and "good" levels of competition and integrity. This book came together as we started to see the links and crossovers among themes.

We believe these themes are leading us in a new direction, one that will not only be morphed by new technology, but also will result in a different way of operating globally in business. As we enter an era of post-globalization and settle into an era of mass customization driven by regionalization, competitive forces will continue to determine who will thrive and who will fail. In this chapter, we take what we have observed, and make predictions about the future of supply chain management. So far, these predictions have not yet fully materialized or are in a very early stage in their evolutionary cycle.

Specifically, we will predict some major technological trends and global network issues for the next decade. These projections will almost certainly become a reality. As we wrote this book, these trends became increasingly self-evident. They are:

1. Autonomous supply chains
2. Risk of supply chain hacking
3. Human rights management and illicit supply chains (drugs, slavery, stolen goods, governments)
4. Chain of custody requirements
5. The new connectography and supply chain wars
6. The rise of real-time information and mobility

The LIVING Supply Chain: The Evolving Imperative of Operating in Real Time, First Edition.
Robert Handfield and Tom Linton.

Self-driven supply chains

Ano nuevo state park

Figure 8.1 Northern Elephant Seals. *Source:* Reproduced with permission of iStock

Trend 1: Living Supply Chains Will Become Autonomous

Let's return to Tom Linton's discussion about elephant seals in his Singapore talk, discussed in Chapter 5.

Tom showed a large group of Singapore government officials and investors a picture of a herd of elephant seals at Ano Nuevo State Park (shown in Figure 8.1). Tom pointed out that hundreds of thousands of northern elephant seals that once inhabited the Pacific Ocean were slaughtered for the oil rendered from their blubber. By 1892, only 50–100 seals were left. After protection programs in Mexico and the United States, the seals began to recover and to multiply exponentially, and extended their breeding range as far north as Point Reyes. Today there are approximately 160,000 northern elephant seals.

If you want to see the elephant seals, you can visit them on a beach in California that only a few tourists venture to, the Ano Nuevo State Park, north of Santa Cruz. This is one of a few scattered beaches where you can see the seals – the other significant place is in the Aleutian Islands in Alaska.

Years ago, once the seals were reestablished after near-extinction, researchers noticed that the once-plentiful seals disappeared for part of the year ... but no one knew where they went! They had drifted off slowly, not all at once, so it wasn't a traditional migration. They wandered off one at a time over a month or so, until they were gone.

Finally, some University of Santa Cruz researchers attached GPS devices to the seals to track and map their migratory habits. They found out that in the summer, the seals went to a remote beach in the Aleutian Islands, off the coast of Alaska between the Alaska Peninsula and Russia's Kamchatka Peninsula. There they gave birth to and nurtured their pups, 6 months later returning to California.

But this migration isn't what makes northern elephant seals so interesting. Most migrating animals do so in packs, flocks, or herds. Penguins migrate as a group, as do wolves, elk, salmon, antelope, and the like. Canada geese migrate in their well-known V-formation, with the leader at the point of the V facing the headwinds, allowing the rest to draft behind him, rotating to the back of the flock when he gets tired. These animals follow coastlines, rivers, and other geographic landmarks.

But the elephant seals don't migrate together. *They migrate individually*, on their own. And when researchers tracked them on GPS, they learned that each seal takes its own route to the beach in Alaska. These routes certainly do not form a direct vector, as shown in Figure 8.2.

These elephant seals don't follow a specific pattern and aren't guided by landmarks, rivers, or other features. The Pacific Ocean is very deep at this point, and the seals aren't using navigational aids. So how do they all wind up on the same

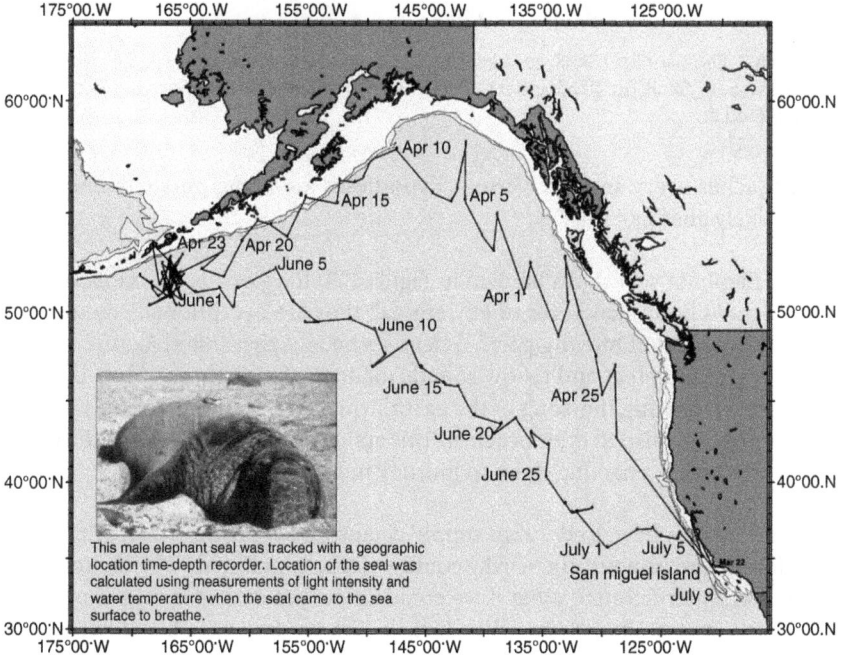

Figure 8.2 The Journey of an Elephant Seal. *Source:* Used under http://www.afsc.noaa.gov/nmml/education/science/studymmsealexample.php

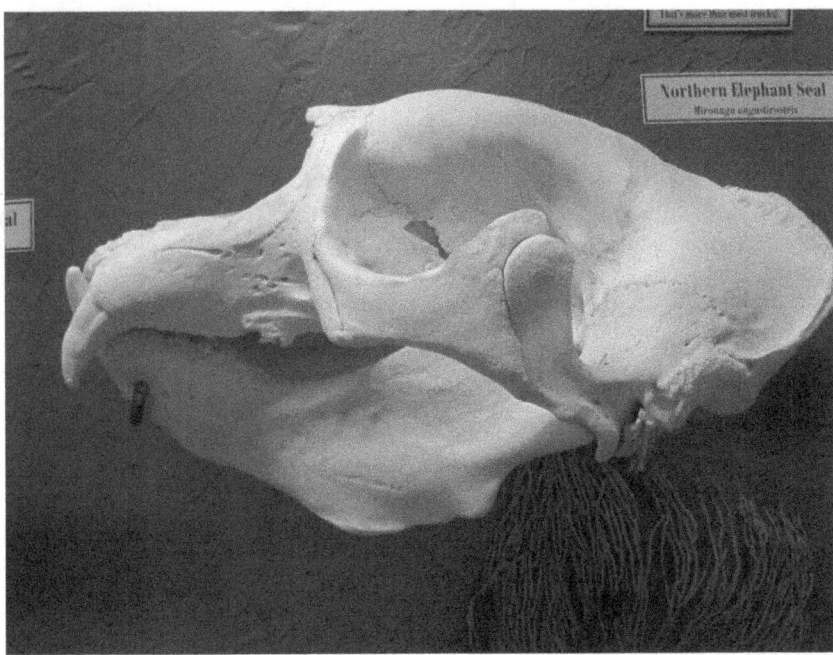

Figure 8.3 Elephant Seal Skull. *Source:* https://commons.wikimedia.org/wiki/File:Northern_Elephant_Seal_Skull.jpg. Used under CC BY-SA 3.0 https://creativecommons.org/licenses/by-sa/3.0/deed.en

two beaches every season? Various hypotheses are being pursued; one of the most likely goes like this:

> Elephant seal skulls (shown in Figure 8.3) have one of the most complicated bone structures of any animal; they are exceptionally dense, with complicated moving parts. Scientists believe that this structure enables them to detect and follow sounds made by the earth. In effect, the seals are following the 'song of the earth,' which guides them not only to their prey, but also to their beaches. This ability to learn the "song of the earth" is genetic, enabling them to journey independently.

What does this have to do with supply chains and real time? If elephant seals can follow the 'song of the earth,' could we teach inanimate objects to follow imprinted instructions? What if we could create autonomous cars, boxes, and packages, and embed them with devices like we find in Uber devices, that show us where the driver is, and tells him or her where we are, and the cost to move to a location? What if we could track every shipment in the world through an autonomous, self-driving supply chain that was in constant communication with other boxes and trucks on its way to its final destination, imprinted with a particular map or song guiding it to its destination? This "supply chain song" is not as far off as you might imagine, and the implications of such a capability are far-reaching. Perhaps, like seals swimming from one beach to another, the future of supply chains might be autonomous, node-to-node movement.

I witnessed a discussion of the future of autonomous vehicles at a BVL conference in Germany by Continental AG's Elmar Degenhart, Executive Chairman of the Board, in a presentation titled "Mastering Challenges through Transparency and Individual Responsibility." He started by noting a few interesting facts: "Every German spends 50 hours per year in a traffic jam – a waste of time and fuel. What we should try to achieve is to keep things flowing and not blocked. The roundabout is a good example of high efficiency, but we also find in our corporations that there are too many bottlenecks in warehousing and workflow, our behavior, how staff and we deal with partners. We may work against one another and waste time and resources."

Dr. Degenhart shared his vision of the future – driverless vehicles – based on technology that is being worked on by Continental. The corporation's vision emphasizes three crucial value streams: innovation, productivity, and profitable growth. Driving innovation means emphasizing to employees that we have to *learn* how to manage businesses and be constantly exploring new concepts that have been untested. Since hierarchies are toxic to innovation, the company has established a network structure. Employees should be able to work and connect with each other across hierarchies without informing their superiors. If they want to move fast to drive innovation and industrialize new concepts, speed is critical.

Continental is emphasizing networking, with vehicles connected with the backend road network and the Internet. Cameras set up in major cities will enable these vehicles to effectively "look around the corner" as they approach an intersection, and determine whether other vehicles are approaching. Their systems will increase visibility beyond what is immediately in front of the vehicle, to seek and capture possible risks. Technologies will change the functions of the car, controlling its speed, trajectory, and route. Continental envisages a three-stage model for vehicle automation: semi-automated (2017), partly automated (2020), and fully automated (2025). Running alone at a speed of 30 km/hour will be the first stage of automation. In this scenario, passengers will not have to steer, and the vehicle will have automated start and stop sequences. Drivers will be able to use their time in the vehicle more productively, to read, work on the Internet, or be on their smart phone. This vision is not just a fantasy – the technology is already available. The innovation in this case is already in the industrialization process at Continental.

The capability of the elephant seals to navigate their way across the ocean to their final destination is not unique in nature. In his book *The Homing Instinct*,[1] Bernd Heinrich provides multiple cases discovered in the natural environment of living creatures that despite the minute dimensions of their brains, find their old homes after years of wandering in the vastness of oceans, unfamiliar woods, and mountainous terrains. Humans are not equipped with the same abilities, relying on maps, compasses, or GPS devices to do so when in unfamiliar territory. Heinrich begins by sharing the story of a pair of cranes (that mate for life) that travel from the southern reaches of Texas, 5000 kilometers away, to Alaska, landing in a small pond that was the place of their birth. They make this migration every year, perform the same mating dance, and give birth to their young. He also describes the same homing characteristics found in Suriname frogs, honeybees, bar-tailed godwit birds, and Monarch butterflies. What makes these creatures able to find their way home?

What does that mean in terms of entities in supply chain networks? Intelligent transportation services (ITS) will become a multi-billion-dollar market, focused on mobile goods and interconnected logistics through communication technology. A highly complex structure will emerge that will enable companies to save costs and time, and will promote a more sustainable logistics value chain that saves lives. Safety and security is critical to this innovation, which will be designed for the supply chain of the future. Active tracking will become a way of monitoring the movement of all things, in the same way we use enterprise and Cloud software today. Over time, we believe that technologies will find a way to create "homing" devices that will enable packages, materials, and objects to become self-directing, leveraging the ability of an open market willing to transport and handle material that is bound for a specific destination, using open source technology. Of course there are multiple issues related to security, chain of command, and other factors, but the notion of a "homing instinct" for supply chains is an appealing one that we believe will one day come to fruition.

Trend 2: Supply Chain Hacking Will Increase

With the movement toward greater autonomy, an increasing number of decisions and transactions will be made by computers, not humans. Adding to this risk in machine-led transactions is an increased risk of hackers jumping into the software and introducing malware and code that drives negative and even dangerous outcomes. Loss of human autonomy must be countered by measures that hunt down hackers.

---

1 Heinrich, B., *The Homing Instinct: Meaning and Mystery in Animal Migration*, Houghton Mifflin, New York, 2015.

As the world becomes more and more connected electronically, a new supply chain challenge is born: combating data theft and hacking. According to one estimate, some 80 terabytes of data per minute now enters and leaves the United States, and servers are located in every country around the world. Further complicating the issue, local laws governing data and code security change according to individual countries' laws.

Supply chain security will also prove to be a major challenge. Research suggests that the likelihood of hacker entry points is directly related to human weak points. Exhibit A is Edward Snowden, who leaked numerous NSA documents to the public. As a result, security of individuals tasked with managing supply chains will likely increase, and software vulnerabilities will become increasingly important. Recently, the head of the Innovation Institute in the Department of Defense visited the Pulse Center and noted the importance of addressing the way in which products move in and out of ports. Emerging technologies also will be able to actively track assets anywhere in the world, and measures will be created to notify executives if containers or packages are going to the wrong place. In addition, security measures related to logistics parties (DHL, UPS, FedEx) will increase. Should these providers be somehow "knocked out," companies still will be able to track their shipments, whether they are in a warehouse, in a customs house, or in a port, with no reliance on third parties.

Trend 3: Improving Human Rights and Combating Illicit Trade Will Become a Core Goal of Supply Chain Management

Pierre Mitchell of Spend Matters shared an interesting story:

> An anthropologist proposed a game to the kids in an African tribe. He put a basket full of fruit near a tree and told the kids that whoever got there first would win the fruit. When he told them to run, the kids all joined hands and ran together, then sat together enjoying their treats. When he asked them why they had run like that, as one child could have had all the fruits for himself they said: "UBUNTU, how can one of us be happy if all the other ones are sad?

Creating happiness may seem like an odd theme to bring up in a book on the future of supply chains. However, for the same reason that we discussed the importance of supply chains being "good" in Chapter 7, we emphasize here that the "happy quotient" will become increasingly important to private companies operating the supply chain. This means not just that you declare your intentions on your website as do-gooders, it requires real action. In specific terms, it means closer integration of the supply chain private sector with the international intelligence community to work together to drive out non-compliant human rights violations, and to combat the strength of illicit supply chains.

The evolution of global trade agreements such as those found in the Trans-Pacific Partnership (TPP) in the future will expand the effort for combating illicit global trade. Paradoxically, by creating the foundation for free trade, agreements such as the TPP are not representative of the conventional thinking around free trade. Opposition to free trade and global trade agreements typically is based on the belief that things need to be as they were, and that we must recreate the past. One prime example of this is the argument against NAFTA, which contends that many manufacturing jobs moved to Mexico due to lower labor costs, and that Americans need to establish higher protections to ensure that these jobs return. In reality, the major reasons for Mexican sourcing decisions involve transportation costs and closer working relationships with suppliers.

Future versions of the TPP will have major impacts on the evolution of the LIVING supply chain.[2] The goal of the TPP was to have a "comprehensive and high-standard" agreement that eliminated tariff and non-tariff barriers for trading goods (including agricultural) and services (including financial), addressed trade issues not present in existing FTAs, and established rules for economic activities across the TPP partner countries. There is a need for a comprehensive framework for bilateral, regional, or multilateral (e.g., WTO) negotiations. Issues such as governance, dispute settlement, and due process will require buy-in from various government and private organizations. Such frameworks, although included in the TPP, will likely emerge in future trade deals in the years to come.

Frameworks such as the TPP have major ramifications for supply chain performance, especially in situations where supply chain components fall within the participant countries. Further, policies related to government procurement, state-owned enterprises, intellectual property rights, rules of origin, transparency, competition, trade remedies, and regulatory coherence are all elements of the TPP that can be detrimental to supply chains, and which future agreements must control for.

Future agreements, like the TPP, will also need to address cross-border data and information flows. A requirement of the TPP was to remove some nations' requirement for servers to be located locally to supply citizens with data. This requirement has led to the theft of servers and data due to poor security and ineffective policing. Agreements may also remove some nations' requirement that servers share their highly secure code with the local government, a policy which has created security issues in countries with a history of corruption. The

---

2 https://scm.ncsu.edu/blog/2014/02/21/what-is-the-trans-pacific-partnership-tpp-guest-post-by-arun-gupta-phd/

TPP also allows for secure cloud-based IT services and controlled data access, and provides the data owner with full authority over who gets access to the data and what level of data users may access. These changes represent progress on supply chain hacking; however, the fight will continue to be tough as new technology and better-equipped hackers enter the fight.

But what happens now that the US government has publicly stated that the United States will not ratify the TPP? Do things then remain in the status quo? Absolutely not, and this is where a knowledge of global trade agreements is critical.[3] There are nations in southeast Asia that have been asked to join a similar trade agreement called the Regional Comprehensive Economic Partnership (RCEP), which is China-led that excludes all nations outside Asia. There is an overlap of countries that are party to both the TPP and RCEP, however for those nations, such as Japan, Vietnam, Malaysia, Australia, New Zealand, Singapore, and Brunei, most have gone on the record saying that they see the United States-led TPP as the most critical and inclusive, and will put the RCEP on hold pending the decision on TPP. As the TPP dissolved, this has created a great opportunity for China to take the lead in Asia trade via the RCEP, leaving the United States on the sidelines. Supply chain leaders now need to relook at their structure, to understand how the RCEP will further restrict trade with Asia, both in manufacturing product, but also in exporting product from the United States into Asia.

Today every company will do what it can to maximize the benefits of free trade. As the rules of global trade change, via free trade agreements or new barriers to trade, each company will need to evolve its supply chain to maximize opportunities and protect itself. Individuals must make the same adjustments. If free trade opens with Vietnam for textiles, for example, an individual American who makes T-shirts will need to evolve his or her skill set to maximize income in the new environment. Those who don't will be stuck in an ever-challenging situation. The evolution of an individual and his or her skill sets is well covered in Jason Schenker's book *Recession-Proof: How to Survive and Thrive in an Economic Downturn*. So, to embrace free trade and allow market forces to identify the most efficient ways to design supply chains will always result in business growth and profits at the expense of those who stand still and fight change.

One consequence of globalization is that counterfeiters may be able to quickly find a customer for a product that no one would suspect was faked. A legitimate supply chain is a vital insurance against illicit goods. Neither INTERPOL nor any other law enforcement agency, can achieve this in isolation. Hence, INTERPOL has partnered with more than 40 industry sectors and

---

3 https://scm.ncsu.edu/blog/2016/06/16/why-global-trade-agreements-must-be-part-of-your-supply-chain-planning-guest-post-by-tim-barnes/#_ftn2

a number of cross-industry associations and representative bodies that offer financial and operational support.

One of the most notorious forms of illicit supply chain management is human trafficking. Immigration crises in Europe, the Middle East, and Latin America are extending all over the world, giving rise to supply chains that are being appropriated for moving human beings. Incidents of trucks and containers full of people in horrible conditions leading to deaths and suffering are becoming more prevalent. The private sector must work more closely not only with INTERPOL, but also with NATO, the World Bank, and the United Nations to combat these activities.

One of the most important innovations in supply chain management to emerge in the last 40 years is outsourcing. Instead of just managing their own organization, supply chain managers have focused on managing their end-to-end supply chains, often relying on specialized companies to perform this task. This shift constitutes an evolution from company thinking to supply chain thinking. In the 1970s, Nike was one of the first companies to embrace supply chain management, and to recognize the benefits of outsourcing production to lower-cost country suppliers. Indeed, Nike also led the charge to sustainable supply chains when they discovered the important impacts on the brand when labor codes were violated.

While supply chain management was initially designed to make products more efficient, this transformation is now likely being repeated to make products more sustainable – and more transparent. For example, labels that were linked to a single brand (company thinking) are being replaced by digital maps that visualize the end-to-end supply chain (supply chain thinking). While consumers have to trust the controlling body behind a label, supply chain thinking enables consumers to become their own controlling body. This transformation requires data about suppliers' suppliers, but becomes realistic as transaction costs to map the end-to-end supply chain are increasingly reduced due to smarter technologies, newer standards, and improved analytical algorithms. Will this transformation make fairer products more and more affordable?

The implication is that supply chain managers also will need to become much more analytical, and to employ individuals who understand the commercial realities of supply chains, and who can interpret these insights to computer programmers. These individuals will need to construct non-relational databases capable of storing many types of data that together can analyze control functions in the supply chain that assure compliance to codes of conduct. These analytical control functions will require the capability to capture complex human behaviors and measure them in a format that assures consumers that a company's supply chain is more than a representation of what it *intends*. You can't get that from a label.

Such measures will undoubtedly require horizontal collaboration among industries to establish standards that apply to industries such as apparel, food, electronics, and others that are migrating to least-cost countries. These standards require executives with deep insight into these issues, and who will establish norms that ensure that companies operate with integrity and can maintain and improve competitiveness. Indeed, we may find that companies at the vanguard will establish a new form of competitiveness, especially if the customer values it.

Trend 4: Chain of Custody Will Become a Dominant Force for Designing Federated Supply Chains

With the natural increase in attention to where products and services originate, combined with the need to become more aware of parties using our products and services for illicit purposes, the chain of custody will become a requirement for doing business. The supply chain today is full of "gray areas" where shipments disappear from sight; these black holes will become the focal point for scrutiny.

A good example here was shared by a senior logistics executive who spoke in my class on the roll-out of a new product such as an Apple iPhone:

> Security is one of the most challenging components of a product roll-out, because the manufacturer wishes to be able to deploy a product roll-out simultaneously across the entire country, in California, New York, Chicago, Shanghai, and everywhere in the world. This makes it extremely challenging for logistics providers. Some companies emphasize the same "experience" for all their products, and this was one of the toughest parts of meeting their logistics requirements on new products. This can be challenging as customs clearance becomes critical. One of the benefits our services is that we have our own people in customs, and they can get the material through much easier than a third party can.

> One of the biggest differentiators for us is that for demanding customers, every transfer point has to be electronic and real time – and there is a cost with the demands for the tracking and tracing of the shipment. Real-time commitment is critical. If you can't provide real-time tracking, you won't even be invited to bid. This is all done by real-time scanning with agreed-on scan points, including the transfer from their dock at the plant, transport to the airport, turnover to the carrier, loading onto the plane, and another transmission on wheels-up (showing if the plane is behind), and the technology wrapped around all these scans and systems has a cost to be wrapped around that. Liability insurance is another issue: Will it be for each container, product in the container, or the entire aircraft? If an

entire aircraft goes down, there is a cost to providing that insurance. If we don't use our own airline, we have to buy insurance.

Once the plane lands, we move the product from the airport to the factory, and in some countries, need to worry about security of drivers, and prevention of hijacking. The route has to be approved, and in some parts of the world, we provide chase vehicles with the trucks so there is no hijacking. These kind of complications makes simultaneous product release at stores very, very complicated!

A chain of custody for food and pharmaceuticals is even more critical. By some estimates, as much as 80% of pharmaceutical products in remote regions of Africa are deemed to be counterfeit. The recent set of events around food contamination at Chipotle and other restaurant chains is causing consumers to be that much more aware of the origins of what they ingest.

While companies have been talking about "integrating supply chains" since the 1990s, this concept has limits. Integrated supply chains were largely a combination of functions in companies that expanded the role of business-to-business (B2B) and electronic data interchange (EDI) technologies, with standards and protocols that emerged in the 1980s. As companies become more connected electronically through global communication standards, the ability to exchange information through the Internet has grown quickly, and most companies have been integrated, with a few exceptions (hospitals and utilities, for example).

But federated supply chains (FSCs) will dramatically improve the likelihood of increased supply chain security. Why? Because having people on the lookout for misdeeds is the single best way to prevent fraud and illicit trade. Federated supply chains are composed of individuals linked in a common purpose. That purpose may have a lot to do with the removal of undesirable elements from the chain of custody, and to ensure that those suppliers and partners who are part of the supply chain have a common set of morals, principals, and high integrity aligned with the principles described in Chapter 7. Federated supply chains are closely tied to being good global citizens, "doing the right thing," and driving to a common set of operating principles that is fostered by open trust and dialogue. Suppliers and customers in a federated supply chain have high transparency, which leads to greater trust. Indeed, if you are in an FSC, you should have nothing to hide, and will gladly open your factory to customers and to technologies that allow them to see what is going on in your facility. In the end, people in a federated supply chain will win together, or alternatively, die together. Think again about the trophic cascade, the Samsung Galaxy 7, and what is happening to others in the supply chain who depend on one another for their mutual survival.

Much activity is being driven by increasing calls for government oversight and corporate sustainability initiatives; not surprisingly, these federations are composed of both parties. This reflects the increasing notion that governments are indeed an integral part of the supply chain. Some choose to ignore this fact – at their peril. Government regulation is an increasing force to be reckoned with.

Government integration is already happening. Federated supply chains that include government entities extend collaboration, and may span several tiers in both directions (up and down the chain). Apple, for example, requires its suppliers to fit its federation of global operating standards. Almost every Fortune 500 company has something similar. Much of this activity started with the EICC and the UN Global Compact, as well as the Dodd–Frank Act, the California Transparency Act, and multiple UN and government rulings related to human rights, conflict minerals, environmental performance, emissions standards, use of bio-based products and biofuel, EU government rulings, trade and customs regulations, and individual country rules. (For instance, the EU has limited the use of genetically modified food, even though it is almost impossible to trace source and origin of organic vs. GMO food in many food supply chains). Other organizations, such as the Sustainable Apparel Coalition and others, have emerged to promote industry-specific standards.

We are likely to see much more in the way of government–industry collaboration around federated supply chains in the years ahead, due to the need for the industry to "get a seat at the table" when it comes to setting policy, regulations, and supply chain standards. Executives need to be proactive to shape government regulations, rather than sit back and react.

Trend 5: Supply Chain Wars

In the new book *Connectography: Mapping the Future of Global Civilization*, Parag Khanna discusses the "new supply chain wars." Khanna discusses how multinationals have become deeply connected and exposed to the emerging markets that have become their main competitors. But as countries like China become wealthier and export more of their low-cost jobs, they too will favor openness over protectionism and a level commercial playing field.

Central to his argument is that global supply chains have become more complex, but also have merged into a comprehensive whole. For example, America's import content of exports is relatively low (15%) but increases to 40% if one takes a full-cycle view of downstream distribution and sales as being included in the end-to-end supply chain view. Even World Trade Organization chief economist Patrick Low describes these "hybrid value chains" as different: "The physical and the digital, the manufacturing and the services, and the value-added from intangible factors such as competence and reputation are simply not captured by today's statistical methods."[4] Products should carry the label "Made Everywhere."

One of the best examples of this is Apple, which is often criticized for producing too many of its products in China at FoxConn. Apple CEO Tim Cook recently said, "I don't think we have a responsibility to create a certain kind of job. But I think we do have a responsibility to create jobs."[5] In fact, Apple is now going to produce one of its iMac lines in Texas, but most of the parts for these products will be imported from all over the world. Even China imports 34% of its electronic components in producing its information technologies. The point is that import and export is a key part of this global trade – but this pattern is being threatened.

Khanna suggests that one of the single biggest threats to current global trade is the combination of 3D printing and sharing economies in which goods will be consumed as services. Moreover, he predicts that local prototyping and mass production could bring about a severe long-term contraction in global shipping, inventories, and warehouses. Replacement parts for airlines, equipment, appliances, etc. could be produced essentially on demand. If this is the case, technology won't eliminate supply chains, but will "morph" them, as raw materials such as organic matter or plastics will need to "feed" 3D printing. In addition, the people who design the software and the printers will lead the market.

One of the most compelling insights of this future view of supply chain wars is the formulation HORIZONTAL + VERTICAL = DIAGONAL. According to a 2012 article in *Bloomberg Businessweek*, "Competitors want to be horizontal nodes of production and distribution and vertical hubs of value creation – together propelling themselves diagonally up the ladder of economic complexity" (p. 158). In this formula, countries with no resources can become transshipment points that smooth out supply chains. For example, Singapore has no raw materials but generates massive profits from its transshipment port. When countries impose sanctions, higher royalties, port access restrictions, anti-corruption witch hunts, and other "tug of war" tit-for-tat measures, the global economy will be impacted by this "horizontal resource mercantilism." In the same manner, "vertical tug of war" occurs when countries grab the most technologically sophisticated and financially profitable segments of strategic industries. Eventually, countries that are lower on the food chain will expand and ascend up the value chain to take over those industries now populated by Western countries. In places like India, companies think of "copyright" as "right to copy"! And keeping the "R" in "R&D" out of countries like China is not a formula that Western companies have been able to work out yet.

---

4 Interview with Parag Khanna, July 18, 2016.
5 Tyrangiel, J., "Tim Cook's Freshman Year: The Apple CEO Speaks," *Bloomberg Businessweek*, December 6, 2012.

Companies need to pay more attention to the global dynamics emerging around these supply chain wars. One of the most difficult ways to "copy" these forms of transgressions is creating a LIVING supply chain that functions through collaboration, velocity, and adaptation. These are learned activities that are difficult to replicate.

Trend 6: The Rise of Real-Time Information, Digitization, and Mobility

In 2016, the World Economic Forum, well known for its annual meeting in Davos, Switzerland, selected "Mobility" as one of the cornerstone councils as it looks toward the next 3 years. Technology and global connectedness is driving new forms of communication and movement. Whether it be emigration, immigration, or the shifting fortunes of individuals, companies, or countries, information and mobility are often drivers of change.

When we look at the state of supply chains today, we only need to look at analogies in nature to see what they will become. Faster will win over slower, better will succeed over corrupt, lower cost will lead over expensive, and companies and countries that lead with sustainable and human-centered outcomes will prevail. Nature has shown us the way.

Real-time information or information that is not batch- or report-based but delivered immediately to users will drive dramatic productivity improvements. Data latency caused by man or machine will be driven out and "the Cloud" will live up to its promise of information everywhere – on mobile devices or in the office.

New levels of automation will lead to labor needing new places to go. This shift will lead to demand for technical skills to service the new economy and "good" will drive demand for low-energy supply chains that will require shorter, faster, and more compliant ways for moving goods.

The biggest change will be in the "Internet of Things," which will drive "computing at the edge." This is also known as "distributed computing" and "distributed analytics," which involves computing data at the source of collection, which will increasingly be in machines and equipment. Smart sensors are emerging in the sub-$5 range that will capture data on shipments' temperature, location, and velocity.

A great example to consider is the collection of tire pressure on a moving truck. Sensors in the tires will capture tire pressure every millisecond – but there is no need to dump all of this data into a centralized data center! Smart sensors combined with distributed computing on the truck will collect first-pass data, and generate summary statistics, such as the fact that the tire will last 362 miles before a flat. Sensors combined with a local computer can provide key analytics, and when multiple sensors interact, they can provide clues as to what is happening in the supply chain. For instance, vibration sensors combined with the tire sensors may have a strong correlation with theft, and analysts can determine that if they know what they are looking for. In another case, a truck pulling up to a loading dock in a distributed computing model will interact in the cloud with systems at the loading dock. A notification will be sent regarding the number of loads ahead of them at the dock, and the driver may be notified to slow down, burn less diesel, or take a break for a meal, as their slot at the dock has been pushed back. These types of interactions will require that cloud edges need the ability to discover each other and communicate. For this to occur, standards will need to be established, just like Ethernet cables and Internet protocol standards were agreed on for telecommunications.

Such technological evolutions will create service provider niches that will form the basis for commercial platform creation and evolution, but also the potential for extinction of existing service providers through disintermediation and reintermediation. New technology has the potential to drive innovation and new platforms, but waves of digitization also can cause creative destruction of existing players that are too slow to keep up. In other cases, lawyers are quick to object with security concerns – just as they were with personal computers, personalized apps, and voicemail. Waves of digitization will continue to reshape the environment we live in. So how will digitization change your life?

Many companies are in the forefront of driving analytic insight and transparency throughout the supply chain. One of these is IBM's Transparent Supply Chain (TSC), an analytics based platform that seeks to enable end-to-end supply chain visibility, orchestration, and collaboration for the supply chain. Internally, the platform has transformed how work is done in IBM's globally integrated supply chain by making it easier for colleagues to work together and collaborate across multiple time zones. Through the TSC, all the teams have a single trusted source of information, aggregated Key Process Indicators (KPIs), Mobile alerts, analytics, and social collaboration tools to solve business challenges. Information and data from social media (Twitter, Facebook, etc.) is also integrated to provide a powerful context based information source for a range of supply chain decisions.

The current implementation touches all of IBM's global hardware manufacturing sites providing a single view of one global hardware manufacturing team rather than silo-driven activities in Poughkeepsie, New York; Singapore; Vác, Hungary; and Guadalajara, Mexico. It also extends to partner led operations such as the Central Distribution Centers (CDCs) in Germany, and The Netherlands, where the logistics activities are predominantly led by IBM's Third Party Logistics provider (3PL). The current implementation can facilitate the receipt of supplier and other partner provided information on the hardware products as well as the movement of goods. The TSC initiative is using the Agile implementation approach and is 2.5 years into its approximately 5-year implementation plan.

The TSC also is beginning to leverage the Watson cognitive analytics technology, which combines transparency with "big data" search methods. This approach has several visionary goals:

Create a modern supply chain that is transparent, intelligent, and predictive: Business expectations have changed, and by establishing greater visibility into supply chain data and processes and leveraging fast-emerging cognitive technologies, supply chain organizations can both predict and mitigate disruptions and risks and deliver even greater value to the business.

Establish greater transparency and visibility: Develop greater transparency and visibility by establishing a single, shared view of supply chain data and intelligence across all suppliers, partners, systems, and processes. Such visibility should include both internal and external sources of data – and both structured and unstructured data. Provide the supply chain organization with data and intelligence that gives the complete context of and perspective on the impact of, business decisions.

Predict and proactively mitigate disruptions and risks: Leverage the latest cognitive technologies to create greater transparency and comprehensive visibility into supply chain processes – and potential disruptions and risks – so that the organization can quickly and proactively mitigate those events.

The capability and intelligence needed to deliver optimal performance: Watson Supply Chain elevates the supply chain organization's existing systems and capabilities to provide greater visibility, transparency, and insight into supply chain data and processes. Watson Supply Chain embeds cognitive capabilities to empower organizations to better predict and mitigate disruptions and risks, as well as drive collaboration and innovation, while reducing costs.

Beyond the LIVING Supply Chain

The LIVING supply chain and the imperative of operating in real time is a requirement for the supply chain we know today and for the near future. The supply chain of the future, or as we suggest, the federated supply chain circle of the future, will incorporate technology with responsibility and provide trusted transparency and efficiency way beyond what we have today.

Supply chains have remained unchanged since the dawn of industrialization. Material has been transacted and moved distances to be assembled into varying levels of products or structures. People have managed that process with experts in planning, sourcing, logistics, and materials. Systems have been designed to make that process increasingly efficient and cost effective. However, the truth is that many of the processes that drive it are antiquated and built on 19th century rules and processes. Processes that lead to successful mass industrialization and military conquest will not work well in the future that lies ahead.

That is about to change.

The shift away from globalization, driven by mass customization of products closer to the point of consumption, is changing the distances in supply chains. The transactional component, driven by a need for greater transparency is looking to "block chain" technologies pioneered by Bitcoin to provide the 'trust but verify' solution missing in the multilayered world of business partners. A block chain is a block of transaction that forms a common ledger of truth. In this new world, everything can be known and the very idea of social and environmental responsibility will be verified. In 2016, IBM launched this shift with Block chain technology into supply chain.[6]

The notion of block chains is congruent with the focus on greater transparency, especially regarding consumers' need to understand the origins of goods guaranteeing the integrity of certificates that claim to document the source or origin of food and products, or documentation of "chains of custody" remains rudimentary and difficult to verify. As noted in a recent white paper, no single organization "… can be trusted to broker all data about every product's supply chain … relying on one party (or even a small collection of cooperating parties) creates an inherent bias and weakness in the system."[7] However, the emerging technology of "blockchains" present a whole new approach. The blockchain platform is a recent development in the field of computer science, which uses a global peer-to-peer network to provide an open platform that can deliver neutrality, reliability, and security. The origins of blockchains were originally as a solution underlying Bitcoin, but the approach now does not require any particular behavior on behalf of participants, including honesty or integrity. Instead, the idea of a blockchain is determined by consensus, or a defined convention for how to execute and administer business logic, which unambiguously discovers the state of the system, including the current level of stock or the origin of a particular certificate, not from a single authority by independently applying common rules and publishing data openly. These new forms of digital security will emerge as a critical foundation for assuring supply chain sustainability and origins/traceability of products.

There is also a virtual reality emerging in supply chain where a product is constructed across an extended enterprise that may include several companies acting as one. If the ledger is common, why not have a common supply chain organization? The commercial limits defined by the Uniform Commercial Code (UCC) of how buyers and sellers behave may need a new set of terms

---

6 http://www.wsj.com/articles/ibm-pushes-blockchain-into-the-supply-chain-1468528824
7 https://www.provenance.org/whitepaper

and frameworks to define how collaboration changes responsibilities of different players in a supply chain. The root of how buyers and sellers work may need a rethink, and standard legal contracts which emphasize indemnification and limits of liability will need to be completed redesigned. If companies co-source, co-manufacture and share a common system the traditional rules that govern commercial relationships will need changing. New technologies driven by emerging capabilities with Augmented Reality (AR) and Virtual Reality (VR) will transform how we as humans interact with demand and supply systems.

Likewise, with the rise of track and trace technologies[8] in logistics, the visibility into where things are continuously will change how we view inventory, liability, and network design. Materials will move by autonomous trucks, trains, and possibly planes (drones) as regulatory systems adapt to changing technologies. Existing industries around premium transportation, third party logistics providers, and distribution will need to adapt to this change. Uberization and the rise of a shared economy are evidence that technology disrupts established models. Uber single-handedly changed how people view personal transportation. Will the same shift happen in the commercial world of transportation? Will parties that distribute and manage supply chains for others be disrupted when the core reason for their existence (managing net working capital, supply, and support) is replaced by a common supply system making their advantage obsolete?

As supply chains move past descriptive (what happened) and the diagnostic (why did it happen), software, and systems will become more cognitive. The thinking part of supply chains tools will allow for a more predictive (what will happen) and ultimately prescriptive (what should I do) capability. As this occurs, machines will replace people currently calculating and making transactional decisions. The labor needed in supply chains will require increasing and levels of skill as decision-making becomes reduced to choosing between various financial outcomes.

Prof. Klaus Straub has termed this next phase of change "Industry 4.0." In this era, the very construct of how things get made is predicted to change fundamentally. The rise of ubiquitous sensing objects, built by 3D printing machines and operated by robots is now realistic.[9] The bigger issue supply chain leaders will face in the future may be around the ethics of what should be done versus what can be done and how we decide what and how we want machines to make decisions previously made by humans. Prof. Stephen Hawking, the renowned

---

8 http://blogs.gartner.com/it-glossary/track-and-trace/
9 https://scm.ncsu.edu/blog/2016/08/26/seeing-is-believing-debunking-the-myths-of-3d-printing-at-materialise/

astrophysicist told an interviewer that artificial intelligence could "outsmart us all" and that there is a "near certainty" of technological catastrophe.[10]

Supply chain management without human emotions may create the most efficient supply chains in the world, but if we don't actively manage these transitions, supply chains may evolve into a system without the soul that supply chains have today.

Conclusion

This chapter points to the current trajectory of technologies, which all point toward a real-time, LIVING supply chain of the future. These trends are all being experienced by Flex, as it is one of the most cutting-edge supply chain companies working across not just a single vertical, but indeed across all the major global industries, with the exception of financial services. One of the most important developments will involve looking at how autonomous supply chains will evolve. Elephant seal migration is used to suggest that supply chains are driven by a "song" that will direct all traffic and objects to their ultimate home location. What will happen when a package or box embedded with a living electronic chip enabled by Wi-Fi and GPS is embedded with a "song" that drives it to its ultimate location? What if we can track every shipment in the world, and teach objects to be in communication with other boxes, trucks, and transportation vehicles, and to be programmed to achieve a final destination? What will be the impact of additive manufacturing, which will enable objects to be produced on-site at a molecular level, and eliminate the need for transportation altogether? And finally, how will this reshape the global network and flow of business, as we are able to produce products on demand anywhere in the world, to drive out working capital and produce customized requirements? The impact of these trends on the global economy will be massive, and are likely to occur in a much shorter time horizon than anyone believes possible.

The following questions should drive strategic discussions and planning workshops to engage not only SCM executives, but all parts of the business, as organizations seek to develop future-driven business strategies.

1. What is the shape of your supply chain? Is it slow and not very visible? At what key points is visibility is an imperative?
2. Do you have visibility of visualized data in your supply chain? It is important to recognize that imperfect data visualized immediately is better than perfect data processes in a batch environment that arrives too late or that is not effectively visualized to render a decision in time. Sometimes you just have to get comfortable with changing engines while flying! Launching the

---

10 http://www.ft.com/cms/s/2/49c179b4-7ae8-11e4-b630-00144feabdc0.html#axzz4LZHnm5k6

real-time information approach requires learning by doing, piloting, and learning by trial and error. The adage of "You can't fix what you can't see" is critical here in creating velocity in the supply chain.

3. How many days of supply (DOS) does your supply chain have? Deep financial understanding of this measurement is necessary to improve asset velocity and accelerate free cash flow.

4. How much labor is in your supply chain end-to-end? Where can you take out the need for manual labor and automate with new tools?

5. What is the speed of your supply chain? Asset velocity at each stage between nodes must be understood to being disrupting time, as time is cost.

6. How many active part numbers are in your supply chain? Beyond SKU reduction, managers need to kill off "vampire data" that slows everything down.

7. How interactive is the data in your supply chain? Can you drill down into your supply chain to see and visualize what is going on, which allows you to repair it, manage by exception, and remove unnecessary "white space" between your nodes?

By thinking through these questions and engaging in debates with your colleagues across your enterprise, you will be taking the first steps toward adaptation to the emerging LIVING supply chain that is evolving and coming your way, and which will be here sooner than you think!

Index

The LIVING Supply Chain: The Evolving Imperative of Operating in Real Time, First Edition.
Robert Handfield and Tom Linton.
© 2017 John Wiley & Sons, Inc. Published 2017 by John Wiley & Sons, Inc.